Power and Influence in the Boardroom

In the last decade there has been an increasing interest in the role of people management in formulating key business decisions. This book offers a counterbalance to the predominant view that Human Resource and Personnel managers have little influence in the strategy-making process.

The research in this volume is based on original studies of sixty organisations. The authors examine the presence of Personnel/HR directors on different types of board in both private and public sectors, and in small to medium-sized firms. Through analysis of case studies, they examine:

- The involvement of Personnel/HR directors in strategy formation and implementation.
- Their informal power and influence on decisions.
- The multi-directional nature of strategy information.
- The importance of the attitude of the Managing Director or Chief Executive to the status and role of Personnel/HR.
- The proactive strategies which can persuade the senior management of the importance of Personnel/HR in adding value to businesses.

The book offers guidance to Personnel/HR managers aspiring to raise their status in organisations, as well as an indication of the future development of the role of people management at the highest levels of business. It will be essential reading for all those with a professional or academic interest in Human Resource Management and employment relations.

James Kelly worked for ten years in the building industry, followed by four years as an industrial relations officer in the steel industry. As a senior lecturer at Strathclyde University he has written and lectured widely in Human Resource Management. He is a Fellow of the Chartered Institute of Personnel and Development, and assistant editor of the journal *Employee Relations*.

John Gennard is Professor of Human Resource Management at the Strathclyde Business School. He has written widely in the field of employee relations, and is a consultant to employee and employer organisations. He is also a Fellow of the Chartered Institute of Personnel and Development, a member of the list of ACAS independent arbitrators and editor of the journal *Employee Relations*.

Routledge advances in management and business studies

Power and Influence in the Boardroom

The role of the personnel/HR director

James Kelly and John Gennard

Routledge
Taylor & Francis Group

LONDON AND NEW YORK

First published 2001 by Routledge
2 Park Square, Milton Park, Abingdon, Oxfordshire OX14 4RN

Simultaneously published in the USA and Canada
by Routledge
711 Third Avenue, New York, NY 10017

First issued in paperback 2015

Routledge is an imprint of the Taylor and Francis Group, an informa business

© 2001 James Kelly and John Gennard

Typeset in Baskerville by
HWA Text and Data Management, Tunbridge Wells

British Library Cataloguing in Publication Data
A catalogue record of this book is available from the British Library

Library of Congress Cataloging in Publication Data
Kelly, James, 1936–
    Power and influence in the boardroom : the role of the personnel/
    hr director / James Kelly and John Gennard.
    p. cm.
    1. Personnel management. 2. Personnel directors. I. Gennard, John. II.
Title.

HF5549 .K349 2001
658.3–dc21   2001019665

ISBN 13: 978-1-138-86397-2 (pbk)
ISBN 13: 978-0-415-21760-6 (hbk)

To Ann and daughters Karen Mary and Deborah Moira

Contents

Figures

Tables

Case studies

Acknowledgements

This book could not have been written without the help and co-operation of the personnel/HR directors and chief executives/managing directors who gave generously of their time to be interviewed and to talk to us 'off the record'. We would like to thank them for their access, particularly given their heavy and busy work schedules. We would also thank *Employee Relations Review* for permission to reproduce Figure 2.1 and *Human Resource Management Journal* for their kind permission to reproduce text and tables. The origins of the book stem from the encouragement received from the late Sandy Souter, a leading personnel/HR figure in Scotland, who provided the initial funding for the work.

Inevitably the production of books interferes with family life. We would therefore like to thank our wives (Ann and Anne) for their patience and understanding in this regard.

James Kelly
John Gennard

Abbreviations

BCG	Boston Consulting Group
BMA	British Medical Association
CCT	Compulsory competition tendering
CIPD	Chartered Institute of Personnel and Development
CLIRS	Company level industrial relations survey
EWC	European Works Council
HR	Human resources
HRM	Human resource management
IPP	Investors in people
IRS	Industrial Relations Services
JETRO	Japanese External Trade Organisation
MNC	Multinational company
MOD	Ministry of Defence
NEDs	Non-executive directors
NJIC	National Joint Industrial Councils
RCTUEA	Royal Commission on Trade Unions and Employees' Associations
SEM	Single European Market
SMEs	Small and medium-sized enterprises
TMT	Top management team
TUC	Trades Union Congress
WERS	Workplace Employee Relations Survey
WIRS	Workplace Industrial Relations Surveys

1 Power and influence of the personnel/HR director

The contemporary debate

Strategy is a disputed concept, with different meanings for different people at different times. However, one of the leading British texts on strategy (Johnston and Scholes, 1993) defines it as '… the direction and scope of an organisation over the long term, ideally, which matches its resources to its changing environment, and in particular to its markets, customers or clients, so as to meet stakeholder expectations'.

Within this perspective, strategy is seen to operate at three levels: corporate strategy relates to the overall scope of the organisation, its structures and financing and distribution of resources between different parts of the organisation; business or competitive strategies relate to how the organisation is to compete in a given market, its approaches to product development and to customers; finally operational strategies are concerned with how the various management functions – marketing, finance, personnel/HR, manufacturing – contribute to higher-level strategies. This top down perspective in which strategies are assumed to be formulated by Boards of Directors and then cascaded down the organisation represents the dominant view in most of the academic literature on strategy. This approach to strategy sees it as non-political, being produced by managers who are objective and have only the organisation's interests at heart.

However, for Mintzberg and Waters (1985) business strategy is a continuous process of adjustment to unexpected pressures arising from evolving circumstances often beyond the direct control of the organisation. They argue strategies evolve through a process of discussion and disagreement which involves managers at different levels in the organisation and that in some cases it is impossible to specify what the strategy is until after the event. In effect, actions may only become defined as strategy on the basis of hindsight and a process of post ad hoc rationalisation. This approach, however, recognises that in reality organisations are characterised by a plurality of interests which gives rise to rivalry (e.g. between different management functions), tensions and conflicting goals between stakeholders, together with attempts to attain personal as well as departmental goals. The Mintzberg and Waters approach acknowledges the conflictual nature of organisational life and therefore a political dimension to strategy formulation and implementation. It gives a central place to the exercise of power and influence and to the importance of informal and direct power on strategic decisions.

The contingency approach to strategy suggests it is possible to operate with a range of different personnel/HR practices depending upon the competitive position of the organisation. However, these practices are seen as being aligned with, and downstream from, business strategy. The four main contingency approaches are – the Boston Consulting Group (BCG) matrix; life cycle models; applications of Porter's work on competitive advantage and Miles and Snow. The BCG assumes that personnel/HR decisions are downstream from corporate and business/competitive strategies and are contingent on them as well. Business strategy is seen as determining the HRM policies to be adopted by the organisation. The model emphasises business stars (characterised by high market share and growth), cash cows (mature markets in which the firm has high market share and is profitable but has little opportunity for further growth), wild cats (young businesses with low market share but competing in markets with high growth potential) and dogs (both low market share and low growth with emphasis on cost reduction). It postulates different HR policies to fit these four different strategies. For example, with a wild cat strategy, essential personnel/HR policies would be flexible and team working combined with an open management style.

Storey and Sisson (1993) tried to relate life cycle models of strategy to HRM in an effort to explain why employers adopt different policies in different situations. They use four categories – start up, growth, maturity and decline. In the decline stage, for example, they point out companies will be concerned to reduce costs to survive and HR issues like redundancy policy and practice will come to the fore. Porter (1985) argued that employers have three strategic options to gain competitive advantage – cost reduction, quality enhancement and innovation. Cost reduction entails producing goods and services cheaper than one's competitors whilst a quality enhancement strategy is characterised by producing goods and services at the highest possible quality. Innovation requires groups of highly trained specialists working closely together to produce rapidly changing products and services to remain ahead of the competition. Schuler and Jackson (1999) draw out the personnel/HR implications of these strategies. For example, a quality enhancement strategy requires personnel/HR policies of, *inter alia*, continuous training and development, high levels of employee commitment and carefully controlled recruitment and selection systems.

Miles and Snow (1978) identified business strategies of:

- prospector – typified by the continual search for new product market opportunities and emphasising innovation;
- defender – characterised by a stable product market and emphasising cost efficiency and defence of market share; and
- analyser – operating in both stable and changing product markets and although not market leaders following changes more quickly than defenders.

They also postulate the personnel/HR policies appropriate to these strategies. For example, the prospector strategy requires sophisticated recruitment policies designed to select individuals who possess the relevant skills for the organisation, whilst training and development policies are likely to centre on specific problems faced by the employer.

In the 1990s, the resource-based view of business strategy began to emerge. It is more holistic, giving HR a more integrated and central role in the formulation and implementation of strategy. The resource-based theory's premise is that, under certain conditions, the organisation's resources and capabilities provide the source of a firm's competitive advantage. The key to competitiveness is thus the skill mix and the quality of the top management team who identify the opportunities and the threats in the market place and develop the organisation's strengths whilst minimising its weaknesses. The top management team attempts to shape the enterprise's environment to its advantage as well as defending it from threats.

However, our research is not about the strategy an organisation adopts. It is about the players, and one in particular – the personnel/HR director – in the processes of formulation and implementation of strategy in contemporary work organisations. It is also concerned with the linking of business and HR strategies in this process. The study is based mainly on British data but where appropriate international comparsions are made. In the UK the dominant view is that personnel/HR as a specialist function, does not possess significant authority, power and influence at crucial points in the organisation relative to other management functions, such as finance, marketing and operations management, to influence strategy formulation and implementation. Decisions about personnel/HR policies are seen as downstream from where the key business decisions are made and are contingent on them as well. This pessimistic conclusion is based on a number of criteria, including personnel/HR's formal presence on Boards of Directors, the role of corporate personnel/HR in de-centralised corporate structures, the welfare image of the people management function, the rise of HRM and salaries paid to personnel/HR directors relative to other directors.

The pessimistic view

Personnel's board of director presence

Some argue personnel/HR has little influence because of its relatively low presence on Boards of Directors where it is implicitly assumed, business strategy is formulated. The Workplace Employee Relations Survey of 1998 (WERS), reported in Millward *et al.*, 2000, based on a random sample of 2100 workplaces, showed specialist personnel representation on company Boards of Directors to be 36 per cent, i.e. about one in three Boards have personnel/HR directors. The Company Level Industrial Relations Survey (CLIRS), reported in Marginson *et al.*, 1993 and 1988, revealed personnel/HR Board representation at 30 per cent in organisations employing 1000 or more. An Industrial Relations Services (IRS) survey of August 2000 into small and medium enterprises revealed 27 per cent of such businesses to have a personnel manager, although it produced no specific data on personnel/ HR directors. The Workplace Industrial Relations Surveys (WIRS 1992, 1984 and 1980) contain data on 'any' personnel/HR representation on company Boards of Directors and in 1998 estimated such representation at 64 per cent. 'Any' representation was defined as the presence of a Board member with a portfolio which included personnel/HR responsibilities. Table 1.1 shows the trend, over the last two decades, as reported by WIRS surveys in 'any' personnel Board representation at the Board level.

It shows a rise in presence on main Boards between 1980 and 1984, after which it declines, leading its authors to conclude that the personnel function has generally little power and influence on strategy issues. Millward *et al.* (2000) based on all WIRS and WERS surveys, conclude

> The decline from 71 per cent to 64 per cent of establishments is explained by the changing composition of workplaces. It is new workplaces, rather than established ones, which remain to be convinced of the value of Board level personnel representation in organisational decision-making.

To put the UK position into a European context Brewster and Hegewisch's (1994) European survey records personnel's presence on Boards of Directors as less than 20 per cent in Italy but over 80 per cent in Spain, France and Sweden. An Australian Human Resource survey also reported low personnel representation on company Boards at 18 per cent for 'specialist' representation and 25 per cent for 'any' representation (Fisher *et al.*, 1999). This led the authors to conclude that in Australian enterprises human resource/personnel management influence is relatively low.

The above studies use the presence of a personnel/HR director on Boards of Directors as a proxy for their authority, power and influence in the organisation. Academics, using the CLIRS data (e.g. Purcell, 1991; Marginson *et al.*, 1993; Purcell and Ahlstrand, 1994), have concluded the personnel function is marginal, third order and far down stream from the point of strategic decision-making. Nevertheless they do accept that where a company has a personnel director on its main Board the function is more influential. To quote Purcell and Ahlstrand (1994):

> The 1992 results showed personnel people were more likely to be involved in first and second order strategy where there was a personnel director on the main Board. However judging by the number of personnel directorships (30 per cent) on main UK boards of large private sector companies, the overall trend appears to be a decline in the importance of the central personnel function.

Table 1.1 'Any' personnel/HR board of director presence in the private sector (figures in percentages)

Type of representation	1980	1984	1990	1998
Any representation	73	76	71	64
Specialist representation	–	–	47	36

Source: Millward *et al.*, 2000

De-centralisation of corporate structures

Purcell and Ahlstrand (1994) consider the growth, and dominance, of the multi-divisional company has caused a transfer of HR activities from the corporate headquarters to the divisions and business units of such companies. In an earlier study Purcell (1991) recorded a major shift since 1950 in the structure of the top 200 UK companies towards diversification with the significant growth being in related and conglomerate businesses rather than single product businesses. This is the large M-shaped decentralised company consisting of multiple divisions and subsidiary business units. Such companies emphasise financial control with the corporate centre laying down for some period ahead tight targets and standards for judging subsidiary business unit performance. As Purcell and Ahlstrand state, 'Overall, the prime task in managing the business units (as opposed to marketing products) is to reduce costs and push up margins in the short term'.

The business strategies of such companies are congruent with the short-term financial requirements of capital markets, especially to maintain a rising share price. No attempts are made to shield the business unit from such external pressures. If they are not performing adequately they are quickly sold off. Business unit managers are free to introduce their own HRM strategies and policies, but financial requirements severely limit such autonomy since investment in people is a cost reflected in bottom-line performance. The HR implication is the demise of the corporate personnel department as corporate strategies and policies are abandoned in favour of decentralisation. In such devolved companies there is little by way of corporate HR strategy and what is possible at subsidiary level in HR terms is severely limited.

As Marginson *et al.* (1993) say:

> The 'financial controllers' operate with a small (headquarters personnel) office whilst the strategic planners had a much more centralised, well staffed corporate office. ... Conglomerate or more diversified enterprises have a hands off approach and are less likely to impose administrative standards or policies. They have relatively smaller corporate offices in personnel.

This view assumes the centre becomes significantly less important as an organisation decentralises. This is questionable because the degree of autonomy granted to business units by headquarters varies. Most are expected to apply common corporate wide personnel/HR standards and policy in issues such as pensions, management development, equal opportunities, remuneration of senior executives etc., but areas such as pay determination (collective bargaining), joint consultation and job evaluation tend to be devolved to the business units. It is these last three areas to which Purcell and Ahlstrand are mainly referring when they judge personnel/HR power and influence to be limited as a result of the de-centralisation of companies. Had they looked at a wider range of personnel/HR issues they may have modified their view.

Personnel's role in strategy formulation

Purcell and Ahlstrand (1994) argue that as a third order, down stream function, personnel/HR is more involved in strategy implementation than in its formation. CLIRS sought to establish the extent of the involvement of personnel/HR in the making and the implementation of business strategies by asking corporate personnel specialists to state their contribution. The survey also asked financial specialists how they regarded the contribution of corporate personnel specialists to the formulation and implementation of business strategy. Generally personnel respondents claimed to be involved in drawing up strategic proposals in between one-half and three-quarters of cases, and in the implementation of strategic decisions in between one-half and two-thirds of cases. However, differences of view were evident when comparing personnel/HR claims in relation to their involvement in strategy formation with those of finance specialists' views of personnel/HR involvement in key business decisions. Financial specialists considered personnel specialists to be less involved than the personnel respondents claimed. The authors of the survey comment, 'For example, one half of personnel but only one third of finance respondents said the personnel function was involved in drawing up a proposal for merger and acquisition'.

Marginson *et al.* (1993) note that the presence of a main board personnel director tends to increase personnel's involvement in strategy formation, but with 30 per cent Board presence personnel's strategic contribution was thought likely to be low. They conclude, 'If one of the defining characteristics of human resource management is the explicit link with corporate and business strategies then the survey has failed to find it for the majority of large companies in the UK'.

Notwithstanding this evidence, Purcell (1995) recognises that statistical analysis based on formal structural variables is not sufficient to explain either the presence or absence of personnel/HR director influence in the boardroom. He argues:

> There is no association with enterprise size and other structural variables, except for ownership: large overseas-owned firms in the UK were much more likely to have a personnel director than their UK counterparts ... the decision to have a main Board personnel director is a matter of choice unrelated to size, structure or strategy. Almost certainly it is linked to the views of the chief executive, non-executive directors and the historical experience of the firm.

What matters then is the political processes involved in decision making and that is a central concern of this book.

The rise of human resource management

For some an important factor explaining the alleged relative lack of power and influence of the personnel/HR function on mainstream business decisions is its historical development. Personnel's roots are in employee welfare (Niven, 1967) designed to improve the health, working conditions and quality of working life of employees. In today's organisations this welfare tradition is reflected in managing diversity, friendly family policies, the provision of crèche facilities etc. These are normally the responsibility of the personnel/HR department. The counselling of individuals about personal problems such as drugs and alcohol abuse, AIDs, early retirement due to ill health etc., are also modern day welfare responsibilities of personnel/HR professionals.

However, it is well established that labour management in the 1920s and 1930s and in the 1960s and 1970s industrial relations were major personnel roles (Tyson and Fell, 1986; Purcell, 1988; Storey, 1992). The Royal Commission on Trade Unions and Employers' Associations (RCTUEA, 1968), under the chairmanship of Lord Donovan, considered the root of Britain's industrial relations problems was, *inter alia,* shop stewards undermining the regulative function of industry-wide collective agreements resulting in informal, autonomous and fragmented collective bargaining, unofficial (not given backing by the union national decision-making structures) and unconstitutional (withdrawal of labour before all the agreed stages for resolving disputes have been exhausted) strikes. Such behaviour was seen as contributing significantly to the UK's productivity deficit relative to its major competitors.

The Donovan Commission recommended, amongst many other things, Boards of Directors accept responsibility for personnel and industrial relations reform in their organisations (RCTUEA, page 44, paragraph 179) by the appointment to the Board of someone with this responsibility. Although this recommendation resulted in a growth in the number of personnel specialists there is little or no evidence – other than Armstrong (2000) – as to its subsequent effect on the power and influence of personnel specialists in the formation and implementation of key business decisions. Much of the contemporary literature, however, implies that personnel still continued to confine its activities to operational matters where its activities were fragmented and unregulated (Drucker, 1989).

Personnel's industrial relations role is generally regarded to have declined in the 1980s and 1990s with a reduction in trade union membership and in the extent of the coverage of collective bargaining. The annual reports of the TUC and the Certification Officer show union membership falling from nearly 13 million in 1979 to just under eight million in 1997. This decline, in the view of some academics and consultants, has been accompanied by a rise of human resource management. The nature of HRM has, however, been the subject of extensive debate ranging from the work of Guest (1987) and Storey (1992) who attempted to define it, to those such as Keenoy (1999) who regard it as an ideology defying definition. Generally, the accepted dominant view is that HRM, unlike personnel, participates in strategic level management decision-making. It is seen as integrating HR strategy with business strategies (external fit) and the coordination of various personnel policies (internal fit).

Guest (1987) and Skinner (1987) argued HRM is too important to be left to the personnel department whereas others, such as Storey, maintain that personnel is stuck in an industrial relations role incapable of grasping opportunities to become strategic 'changemakers' and/or what Tyson and Fell (1986) classified as 'architects'. Storey (1992) considers line managers, by undertaking personnel/HR work, both at the policy making and implementation level, are a threat to the future existence of personnel. It is asserted personnel will wither away in the face of such competition. This argument receives support from other academics such as Cunningham and Hyman (1999) and Oswick and Grant (1996) who argue that a consequence of devolving personnel work to the line managers is, even where personnel is represented on the Board, that personnel now has insufficient power and influence to obtain resources to support personnel/HR policies.

Personnel without a business focus

Some contemporary research on the role and function of personnel management highlights its lack of a strategic business focus. Storey (1992), for example, identifies four models of personnel management which he labels tactical handmaiden, tactical regulator, strategic advisor and strategic changemaker. Handmaidens provide an administrative service reacting to line managers' requests for information on personnel records etc. The regulators are occupied with industrial relations dealing with trade unions, the negotiating and administrating of collective agreements and attending to employment issues such as discipline and grievances. Advisors adopt a strategic planning role but leave the decision-making and action to general management. The changemakers are also strategic but are involved in the business decision-making process and in making things happen. The changemaker role is equated with HRM. Storey studied in detail 15 British companies in which only two headquarters personnel departments pursued a strategic changemaker role. Strategic business and HR initiatives came from general, and not personnel, management. In Storey's research the majority of personnel departments were found to be of the regulator (industrial relations) role and thereby little involved in strategic business decisions.

Tyson and Fell (1986) identified three models of personnel management, namely the clerk of works, the contracts manager and the architect. The clerk of works provided routine administrative service to line managers. The contracts manager is heavily involved with trade unions and the making and implementing of collective agreements. In its architect role personnel is engaged in strategic long term planning and is more fully integrated into the business decision-making process. Tyson and Fell argued that with the demise of its industrial relations role personnel's contribution would be increasingly confined to low level administrative work, and only in a few cases to high level strategic work.

Storey and Tyson and Fell's analyses throw further doubt on the role of the personnel function in contributing to business strategy formation. They divide their changemaker and architect roles into two sub-types. In the case of Storey's changemaker the sub-types are a human resource specialist concerned to introduce high professional standards and a business orientation. Tyson and Fell sub-divide the architect into a change agent and a business manager but in both cases they assume the personnel role to be subsumed within the stronger business culture of the enterprise. Indeed Tyson (1995) says 'The business role can be and is performed well by non-personnel specialists'.

In this way Storey and Tyson and Fell regard the personnel function's contribution to business strategies as weak and limited.

Purcell and Gray (1986) also highlight the industrial relations role of the personnel/HR function, viewing it as a buffer between trade unions and management. They concentrate on the corporate personnel department and explain its role in the context of decentralised collective bargaining as ensuring subsidiaries conform to pre-planned corporate budgets. For Purcell and Gray personnel absorbed the pressures from trade unions which deflected them from dealing with the real strategic decision makers at Board level, and which also prevented personnel from adopting a business focus.

The dominance of finance

Armstrong (1995) presents a further warning (or threat) to personnel as a specialist function. He argues increased market competition and the shift of emphasis to cost reduction has given disproportionate power and influence to accountants. Personnel policies such as performance appraisal and performance-related pay implemented by line managers are designed to achieve cost reductions. The criteria for monitoring performance is thus established by finance specialists rather than personnel. This importance credited to finance specialists in HR decisions also received support from the CLIRS survey (1993) which, as we have already seen, reports finance specialists' perceptions of the involvement of personnel/HR specialists in making strategic business decisions as much lower than that stated by personnel specialists.

Personnel directors' salaries

It is a generally held view that personnel/HR directors are the most poorly paid of company directors, reflecting it is claimed their lower status amongst director colleagues. According to the Reward Group survey (1999) the median cash remuneration (excluding non-monetary benefits) of personnel/HR directors was £52,775 compared to £59,049 paid to operations directors, £55,959 to marketing directors and £65,322 paid to finance directors.

Weaknesses of the pessimistic view

Formal structures

Relatively little is known about the behaviour of Boards of Directors, compared with their structures. This constitutes a black hole in the understanding of how organisations work (Brookes, 1979) and how, and who, actually exercises power and influence. There is a need to investigate not only the formal structures and composition of boards, but how board members are selected, the various roles they play, especially that of the chief executive officer, their interaction with each other, the types and styles of Boards and the exercise of power within them. There is also a need to investigate Boards at all levels of an organisation. Chapter 2 contains a more detailed explanation of such Boards (all of which have executive authority and power) so what follows is the briefest of explanations. In the private sector this covers the main corporate PLC Board, the CEO/MD Executive Group, subsidiary/divisional and business units, and the Boards of independent small and medium-sized enterprises (SMEs). The main PLC Board has legal and financial responsibilities in governing the enterprise. The CEO/MD Executive Group is the point at which decisions to grow and develop the business are formulated. Personnel/HR representation on this Executive Group is ignored by those who have a pessimistic view of the power and influence of personnel/HR in the formulation of business strategy. Strategic decisions, but within parameters decided at the corporate level, are also made at the subsidiary and business unit levels. An independent SME Board holds legal and financial responsibilities but is likely, due to its size, to be more closely involved in the day-to-day running of the firm.

The Boards of Directors referred to in WIRS and CLIRS and other surveys are by implication the main or corporate Boards of Directors of private sector PLCs. However the evidence in such surveys regarding personnel Board representation is ambiguous as they do not make explicitly clear the type and level of Board to which their analysis relates. It is shown later in the book that it does not always follow that individuals with the title director are members of a Board of Directors. It is possible that people replying to questionnaires are unaware of this fact. Indeed it is even more likely to be the case if the respondent is located at the workplace and it is on this level that the analysis of WIRS focuses.

Purcell and Ahlstrand's analysis shows a rise in the multi-divisional company with decentralised structures. Financial control is said to dominate the multi-divisional company providing the integrating mechanism between subsidiaries, with little need for corporate level personnel and the integration of corporate level business and HR strategies. This they claim leads to autonomous business units and slimmed down corporate headquarters. This is an overly structural and top down view of strategy formation and implementation. Multinational companies (MNCs) exhibit many structural forms including matrix, heterarchy and network shapes with upward, lateral, diagonal and downwards communications (Dowling *et al.*, 1999). Problems can, however, arise around the staffing, development, transfer and payment of international managers, the solutions to which often require some guidance from the corporate centre. Ferner and Varul's research (2000b) shows, within German MNCs, corporate personnel departments need to be less administrative and more strategic and proactive. In such circumstances the need for corporate headquarters HR coordination and intervention is paramount. Moreover, even in the decentralised financially driven conglomerate as described by Purcell and Ahlstrand, the need for some HR central control is recognised in the form of personnel committees which are usually, but not always, serviced by a personnel/HR director. Although MNCs do not normally carry over their domestic collective bargaining arrangements into their overseas subsidiaries, they are likely to implement in all subsidiaries, regardless of location, common HR policies on issues such as performance management.

It has also been argued (CLIRS, 1993; Purcell and Ahlstrand, 1994) that a weakness of the corporate personnel role is its lack of contribution to the formation of business strategies. This raises questions as to where strategy is made and by whom? CLIRS and Purcell and Ahlstrand analysed Boards of Directors of large companies in the private sector. However, Budhwar's (2000) research demonstrates that personnel/HR directors participate in strategy formation. His research showed that of the 93 companies surveyed 87 per cent had corporate strategies and that in 77 per cent of these the personnel function was involved either at the outset or early, in the consultation process. Another weakness of the view that personnel/ HR makes at best a limited contribution to strategy formulation is the implicit assumption that main Boards of Directors actually make business and HR strategies. Where is strategy made, and by whom, thus becomes an important question. To answer it a more rigorous analysis of Boards of Directors and the behaviour of CEO/MD Executive Groups than currently exists in the literature is required. More knowledge and understanding about what Boards do, how Boards actually operate and how their members interact with each other is essential if the extent of personnel/HR involvement in business strategic decision-making is to be properly assessed. This cannot be achieved, by relying on formal structures

The decentralisation argument is closely aligned to that of those who argue the devolution of personnel/HR work to line management strips the function of its existence. The devolution to the line argument (Storey, 1992) assumes the relationship between those two management functions is one of competition and a zero sum game within which one function gains at the expense of the other. It is contended that devolution to the line results in headquarters' personnel departments losing work and therefore control and influence over HR and business strategy. This argument has also been made forcibly about the public sector by Kessler and Purcell (1996) and by Oswick and Grant (1996). The assumption behind the devolution threat thesis is a negative perspective based on a one-way causation. In the public sector, decentralisation and devolution are seen to hold the threat of reducing the power and influence of personnel, but by the same token they also provide the opportunity for it to develop a new role based less on rule interpretation and the 'you cannot do that syndrome'. The view that line management and the personnel functions compete with each other has also been challenged. Renwick (2000) argues, based on his work with a Scottish utility, that the relationship between HR and line is one of a consensual partnership. There is also evidence which questions the view that functional rigidity exists between line and HR specialists and the reality is the distinction between them has become blurred in favour of flexible roles providing mutual benefit to line and personnel/HR managers (Gennard and Kelly, 1997).

Storey and Sisson (1993) consider that in Britain the industrial relations tradition is so strong that the HRM model, with the exception of a few exemplar companies, is unlikely to exist in anything like its ideal form. They argue, therefore, for a balancing between the alleged individualism of HRM and the collectivism of industrial relations. They say, 'The experience of those managements that have maintained relationships with trade unions above the individual units, however, suggests that the advantages considerably outweigh any disadvantages'. Line managers continue to need the advice and support of personnel specialists, albeit within a changed context requiring a different style.

Finally the assumption that the personnel function is, and has, lacked a business focus has clearly been exaggerated. Back in the mid-1980s Tyson identified the business manager role of personnel management. In 1991 Coulson-Thomas recorded the emphasis placed by boardroom personnel directors on their participation in business decisions as almost every decision has human resource implications. To quote him, 'The personnel director should be a business person first and a personnel practitioner second'.

Ulrich (1997) advocates an understanding of the business as significant to personnel's role in becoming a strategic partner at Board level. In an interview in People Management (Ulrich, 1998) he remarked, 'It is a ticket of admission to the top table. Without this understanding you do not get a hearing'.

Questionnaire surveys

The relatively little personnel power and influence thesis in Britain is based on results from questionnaire surveys. Questionnaire returns tend to contain a bias and exaggerated self-reporting by the respondents. Postal and telephone questionnaires are limited in that respondents may misunderstand the meaning of the question. In addition busy people in modern lean and cost conscious organisations often do not have the time to reply to lengthy and complex questionnaires. A particular problem applies to very senior managers who have even less time and may delegate the responsibility to answering the questions to an assistant or a more junior member of staff who may not possess the necessary knowledge. Moreover, when completed, questionnaire responses are likely to contain degrees of inaccuracy, stemming from many factors including misunderstanding the values attached to the scales, and to no answer replies to key questions.

Weaknesses in self-report questionnaire survey evidence has been highlighted by Bacon *et al.* (1996) in their study of small and medium-sized enterprises. They employed a survey company to interview respondents over the telephone to discover the number of new management policies adopted by small and medium-sized organisations. This was followed up with site visits to 13 of the respondents during which face to face interviews discovered 'over-claiming' by companies relative to the original self-report survey. For example, the survey method had recorded 76 new management policy initiatives for such companies whereas the site visits produced only 53.

Generally respondents are likely to consider their contribution to be more significant than that of other functional directors such as line managers and accountants. Why CLIRS gave anymore credence to the views of financial managers as opposed to personnel respondents in their survey is unanswered. Any groups of managers are prone to exaggerate their own contribution and play down that of the other functions (Guest and Peccie, 1994). Postal questionnaires are of even more limited value in giving actual insights as to who, and who does not, have power and influence in an organisation. Where they are used to investigate such questions it needs to be as supplementary evidence provided by case studies and interviews etc. There are some methodological limitations underpinning the dominant view that personnel/HR directors have little influence on the formulation of business strategies.

The optimistic view

Personnel's board presence

However, there is some research arguing an optimistic picture of the personnel/ HR function's potential influence on the decisions of the main Board of Directors in terms of presence on such Boards. Brewster and Hegewisch (1994) in their European survey show a wide range of personnel Board representation in selected countries from a high of over 70 per cent in Spain, France and Sweden to a low in West Germany and Italy of 30 per cent and 18 per cent respectively. In the United States, Tsui and Gomez-Mejia's (1988) study based on 900 companies employing more than 2000, reported 73 per cent of top HR executives serve on the enterprise's executive management committee (see Table 1.2).

In the UK Torrington and Hall (1998) show a rise in Board presence from 21 per cent in 1984 (MacKay and Torrington, 1986) to 63 per cent in 1994. A survey by Budhwar (2000) of 93 firms shows personnel Board representation in 55 per cent of enterprises in textiles, pharmaceuticals and other private manufacturing.. A Development Dimensions International survey (1999) on HR Board representation recorded a 72 per cent presence compared with 55 per cent in the previous year (see Table 1.3). However these studies are also based on formal structures of corporate governance and questionnaire surveys. They do not provide insights into who, and why, actually exercises power and influence. Board presence is

Table 1.2 Personnel/HR director board presence in international companies (figures in percentages)

Sweden	France	Spain	US	Norway	Denmark	UK
86	82	80	73	66	53	48

Source: Brewster and Hegewisch (1994), Tsui and Gomez-Mejia (1988)

Table 1.3 Personnel/HR director board presence in UK companies (figures in percentages)

Sources	Mid-1980s	Late 1990s
Torrington and Hall	21	63
Budhwar	–	55
Development Dimensional International	–	72

assumed to equate with having power and influence. This as we explain later is not necessarily the case.

Personnel's power and influence on boards

The pessimistic view of the power and influence of personnel/HR management takes low presence on Boards of Directors as a proxy for power and influence. However, there are some who are more optimistic concerning personnel/HR's contribution to strategy formulation where it does have main Board representation. Marginson *et al.* (1993) considers the presence of a personnel director on the Board increased the probability of the function's involvement in changes to work practices. Guest and Baron (2000) and Guest and Hoque (1994) argue that personnel does make a difference to improving business performance. Purcell (1995) reports that where there is a main Board personnel director the function is more involved in business review meetings. Such involvement was recorded at 30 per cent where there was no main Board director, as opposed to 48 per cent where there was such a director. In addition the corporate personnel director was seen as more likely to include local business unit personnel managers in these review meetings. Moreover, Purcell also claimed the existence of a main Board personnel director bolstered the power and influence of the personnel function compared to the finance function. To quote him:

> The presence of a personnel director had a marked effect in reducing the exclusive role of the finance function in the design and administration of profit and share schemes, the provision of information on pay determination, performance related pay for unit managers and for staff.

Corporate personnel committees

Purcell and Ahlstrand (1994) argue, based partly on CLIRS evidence, that corporate personnel control is not necessarily abolished with the demise of the corporate personnel department. They point to the presence of corporate personnel committees which deal with the development and career planning and salary progression of senior executives. Such committees are predominantly controlled by a few top executive directors sometimes without a personnel director presence. Nevertheless such committees are frequently serviced by personnel directors, either acting by themselves or with the assistance of a small corporate department. Fisher *et al.* (1999) in their Australian study report the same institutional arrangement as follows:

> The research does show that 58 per cent of respondents reported that there was a committee of senior executives that met regularly to consider HR matters at the enterprise level. Consequently, the reported poor representation (of personnel directors) on Boards of Directors may not be totally representative of HR involvement in strategic planning.

This point which is developed further later in the book is also accommodated within Brewster *et al.*'s (2000) model through formal, informal and indirect personnel influences on strategic decision making.

Research methodology

This book, therefore, examines the power and influence of personnel/HR directors in the formulation of business and HR strategies in private and public sector organisations as well as small and medium-sized enterprises. To this end, data was sought on:

1   The role and functions of Board of Directors and top management teams in the formation of strategy.
2   The composition and changes in the structure and organisation of membership of Boards of Directors and top management teams etc., and the factors explaining the selection of individuals for membership.
3   The role, functions and management style of the chief executive officer/ managing director in public and private organisations as well as small and medium-sized enterprises (SMEs). This included how they are selected, their career backgrounds, what skills they require of personnel/HR directors, and their attitudes towards the contribution of personnel/HR to the growth and development of the business.
4   The extent of personnel/HR representation on the Board of Directors and top management teams.
5   The profile of the personnel/HR director in terms of age, qualifications, job title, remuneration and involvement in the formulation of business and HR strategies, etc.
6   The career paths of personnel/HR directors to a Board of Directors and/or top management team membership, including their perception of what CEO/ MDs look for in a personnel/HR director.
7   The role and function of personnel/HR directors on the Board of Directors and top management teams etc., in private, public and small and medium-sized enterprises (SMEs).
8   Factors explaining the power and influence of personnel/HR directors on the strategic decisions made by Boards of Directors and top management teams, etc.

The field work to obtain this data was conducted between mid-1995 and the end of 1999 using semi-structured interviews with CEO/MDs and personnel/ HR directors. This interview data was supplemented by a postal questionnaire survey to CEO/MDs of the *Financial Times* top 200 companies, to small and medium-sized enterprises, public sector organisations and to personnel/HR directors.

The interview programme

The interviews with CEO/MDs were structured, *inter alia*, to gain insights into the inter-relationships between the members of the Board, top management team etc.; the process of Board/TMT decision-making; board/TMT styles of operation; the role and background of the chief executive and their relationship with the Board/TMT members; changes in the structure and organisation of the Board; the competencies that a CEO/MD looks for in a personnel/HR director; how they view the contribution of personnel/HR to the Board/TMT decisions and the factors enabling personnel/HR directors to take power and influence and to shape the key decisions of an organisation.

The interview schedule with personnel/HR directors sought information on their career pathways to the top; on their functions as Board/TMT members; on their personal characteristics (i.e. age, qualifications, membership of professional bodies); on their ambitions and motivations; on what skills and competency they perceived CEO/MDs to be looking for in a personnel/HR director; and on the factors explaining their contribution to the key decisions of the Board/TMT.

The authors conducted semi-structured face-to-face interviews with 31 CEO/MDs (including two non-executive directors who were also chairpersons of other companies) and 46 personnel/HR directors employed in a total of 60 organisations in the private and public sectors. Each interview lasted, on average, three hours. Not all interviews were tape recorded as some interviewees objected, whilst in other cases the authors considered the presence of a tape recorder would limit the respondent's openness and thereby the insights to be gained into boardroom and top management teams, interpersonal relationships. In total 11 CEO/MDs and 33 personnel/HR directors agreed to have their interviews taped. Interactions between the interviewer and the interviewee permitted supplementary questioning, clarification and expansion of issues being discussed. The semi-structured interview programme with CEO/MDs and personnel/HR directors provided a more comprehensive and rich understanding of the issues and the interpersonal relationships between the members of the Board of Directors, top management teams etc., than would have been possible with a large-scale postal questionnaire survey. The transcript of each interview was sent to the interviewee who then either signed it as accurate or amended it before doing so to clarify their arguments and points made.

In 30 of the organisations it was possible to conduct interviews with (but separately) both the CEO/MD and the personnel/HR director. It proved impossible to do this in the other 30 organisations due to diary clashes and/or the busy work commitments of both CEO/MD and personnel/HR director. The interviews with CEO/MDs had the added advantage of being a check against any bias and/or exaggeration likely to be in claims made by personnel/HR directors as to their power and influence on the key business decisions of the organisation. CEO/MDs, have responsibility for a Board or TMT's overall performance, and are thus likely to hold a more balanced view of personnel/HR directors' claims to have power and influence than other directors, such as finance or marketing, who are likely to defend their sectional interests.

Gaining access to CEO/MDs is difficult. They are busy individuals and the authors only found it possible to obtain an interview with them through the mediation on their behalf by a third party. The authors had to rely heavily on their network of personnel/HR directors built up over the past 20 years to gain such access. The interview data is not, therefore, drawn from a representative sample of CEO/MDs and personnel/HR directors. Our findings should be regarded as indicative rather than truly representative. Nevertheless the interview programme covered CEO/MDs and personnel/HR directors in a wide range of sectors, including manufacturing, utilities, services and the public sector (see table 1.4).

Postal questionnaires

The main source of data for our analysis was the interview programme. This was supplemented by three small questionnaire surveys – to CEO/MDs of the *Financial Times* top 200 companies, to CEO/MDs of 100 SMEs and to 54 personnel/HR directors. The aim of these surveys was to provide quantitative data and to explore further the ideas and understanding derived from the interview programme. The Top Companies Survey sought to gain further factual information on the presence of personnel/HR directors on Boards of Directors/TMT; the size of Board/TMT membership and their functional composition; the presence of non-executive directors; the career background of CEO/MDs; their style of managing Board/TMT and the extent of personnel/HR director participation in the formulation of key business decisions; the impact of the Cadbury and Hampel Codes of Practice, and the extent of the international activities of the organisation.

Table 1.4 Interviews with CEO/MDs and personnel/HR directors by industrial sector

Sector	CEO/MDs	HR directors
Engineering	2	7
Electronics	1	2
Drink and food	2	4
Chemicals	1	1
Printing	0	2
Steel	1	1
Textiles	4	3
Shipbuilding and repair	2	3
Total manufacturing	13	23
Financial sector	2	4
Utilities	3	3
Retail distribution	1	2
Transport	1	1
Local authorities	7	7
Health trusts	3	3
Universities	1	2
Other public sector	0	1
Grand total	31	46

Financial Times *top 200 companies survey*

The postal questionnaire survey to CEO/MDs of the *Financial Times* top 200 companies only drew a usable response rate of 13 per cent. However, 28 CEO/MDs of these companies returned uncompleted questionnaires informing the authors by personal letter that it was either company policy not to complete questionnaires or that they were too busy to do so. To quote two such instances both from large British owned multinational companies:

> In recent times the increase in requests to participate in questionnaires and surveys has grown enormously and is now at a level where our staff are no longer able to cope with them without serious interference to their normal work. We have, therefore, been obliged to adopt, reluctantly, the policy of not becoming involved in questionnaires, surveys and returns – whatever their nature or extent – unless a statutory requirement. We regret that we are unable to assist you.

and

> I am sure you can appreciate that Mr X continually receives appeals for questionnaires and surveys to be completed, and he has therefore, asked me to let you know that, regretfully, he must decline as he simply does not have time for such requests.

Small and medium-sized enterprises survey

The SME survey provided a benchmark against which to judge their position relative to the larger company and to gain insights into the development of personnel/HR directorships in organisations in the early stages of the growth cycle. The SME survey provided information on the ownership of SMEs (e.g. family owned, partnership); the size and composition of their boards and the presence of personnel/HR directors on these bodies; the career background of the CEO/MD and the management style in running the Board/TMT; the extent of personnel/HR participation in the formation of business strategies; and the contribution to business decisions CEO/MDs most valued from their personnel/HR directors. The sample of SMEs was selected from the *Personnel Managers Yearbook* (1998). Smaller organisations were excluded as the yearbook limits its coverage to firms employing 100 or more and because it was considered few, if any, personnel/HR directors would be represented in firms employing 99 or less. The table below shows the distribution of the sample and the response rate by ownership of enterprise (see Table 1.5).

Personnel/HR director survey

A postal questionnaire was also sent to 54 personnel/HR directors in the private and public sectors resulting in 42 useable responses. The questionnaire collected

Table 1.5 Ownership of small and medium-sized enterprises (SMEs)

Ownership	Number	Number of responses	Percentage response
Private limited company	58	20	34
Public limited company	12	5	42
Family	23	3	13
Partnership	9	3	33
Mutual	8	3	33
Total	100	34	34

information on the presence of personnel/HR on the Board/TMT; on their length of Board membership; on their job title and job responsibilities; on to whom they reported; on their participation in non-personnel decisions; on the extent of their participation in key business decisions; on their assistance to non-executive directors; on their academic and professional qualifications and on their career pathways to directorships.

Data from multinational companies

Chapter 7 is based on data from the 200 top companies' survey and the interview programme with CEO/MDs of which 23 held such a position with a multinational company at corporate head office or at a UK subsidiary of such companies. In addition the sample of independent SMEs included 16 who had significant international trade. Interviews were conducted with eight senior corporate level MNCs executives and 15 senior executives at the subsidiary level of MNCs. Data was also obtained from the interview programme with personnel/HR directors of whom 31 were employed at the corporate head office of a MNC or at a UK subsidiary of a foreign owned multinational. All the MNCs at corporate level were British owned, but at subsidiary level there were six from the United States, two from Norway and one each from Japan, Canada, Australia, Switzerland, Ireland, France and the Netherlands.

Data from public sector organisations

The data for Chapter 8 was obtained from the semi-structured interview programme with CEOs of whom 12 worked in the public sector, and personnel/HR directors of whom 14 worked in the public sector. Nine of the CEOs and personnel/HR directors worked for the same organisation. The data from the interview programme was supplemented by postal questionnaire responses from 13 personnel/HR directors working in the sector. The public sector organisations included local authorities, Health Trusts, universities, water authorities and rail transport.

Other sources of data

Participant observation, as a research method, was rejected as impracticable in view of difficulties in gaining access to attend a representative sample of Board meetings. Furthermore the intrusion of a 'strange' observer into boardroom meetings was likely to alter the behaviour patterns of Board members relative to the typical situation and thereby giving false impressions, and little insight as to how, and who, makes key business decisions.

The authors also drew on primary data provided by the case study organisations in the form of minutes of Board meetings, annual company reports, company newspapers and, on occasion, sight of private correspondence.

The changing environmental context

All 60 organisations operated in a rapidly changing economic, political and technological environment. The economic context for the private sector organisations was increased product market competition stemming from intensifying international competition. Competitive pressures also existed between subsidiary companies (businesses) within the same group for resources from the parent company which in many cases played the role of banker to its constituent companies. The overriding objective for subsidiary companies was to be favoured in resource terms, by corporate headquarters over other subsidiaries, by contributing significantly to profitability of the parent company. However, in the subsidiaries the direction of influence was not just downward from corporate headquarters. Local managers, committed to the survival of their business unit, had opportunities to persuade corporate level to grant them greater local autonomy to improve their financial performance.

For public sector organisations the context was central government, through funding changes, privatisation, compulsory competitive tendering and contractorisation exposing them to market pressures. Privatisation and liberalisation removed the monopoly supplier position of the former nationalised industries which now had to behave in a commercial way. The local authorities were not only coping with compulsory competitive tendering but with major reorganisation to create a unitary system of local government. The health service Trusts operated an internal market, based on the separation of providers and purchasers, including contractual arrangements specifying performance objectives and targets. These contexts emphasised flexibility, performance management, value for money and cost effectiveness.

The political context in which the 60 organisations operated was one of a government accepting the market as the most efficient allocator of goods and services and the best means of providing freedom of choice based on individual responsibility. The liberalisation of product markets and a reduction in public sector provision were the drivers of this policy. Where it was seen as feasible, or appropriate, private business management ideas and practices were being 'imported' into public sector organisations.

The private sector organisations, including the former nationalised industries, had adopted business strategies designed to achieve, *inter alia,* product market competitiveness, grow the business and enhance competitive advantage. In a ship-building company (a foreign-owned subsidiary) the directors saw its productivity deficit relative to their competitors being offset by greater utilisation of existing employees. A drinks firm (a subsidiary of a domestic multinational) sought to maintain its competitiveness over other subsidiaries in the Group by persuading the corporate board to provide resources to finance an investment in new production techniques which would take its operations from the 'nineteenth century into the space age'. The privatised utilities sought to enhance competitive advantage through product diversification (e.g. adding to electricity supply the provision of telecommunications and water services), the penetration of international markets, organic growth, mergers and takeovers and joint ventures. To achieve their business objectives the private organisations empowered the business unit directors to develop them but within constraints set by the corporate headquarters.

All organisations were seeking to change organisational culture and employee attitudes. The majority of private organisations were persuading their employees to be more cooperative and to understand better the needs of the business if it were to survive and their job security be enhanced. In public sector organisations and the former nationalised industries the desired culture change was from a public service ethos to a more commercial one, with set performance targets to deliver service outputs at reduced costs. The HR context in all 60 organisations was the need to reduce workforces, implement flexible working practices, recruit staff with new attitudes, secure a training and development culture, introduce appropriate pay and reward systems, business oriented consultation and information giving machinery, and, in unionised firms, reform collective bargaining arrangements.

2 The board of directors and top management teams

Research in the 60 organisations revealed that private sector Boards of Directors exist at three levels, namely corporate, subsidiary and business unit. The large private sector company normally has a corporate head office overseeing a number of subsidiary companies (sometimes also called divisions) which in turn are often divided into smaller companies called business units. For example one of the organisations cooperating with our research had its corporate headquarters in Edinburgh but had a number of subsidiary divisions in brewing, retail and leisure and which in turn had business units within them.

In the public sector the research showed there were Boards of Directors in National Health Service Trusts whilst in local authorities and universities there were top management teams (TMTs). However, in both the private (at both corporate and subsidiary levels) and public sectors the research revealed the existence of an Executive Group, chaired by the CEO/MD, whose membership was selected by that person. One of the Group's functions was to devise the organisation's strategy and take it for approval, amendment or rejection to the Board of Directors or in the case of local government to the Council. Following approval of the strategy the Executive Group then had responsibility for its implementation (see below).

Public limited company boards

The main PLC Board of Directors is a legal entity with its members carrying responsibilities for the company's aims and functions in accordance with its Articles of Association as registered under the Companies Act (1985). Main Boards of Directors are accountable to the company's owners, namely the stockholders. In modern capitalist societies accountability is largely financial with the Board of Directors taking responsibility to ensure the sufficient generation of profit to pay dividends, to increase the share price to retain existing and to attract new share-holders and to prevent a hostile take-over of the company by another company. Normally this means fulfilling shareholder expectations as determined by competition in the financial markets between alternative sources of savings. In exercising its responsibilities the Board is the official entity which monitors corporate policy and approves longer-term strategies. Strategic decisions can cover areas

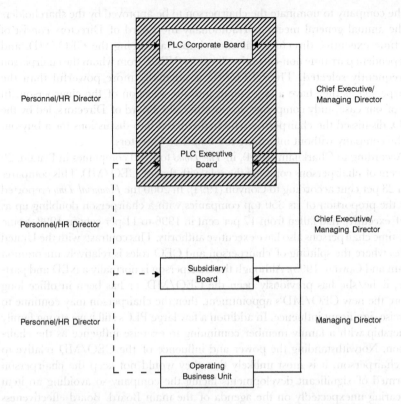

Figure 2.1 Boards of directors at various levels and links through CEO/MDs and personnel/HR directors.

Note: Shaded PLC box represents close interaction between corporate board and executive group. Unbroken line is CEO/MD membership of higher board. Personnel directors responsible to CEO/MD of their own unit however have a broken line to more senior personnel directors and corporate level.

such as dividend distribution, the percentage of retained profits to be reinvested in the business, major capital expenditures, corporate assets growth, sales and market penetration at home and overseas and the means to develop the company for example organically or by merger and acquisition or both.

However, our research revealed that it is not at the Board level that business strategy is formulated. This is done by the CEO/MD Executive Group which then takes the strategy it has devised to the Board for approval. The power house for developing and growing the business is not the Board but the CEO/MD Executive Group. The role of the CEO/MD Executive Group is analysed later in the chapter.

Parent company Boards of Directors are formally led by a chairperson elected by the shareholders at the annual general meeting of the company. The chair of the Board of Directors is formally the person who matters most in terms of authority, power and influence. However, in practice, it is usual for the directors of the company to nominate the chairperson to be approved by the shareholders at the annual general meeting. Traditionally the Board of Directors consist of full-time executive directors, the most important being the CEO/MD, and independent part-time non-executive directors (NEDs) from whom the chairperson is frequently selected. The CEO/MD is normally more powerful than the chairperson as they have a large input into the selection of the chairperson. In one of our case study companies, for instance, the Board of Directors, led by the CEO, dismissed the chairperson who had entered into discussions for a buy-out of the company without informing the Board of Directors.

According to Charkham (1994), in *The Times* top 100 companies in Britain, 26 per cent of chairpersons combine the role with that of CEO/MD. This compares with 23 per cent according to Conyon (1994). In 2000 the *Financial Times* reported that the proportion of its 350 top companies with a chairperson doubling up as chief executive had fallen from 17 per cent in 1996 to 11 per cent in 1998. Some part-time chairpersons also have executive authority. This contrasts with the United States where the splitting of chairperson and CEO roles is relatively uncommon (Aram and Cowen, 1995). Although the chairperson is normally a NED and part-time, if he/she has previously been the CEO/MD, or has been in office long before the new CEO/MD's appointment, then the chairperson may continue to exercise significant influence. In addition a few large PLCs still have strong family ownership with a family member continuing to exercise influence as the chairperson. Notwithstanding the power and influence of the CEO/MD relative to the chairperson, it is most unlikely that they would not keep the chairperson informed of significant developments facing the company so avoiding an item appearing unexpectedly on the agenda of the main Board. Board effectiveness depends on a strong trust relationship between chairperson and CEO/MD. It is commonly held that the chairperson's job is to chair Board meetings, whereas the CEO/MD's job is to run the company successfully.

The literature on boards of Directors has discussed over a number of years a divergence of interests between Board of Directors and shareholders (Pahl and Winkler, 1974; Gordon, 1966; Burnham, 1962; Berle and Means, 1932). It is argued for British companies that shareholders interests are maximised by short-term stock market gains. This is often seen as in conflict with the interests of full-time directors whose goals are likely to be longer term, for example, the growth of company size rather than short-term profits. The Board of Directors, traditionally dominated by full-time executive directors, therefore are said to manipulate organisations in their own interests and not that of shareholders.

Generally, large PLCs are regarded in the business world as more prestigious and are likely to pay higher salaries and offer greater personal standing than smaller companies. On the question of rewards a *Management Today* survey (1999) showed CEOs received remuneration packages far in advance of other directors and employees of their companies. Indeed the survey reported some CEO/MDs have share option packages up to eight times greater than their annual salary. The highest paid CEOs were found in the United States followed by Britain and France, Australia, Japan, Germany and Sweden in that order. The financial rewards of

CEO/MDs became a cause of public concern in Britain in the 1990s and led to the establishment by the Confederation of British Industry of the Greenbury Committee (1995) to investigate the remuneration levels of directors in large PLCs. Greenbury recommended a Code of Practice to contain the following:

- Remuneration committees to report separately from the board.
- Details of remuneration include full pay and bonuses for each director, including pensions, to be made public.
- One year notice periods to terminate the directors contract to be the norm with two years the maximum.
- Greater emphasis to be placed on the provision of long-term bonus schemes rather than options and annual bonuses, to be accepted in a vote of shareholders.
- Bonuses to be based on demanding performance criteria.
- Directors' pay increases should be 'be sensitive to' pay rises elsewhere in the company.

However, despite Greenbury's desire to exercise increased control over CEO/MDs remuneration through NEDs, critics have pointed out that many NEDs of companies sitting on remuneration committees are also executive directors in other companies. Since remuneration committees are concerned with parity etc., executive directors are in a position to influence their own reward package through their behaviour as NEDs of other companies' remuneration committees. This reduces the motivation of NEDs to limit the pay of executives in one company as they in turn can influence theirs as executive directors in another. This divergence of interests between shareholders and executive directors continues as a matter of public concern in Britain where Cadbury (1992) and Hampel (1998) Reports have espoused boards to appoint more independent NEDs to achieve a better balance of power between the two. In 1999 the DTI issued a consultative document on directors' remuneration to which the TUC responded (TUC General Council Report, 2000), by recommending, amongst other items, that performance criteria should take account of the long term so as to encourage investment and organic growth. A review of boardroom remuneration by the Hay Group (2000) indicated a greater interest in long-term financial plans for executive directors based on a balanced score card-taking account of broader criteria including financial, customer, process and people related issues. It was felt that by taking a longer-term view of bonus plans the interests of stockholders and executives could be better integrated.

The purpose of the Cadbury Report (1992) was to ensure greater transparency in public listed companies and to increase shareholder influence over executive management. It proposed the appointment of a minimum of three NEDs and the setting up of sub-committees of the main Board of Directors to be chaired by a NED (Pettigrew and McNulty, 1995). The Stock Exchange's Combined Code recommends NEDs should comprise 33 per cent of Board members. According to the Institute of Management (1999) on average Boards have 40 per cent NEDs and 60 per cent executive directors. Cadbury's proposed sub-committees of Boards included audit and remuneration, although many companies have established in addition a nominations committee. NEDs bring to the Board of Directors a plethora of experience and skills including knowledge of 'city finances', domestic and international markets, suppliers of products and services, specialist technical knowledge, broader experience of business and domestic and overseas government relations. Their selection is dependent on the circumstances of the particular company and the existing skill mix on the Board of Directors. Audit committees arose out of The Stock Exchange concern over the misreporting of company financial returns. Nominations committees, chaired and composed of NEDs, are to provide greater objectivity and transparency in the recruitment of senior executives including NEDs themselves. In this way it is hoped to reduce the ability of CEO/MDs to appoint their own friends to the Board.

The size, and composition, of main PLC Boards is becoming larger. Brookes survey (1979) showed a mean of 7 members with a range from a low of 2 to a high of 20 whilst Conyon and Mallin (1997) report the average size of the main Board of *The Times* top 100 companies to be 12 directors and that for the top 250 to be 9. Our questionnaire survey, based on the top 200 companies, showed a mean size of 10 for a main PLC Board with a range of 8 to 20. The interview programme with corporate executive directors put the average size of Board at 10. This increasing size reflects the complexity of the contemporary company, together with changes in public policy espousing additional NEDs on Boards. The top 200 companies survey revealed a 50 per cent split between executive directors and NEDs. However two of the nine companies in the interview programme had a majority of executive directors and two a majority of NEDs, indicative of the diversity to be found. All our surveyed companies had more NEDs on the Board than the minimum three advocated by Cadbury.

Regarding director age and length of board service our main PLC Boards survey produced a mean of 54 years with a range of 48 to 58 and 6 years for length of service. The dominant length of service varied between two and five years with 58 per cent of respondents having five years or less service on PLC Boards.

In addition to NEDs our questionnaire survey and interview programme revealed a main Board typically comprising executive directors, the CEO/MD, the finance director, and the MDs of operating subsidiaries. The presence of a director of marketing and/or personnel was less common. For publicly quoted companies the appointment of a finance director is a requirement for London Stock Exchange listing. Table 2.1 shows, from our research, for main PLC Boards the executive director composition by management function.

The dominance of the top three is as expected. Some of the company secretaries were also responsible for finance. Personnel/HR and marketing at 4 and 7 respectively were less well represented on the parent Boards.

The main sub-committees of parent PLC Boards of Directors included audit, remuneration and nominations all chaired by NEDs. Audit committees receive, monitor and comment on reports covering the company's financial performance.

Table 2.1 Functional composition of executive directors on parent PLC boards of directors

PLC parent board	Total
CEO/MD	26
Finance	24
Operations	19
Company secretary	9
Marketing/sales	7
HRM	4
Information technology	4
Others[1]	2
Total quality	1

Source: Questionnaires

Note: 1 Others included strategic development, commercial, change management and property.

Remuneration committees are concerned with the salaries, bonuses and non-monetary emoluments of executive and NED directors. Nomination committees deal with appointments to the position of Board membership. This can involve recruitment from the external market and/or promotions within the company. These sub-committees are responsible for their work to the whole Board of Directors via the chair of the Board. The role of the personnel/HR director in these committees is analysed in Chapter 3. Despite the Cadbury Report our interview programme revealed that in six Boards, CEO/MDs were members of the nominations committee and in one case, of both the appointments and remuneration committees. In another company there was a joint nominations and remuneration committee but it was chaired by an NED. Conyon and Mallin (1997) also show in their review of compliance with Cadbury that by 1995 49 per cent of 297 companies surveyed had still not established a nominations committee. This compared with only two per cent for audit committees and two for remuneration committees.

Pettigrew and McNulty (1995) and McNulty and Pettigrew (1996b) in discussing the power and influence of NEDs on Boards expressed concern over their ability to do so effectively. They postulate that the Board context and structures (including access to managerial expertise and resources) into which the NED enter has been decided previously by the history, culture and executive directors past and present and therefore NEDs rely more on 'relationship influence' and the 'will' to use it. Notwithstanding this the appointment of too many NEDs is likely to cause the Board to become bogged down in discussion and to lose some of its effectiveness. However, too many executive directors relative to NEDs carries the danger of the board not giving sufficient attention to the advice and broader business experience of NEDs.

Divisional and/or subsidiary companies

Our research covered 23 subsidiary companies and showed they had a mean top management team (TMT) size of eight directors with a range of five to fourteen. Although titled 'directors' they did not carry the same legal responsibilities as did the parent PLC executive directors and NEDs. It was not uncommon, however, for these subsidiary companies, TMTs to have NEDs. Unlike those on PLC Boards they were not independent as they were employees of the corporate body representing that interest on the subsidiary company TMT. Examples include the local public transport company TMT, about to be privatised, which had on its TMT the chairperson and another director from the main corporate Board. In the private sector a long-established Scottish textile company's (owned by a major multinational company (MNC)) TMT had a chairperson and one NED in membership who were executive directors of the corporate body.

The research revealed considerable diversity regarding the status and relationship of subsidiaries to their corporate headquarters. Several of the businesses were registered in the UK and the Irish Republic as limited companies for legal and tax purposes with their own Board of Directors, although the parent company was sole shareholder. Many subsidiaries were foreign owned operating in the UK. Other UK businesses had long histories often identified with particular geographical areas. Some as profit centres had considerable autonomy of marketing and sales strategies whereas others were simply cost centres operating with responsibility for marketing, sales and distribution lying elsewhere. The latter, as manufacturing units, operated within cost structures laid down by the parent company. All to a greater or lesser degree were constrained by corporate policies in financial, marketing, purchasing and personnel areas.

The corporate strategy literature emphasises a top down approach to strategy formation and implementation thereby playing down the importance of strategy formation in subsidiary businesses. Such emphasis ignores the complexity of decision-making as a political process with organisational actors coping with external environmental uncertainties. Contemporary organisations are potentially unstable with multiple values and interests, markets, technological and political influences causing a continuous stream of new ideas, interventions and reorganisations to amend and challenge established strategies (Mintzberg and Waters, 1985). As a result upward, horizontal and diagonal influences on strategy are apparent as subsidiaries cope with contingencies arising from particular internal and market pressures, feeding these upward, inwards and outwards to and from the corporate centre. This has been acknowledged in the work of Purcell and Ahlstrand (1994) and Ferner and Varul (2000, a) who argue that subsidiary companies have to have the business strategy they devise approved by the corporate centre, which then monitors the outcomes of the subsidiary's strategy.

In our research most subsidiaries of manufacturing companies reported not only on problems arising from the implementation of strategies decided higher up the organisation, but also on initiating their own solutions to problems. Several had introduced team/cellular working practices and others HR and quality initiatives. If successful these new working practices were discussed at the higher organisational level and if accepted rolled out to other subsidiaries within the corporate group. However, not all subsidiary strategic initiatives resulted in improved corporate collaboration as some had been undertaken in competition with other subsidiaries within the corporate group. In some cases the corporate centre was regarded as distant and therefore local Executive Groups of directors

---

Case study 2.1

This case is based on a large international multi-divisional company in the brewing and distilling industry. Questions are asked at the end of the case to which specific answers are provided at the end of the chapter.

A subsidiary company's strategic initiative and the HR function's contribution

During the early 1980s the Group suffered a decline in profitability causing concern as to the future viability of one of its subsidiaries – company A. The CEO/MD of the PLC Group threatened to build a 'greenfield site brewery' in north west England where company A sold over 40 per cent of its output. Company A's TMT recognised that in a multinational corporation the corporate head office could move the product around various sites in search of profit. In the early 1980s company A had contributed around 67 per cent of Group profits. In 1984 the TMT of company A initiated a business plan for the 1990s and beyond, which would diversify its product range. The business strategy also necessitated securing £150 million from the Group to invest in new technology, which in the words of the managing director 'would take the brewing operation from the nineteenth century into the space age'. This business plan, *inter alia*, included that over the period 1980 to 1989 the subsidiary's labour force would be reduced from 4,000 to 900.

The company A MD made representations to the parent Board, and secured the necessary new investment. The personnel director's role was significant. He had, for many years, participated in shaping the strategic direction of the business. Its three previous MDs had held the position of personnel director at company A which had a TMT of five directors including both the MD and personnel director. The five directors constituted a Managing Director Committee which shaped the business plan in which the people implications had received full consideration. The plan encouraged a more participative style of management (traditionally company A had a long history of paternalism), extensive investment in training as new technology changed process workers' skills from hands-on to knowledge based, and job enlargement. Craft workers required training to cope with the new technology. The local personnel directors, past and present, had shaped the culture of the business over the last ten years by inculcating in both management and employees an attitude of acceptance of continuous change. The

---

Case study 2.1 *continued*

implementation plan was driven by the personnel department which had responsibility to co-ordinate and negotiate changes with trade unions and engaged the personnel director of the subsidiary in chairing the Brewery Council, a joint management and trade union body. The implementation of the new business plan brought improvement in profits to both company A and the Group whose share value also increased. The motivation and enthusiasm for devising and implementing the business strategy stemmed from the company A's directors determination to retain production on the present site rather than see it transferred to business units elsewhere.

Questions

Q. 1   Explain the motivation behind local subsidiary management's business strategy initiative. How was Group approval achieved?

Q. 2   Why was the personnel director a major player in devising this strategy?

---

concerned with their own survival initiated policies, subject to approval by corporate headquarters, which often incurred considerable capital expenditure. An illustration of a subsidiary company strategic business initiative in which the personnel/HR function played a significant part is described in the case study below.

Boards of directors in small and medium-sized enterprises

Definitions of SMEs contain two criteria, namely numbers employed and independent owners who determine their own policies (Bacon *et al.*, 1996). The criteria of independence (namely the absence of control from public shareholders and a higher level of executive authority) is important as it prevents confusion with the many small companies which are divisionalised and/or decentralised organisations of large companies. There is no agreement in the literature on the numbers of employees that constitute an SME. The numbers vary from enterprises employing less than 25 to those employing just less than 500. The Workplace Employee Relations Survey (1998) reduced the size limit for firms to participate in the survey from 25 to between 10 and 24. The European Commission identifies 'small' as a company with between 10 and 99 employees and 'medium' companies employing between 100 and 499. The UK Department of Trade and Industry' s criteria for the small firm is the employment of between one and 49 employees and for medium size the employment of between 50 and 249 employees.

Our researches showed the size of SME Boards of Directors to be smaller than PLC boards. The SME mean size of Board of Directors was six with a range of three to fourteen. This compares with a mean of ten with a range of eight to twenty for PLC Boards of Directors. The smaller Boards of Directors in SMEs is

Table 2.2 Functional executive directors' presence on SME boards of directors

Functions	SME board numbers
CEO/MDs	34
Finance	31
Operations	29
Market/sales	28
Company secretary	17
Others[1]	16
Personnel/HR	15
Information technology	6
Total quality	5

Source: Questionnaires

Note: 1 Others include technical development, business development, fleet, security, head of strategy and research and development.

the result of their smaller size and greater financial stringency. The functional composition of executive directors on SME Boards as revealed in our survey is shown in Table 2.2.

As with the PLC Boards the most frequently represented are the CEO/MD and the directors of finance and operations. At 15 (44 per cent) personnel/HR representation on SME Boards is higher than on main PLC Boards of Directors (15 per cent). The smaller employment size of SMEs compared to PLC Boards means there is less scope for functional specialisation and formalisation in SMEs (Newton and Hunt, 1997).

SMEs, unlike publicly listed companies, do not have to engage NEDs, and are not subject to the Cadbury Report (1992). Nevertheless several of the sample companies did have NEDs.

Mileham (1996) argued that many SMEs are not professionally managed and that the engagement of good independent NEDs brings to their boardroom professional business expertise which can improve their long-term planning and networking with the wider business community. A survey by British Telecommunications for the *Sunday Times* Enterprise Network (*Sunday Times*, 17 September, 2000) found that 72 per cent of middle market firms thought the use of NEDs benefited the company. The main benefits were seen as external experience (54 per cent), impartiality (38 per cent) and market understanding (20 per cent). However, only 53 per cent of CEO/MDs of smaller companies considered NEDs brought benefits to the company compared with 88 per cent for CEO/MDs of larger SMEs. The same survey reported NEDs to have on average 18 days contact with the company and to receive fees in the range of £12,000 to £15,000 per annum. In some companies included in our survey NEDs were given share options but there were those who opposed such a practice claiming it can raise questions about the independence and the objectivity of the NEDs' advice.

Top management teams in public sector organisations

The mean size of TMT in the public sector organisations surveyed was ten. However, director representation varied markedly between the different organisations making up the public sector. Top management teams in local authorities were generally larger than in the civil service, universities and in the Health Trusts. In local government TMTs do not formally make policy as this is the responsibility of the elected councillors. Council committees are chaired by members of the Council. The most common Council committees were education, social work, housing, road maintenance, refuge collection, parks and leisure, etc. The management officer structure of local authorities mirrors the organisation of committees with a director servicing the work of the committees. In the local authorities participating in our research there existed Council Management Teams which were in effect TMTs. The purpose and function of these teams was to devise policy options for consideration and debate by the councillors. After approval of a policy, the management team was responsible for its implementation. The TMT was also responsible for the interpretation and implementation of new central government relevant legislation and for advising councillors on the potential options, especially sensitive when the political control of the council is different from that of the central government making the said legislation.

In large local authorities the TMT consisting of CEO and all heads of department can be very large. The average, for the nine authorities investigated, was 14 officials in the TMT, although this ranged from eight in a small authority to 30 in the largest. Personnel directors as heads of department have traditionally had a presence on the TMT. CEOs reported the difficulties in trying to manage groups of this size to produce effective strategy and policy. In these local authorities our research revealed the existence of 'inner cabinets' consisting of the CEO: three or more senior directors met frequently to establish strategic and related policy directions, and their resource implications, before putting it to the full TMT. Members of the 'inner cabinet' normally comprised the largest departments, plus directors with vision from smaller departments. In the majority of our participating local authorities, personnel and finance directors were in membership of the CEO's 'inner cabinet'. This like the CEO/MD Executive Group in the private sector was the point at which key business decisions were made and then taken forward for approval at the appropriate level in the local authorities's decision-making structure.

In 1993 Hospital Trusts were introduced into the National Health Service. To a degree the private business sector model was copied with the introduction of Trust Boards of Directors consisting of both executive directors and NEDs (Ferlie *et al.*, 1996). The chairperson, a part-time NED, and other NEDs are appointed in Scotland by the Health Minister of the Scottish Parliament and in the rest of the UK by the Secretary of State for Health. The number of Trust Board executive directors is set out in the 1990 Health and Community Care Act, e.g. CEO, medical, nursing, finance, whilst another director such as operational, contracts and/or HR may be appointed by the Trust Board itself. In the five Trusts four had appointed a personnel/HR director to the main Trust Board. Our research revealed a mean Trust Board size of 11, normally six NEDs, including the chairperson, and five executive directors. The purpose and function of the Trust Boards was to approve and monitor the work of the CEO Group (see below), to hear proposed policy changes, make suggestions, amend and approve them. Our research in the five hospital Trusts also revealed the existence of a CEO Executive Group membership of which was by invitation of the CEO. As in the private sector, it was in this group that strategy was formulated and then taken to the Trust Board for approval, rejection, reference back etc. In all the Trusts there was a personnel/ HR director in membership of the Executive Group. Given the financial stringencies imposed by government much of the strategic activity was aimed at finding ways to improve performance and reduce costs.

In Britain the university sector has also undergone significant changes, in that over the last decade there has been a large increase in student numbers but within a context of tight financial control. As institutions, in which a Senate comprising academics decides academic policy and a Court, consisting of academics and representatives of the local community, controls the finances and staffing policies, the scope for a specialist personnel function has been limited. Nevertheless the numbers employed in personnel/HR within the university sector has grown. Within universities environmental changes have made this system of governance inappropriate and has led to the establishment of University Management Groups/ Executives made up of senior academic officers who meet more regularly to devise strategies and policies for the growth and development of the university and which are then taken to the Senate and Court for approval.

In the pre-1992 university included in our sample, the personnel director was not a member of its University Management Group/Executive but his attendance was required when an HR issue was under discussion, which was very frequently. The university finance director had the same status. At the post-1992 university in the sample the personnel director held the title senior Vice Principal, had responsibilities for overseas marketing and was a major player in the TMT.

The chief executive officer/managing director groups of PLCs

The HRM literature has little to say about the workings of Boards of Directors, taking them as a given with little or no investigating into their processes of business and HR decision-making. However, an exception is the work of Brewster and Larsen (2000), based on Elsik's (1992) model, and which is discussed in the next chapter. There is even less literature which analyses the social interaction between key players based on a model of organisational politics and relationships of dependency. As we have already pointed out our researches identified the existence, in both private and public sectors, of a CEO/MDs Executive Group which was the actual location at which strategic decisions were taken after which they were presented to the Board of Directors or appropriate bodies (e.g. a local Council) for approval, amendment or rejection. This Group was the power house (the heart beat) for the development of the business, the local authority and health trusts etc.

The Executive Group usually comprised a number of full-time executive directors. In the private sector it also included a number of individual's having the title director but not membership of the Board of Directors. In both the private and public sectors all members of the CEO/MD Executive Group were appointed by the CEO/ MD often in consultation with chairperson and other members. It was the Executive Group that formulated the organisation's business and related strategies including HR to achieve competitive advantage. The CEO/MD Executive Group developed policy and strategy, engaged in planning and budgetary considerations and implemented these in pursuit of the organisation's success. In both the public and private sectors the Executive Group commanded the detailed knowledge and expertise necessary for making the business a success. In local authorities these functions were performed by the 'inner cabinet' system described above. Table 2.3 shows the composition, by management functions, of the CEO/MD Executive Group present in our private sector case study organisations.

The three most common management functions represented on the Executive Group (namely CEO/MD, finance and operations) were the same as those found in private sector main PLC Boards. However, both personnel/HR and marketing have higher representation on the CEO/MD Executive Group compared with their presence on main PLC Board whilst the opposite is the case with financial directors. The interview programme revealed that in both the private and public sectors finance directors were often considered by CEO/MDs to be the most locked into their function, and relatively more problematic in terms of integrating them into the executive team. As one CEO/MD put it: 'Finance directors are on "tram lines". They emphasise economy and cost efficiency, but not risk and the creative use of resources'.

Compared with the PLC and Health Trust Boards of Directors the CEO/MD Executive Group was smaller in size, met more regularly (once every week compared to the once per month of main Boards) was less formal and had a more flexible business agenda. The members of the CEO/MD Executive Group were also younger with a mean age of 50 (range 42 to 53) compared to 54 (range 48 to 58) for PLC Boards.

Table 2.3 Executive director composition of CEO/MD executive group at PLC level

CEO/MD PLC executive group	Number
CEO/MD	26
Finance	21
Operations	20
HRM	19
Marketing/sales	14
Company secretary	11
Information technology	10
Quality	4
Others[1]	2

Source: Questionnaires

Note: 1 Others included strategic development and property.

PLC Boards, Trust Boards and local authority TMTs perform two main functions. First, they anticipate the future and, second, they monitor the work performance of the CEO/MDs Executive Group. The CEO/MD Executive Group in both private and public sectors also engaged to some degree in both these activities. In reality, however, it is more concerned in looking forward and less involved in monitoring than is the main Board. This is not to argue the chairperson and other NEDs are superfluous to strategic decision-making because they are members of the main Board, which is constitutionally the final authority on approving the strategy. They have thus an input into strategy formation when the Board receives the proposed strategy from the Executive Group. Nevertheless it is the latter body where new ideas grow and develop, are clarified and responsibility given either to an executive director or increasingly to a multi-disciplinary project team to carry out the necessary background research to strategy formulation. When the strategy has been fully developed the chief executive submits it to the main Board for approval. The Board of Directors can then exercise its authority to approve the proposal, question or amend it, delay or reject it. However, in the organisations cooperating with our work the Board approved the CEO/MD Executive Group proposed strategy but only after receiving satisfactory answers to their probing questions. This process is typified by the following quote from the CEO of a major utility, 'Most of the ideas originate at the Executive Group with the really big decisions going on to the corporate Board. The corporate Board can amend and delay by asking for more information'.

Nevertheless in one of our case study companies the CEO Executive Group felt strong enough to ignore the advice of the Board of Directors and proceeded to 'buy' another company. Our findings are reinforced by those of Brannen *et al.* (1976) on employee directors on Boards of Directors in the steel industry and who concluded that the main Board was not the organisational point at which policies and strategies can be influenced. To quote them 'We suggest that the final appraisal of policy suggestions takes place at the CEOs advisory committee'.

Notwithstanding the above argument, the Brookes (1979) research paper 'Boards of Directors in British Industry' showed between 35 per cent and 42 per cent of main board respondents claim to have generated strategic decisions compared to ratifying decisions made elsewhere. Brookes, however, believed the main board of directors had exaggerated their influence. As we saw in Chapter 1 this problem is not uncommon with self-reporting methods, especially with data gathered by questionnaire, where the respondents may claim a positive input but which in reality is not as important as claimed. Brookes also recognised his sample to be biased towards small organisations but reported that as the size of organisation increased, the percentage of main board numbers claiming to generate their own strategy and related policies diminished.

The CEO/MD Executive Group in both the private and public sectors had power because it commanded the company's resources including management expertise, met regularly, was less formal, was continuously adaptable and had the potential to form a cohesive group under the leadership of the CEO/MD. As Legge (1978) says, 'It is with regard to how decisions on policy and strategy are formed, developed and implemented that takes us to the heart of power within organisations'.

There was a relationship of dependency between the main Board and the CEO/ MD Group but it was much in favour of the latter. The main Board with its part-time chairperson and other NEDs, meeting less frequently, did not possess the necessary financial, customer, operational, HR and internal cultural knowledge and expertise to match the full-time Executive. Additionally the processes of social interaction between main Board members and the Executive team were not wholly formal. Generally interaction between CEO/MDs and chairpersons was frequent. It would have been a sign of a deteriorating relationship should an important policy proposal arrive on the main Board agenda without the chairperson's knowledge and earlier consultation on matters important to the Board. This dependency relationship required the CEO/MD and the chairperson to engage in a process of communication, persuasion and accommodation prior to any formal approval being granted by the main Board. The argument of Pahl and Winkler (1974) that the ability of the CEO/MD Group to control the timing and amount of information placed before the main Board are the key to their power fits our analysis. However, our research does not support their view that the CEO/MD Groups manipulate the information to which they have access in order to gain their desired ends. The interview programme with both CEO/MDs and personnel/HR directors revealed both groups believed that such a relationship would suggest a complete lack of trust and was unlikely to lead to the long-term success of the organisation.

Aram and Cowen (1995) offer an American analysis which argues that where main Boards comprise of inquiring NEDs and open minded CEOs there is a greater likelihood of creating economic value and thus satisfying the interests of shareholders. To quote the authors, 'Mutual trust appears to be an extra ingredient that brings competent management and a competent board together to form an effective policy group'.

In our research CEO/MDs keep chairpersons and NEDs informed, prior to and between Board meetings, for example by holding separate meetings with NEDs, having both executives and NEDs participate in two day conferences off site, and through participation in sub-committees of the Board and in project teams with executive directors e.g. on mergers, acquisitions and management including HR problems.

Nevertheless there are occasions when the CEO/MD can 'lose the plot' and be forced to resign by the main Board. Such occasions are likely to arise when a PLC is experiencing difficult times in the form of falling profits and a declining stock price. In such circumstances the relationship between the chairperson and CEO/MD may deteriorate to the extent of strong disagreement, making it possible for the chairperson, with shareholder backing, to dismiss the CEO/ MD. If ownership of shares is widespread this can still prove a difficult strategy to mount, although in recent years the support of a few large institutional shareholders has made the difference. An important consideration in this regard is whether the firm's shareholding has a narrow or broad distribution since the former provides greater scope for institutional shareholders to change the CEO/ MD. Such an incident happened in Britain in 1999 when the CEO of the Mirror Group of newspapers was forced to resign by the institutional shareholders who between them held 25 per cent of the total equity. The institutions considered the Mirror Group shares were not delivering an adequate return, and therefore management was not performing adequately. As reported in *Scotland on Sunday* (31 January 1999):

> Rather than wait for the executive to come up with a new business plan or institute a salvage operation ... the institutions got rid of the old guard to bring in some new blood to knock the balance sheet into shape with a vengeance.

Changes in the types of boards of directors

The academic literature identifies two dominant Board types. First there is the functional Board consisting of CEO/MDs and heads of departments/functions and which is found mainly in dominant single product organisations. Second there are financially driven business focused operational Boards of the multi-divisional company consisting of operational MDs with the support of some functional directors (Purcell and Ahlstrand, 1994). Functional Boards still exist, especially in SMEs and in the public sector, with specialist managers contributing their departmental input to decisions based on technical or professional knowledge and expertise. However, it is our research finding that there has been a metamorphoses in Board management type, with a shift towards more open project-based teams, especially within CEO/MD Executive Groups. The pace and complexity of change is pertinent here in that the CEO/MD cannot be involved directly in the total array of policy formation. Ad hoc multi-disciplinary project teams are therefore set up to investigate and make recommendations to an Executive Group. According to Katzenbach (1998) CEO/MDs cope with increasing workload by delegation and team working. Decision-making which has become increasingly subject to external environmental uncertainty and complexity, now requires greater openness in relationships between directors and a collective awareness of the Board as a team. As Aram and Cowen (1995) put it, 'The key towards a value creating board lies in the development of a more open attitude on the part of the CEO'.

In the contemporary fast changing context both functional and operational Board types are being replaced by the more open collective team boards using more standing sub-committees and ad hoc project teams. This implies executive directors, like all other managers, have to undertake a wider range of duties than was the case a decade ago. Chinese walls or chimneys between operations and functions are breaking down. It was clear from the interview programme with CEO/MDs, in both private and public sectors, that they expect members of the Board and their Executive Group to be business people first and functional and operational directors second. This research finding is developed throughout the rest of the book.

According to Charkham (1994) in Britain the collegiate Board (collective/project team) is not traditional (but is more so in Europe) where the values and attitudes of senior management support individual leadership. Burns (1961) has argued for the necessity of an individual champion with sufficient power and determination to push through organisational change. In contrast the open project team type Board calls for a CEO/MD style which is transparent, open and business focused. Openness of communication including cross fertilisation of ideas between functions, and in the international context between overseas subsidiaries, encourages better decision-making through information research and thorough consideration of strategic options (Dooley and Fryxell, 1999; Katzenbach, 1998; Aram and Cowen, 1995). A Board based on open communications may take longer to formulate and approve strategic decisions, but it is more likely to get it right, and collective responsibility is more likely to be accepted, both of which make implementation easier.

However, the CEO open team group requires qualification as circumstances can arise where single leadership is essential, for example, when the business object-ive is clear but time is of the essence if the company is to survive. In such circum-stances the leadership style is likely to be less open and more dictatorial. There is no time for democracy. Business is not about democracy it is about survival. Expert knowledge is based on a division of management functions, but these are secondary to the business orientation of the Board.

Notwithstanding, today power and influence are more equally distributed between directors, hence CEO/MD Executive Groups are more participative and flexible than the traditional functional TMT or indeed the formal PLC Board. As highlighted by Kakabadse (1991), who asked executives what skills they needed to perform their jobs effectively, the quality of inter-personal relations being rated most significant. Pettigrew and NcNulty (1995) studying NEDs, highlight the social skills of assertiveness, persuasion, collaboration, diplomacy, logical argument, trust and respect to improve their influence in decision-making. The open project team type is seen as most appropriate for achieving organisational innovation (Herriott and Pemberton, 1995) to match the faster pace of environmental change. Kakabadse (1991), discussing TMTs, refers to 'thinkers' who reflect on and integrate the work of the board. McKiernan and Urquhart (1996) in discussing inter-personal relations refer to 'intentional cultures' where board members establish mature relationships based on collaboration and participation to cope with difficult business problems. The emergence of the project focused team at CEO/MD Executive Group level provides the opportunity for the chief executive to develop directors by giving them leadership responsibility as MDs of subsidiaries and other important projects. The selection of directors to lead project teams, often outside their traditional area of expertise, is clearly important for their development as well as that of the organisation.

CEO/MDs their backgrounds and management styles

Given the importance our research has revealed about the influence of the CEO/ MD, it is worthwhile investigating their career backgrounds and management styles as factors influencing their Executive Group's performance. They are full-time executives who chair their Executive Group and are members of the Board of Directors or as in local authorities the top management team leader. The Executive Group (and 'inner cabinet') is characterised by controlling the expertise to run the company, frequent weekly meetings, informal and flexible agendas. CEO/MDs are the highest paid of all company directors and have a major say in the selection of executive directors through their membership of nomination committees. The CEO/MD, as the leader of a cohesive Executive Group, is the most powerful person in the firm. The part-time chairperson and Board comprising of other NEDs are the company's *de jure* apex of formal authority but *de facto* power and influence lies with the CEO/MD.

Our questionnaire surveys sought to identify the functional management experience of the CEO/MD in PLCs and SMEs. Of the 26 CEO/MDs of PLCs, 14 claimed general management experience, five operations/production, three marketing/sales, two finance/accountancy, one engineer and one HR. None had a legal background. Examination of the work and functional background of the 34 CEO/MDs in SMEs also revealed the importance of general management experience at 50 per cent of the total. This was below that for CEO/MDs directing PLC Groups of whom 54 per cent had a general management experience background. This would indicate that SMEs are more likely to have been started up by occupational specialists such as engineers, IT, personnel or marketing/sales people. The SME sample revealed a higher proportion of CEO/MDs with a finance and legal background. Our research suggests an important criterion for appointment to CEO/MDs is broad general management experience.

White *et al.* (1997) examined the hypothesis that the career specialisation of the previous CEO and the corporate strategy of the company will determine the career specialisation of its successor. They drew on the work of Pfeffer and Salancik (1978) on resource dependency theory to suggest that CEO succession acts as a means to adapt an organisation to its environment by a rational selection process that ensures the necessary professional and personal characteristics faced by the organisation. Pfeffer and Salancik also suggest that inter-personal attraction can lead to organisation inertia through which individuals, dominant within the organisation, institutionalise their functional specialisms and strategic choices in ways that ensure the continuation of their dominance. White *et al.*'s results show the previous functional specialisation of the CEO and the corporate strategy of the company did not bear out their hypothesis. They conclude that the pace and degree of environmental change is such that enterprises which successfully adapt to this uncertainty tend to select CEOs who are from different professional backgrounds to their predecessors.

An illustration is provided by Marks and Spencer who, in 2000, replaced their CEO with a new executive chairman. The British retail company had been experiencing difficult times in the financial markets that were seeking to see an improved share price performance. The CEO was favourably disposed to personnel having included a personnel director in membership of the Board of Directors. Over the years the company had built up a reputation in the HR world for progressive personnel policies. The new executive chairperson took a stronger commercial line and regarded personnel policy as a lesser, but still relatively high priority, necessary ingredient for business success. The board was reduced in size from seven to four with the personnel presence being removed. However, the chairperson invited the personnel director to be a member of the Executive Group (*People Management*, 2000).

Organisations in the 1990s were most likely to appoint CEOs with a general management, finance or legal background and who had multiple company experience. Our research supports this proposition regarding general management experience but not for finance and the law. In other words to graduate to the position of CEO accountants, lawyers, marketers and HR professionals etc., who specialise wholly within their function, without gaining a broader management experience, are unlikely to get to the top of the organisation (see Chapter 4).

Moreover, this broad CEO/MD career experience is likely to encourage a more open and participative Board as CEO/MDs are more likely to appreciate the totality of the management process and thereby encourage general business contributions from all heads of operations/functions. Rapid change in the corporate environment of organisations provides opportunities for executive directors with new ideas and a preparedness to adapt to secure the CEO/MD position. This environment with its emphasis on competitiveness and financial stringency ought to favour CEO/MDs with a finance background, but in fact favours those with a generalist career background.

Our questionnaire survey asked CEO/MDs if they had changed the strategic direction of the enterprise since taking office. At the PLC level 80 per cent answered in the affirmative. This is supportive of the White *et al.* argument that successor CEOs are likely to possess functional and professional backgrounds different from that of their predecessors. We reduced to three the diversification strategies pursued by the boards of the PLCs and 34 SMEs included in the questionnaire surveys. The PLC results showed 64 per cent to be multi-product related firms with sales distributed between businesses being such that no one business was responsible for more than 95 per cent of the total. Single business strategies accounted for a further 20 per cent defined as not less than 95 per cent of sales from one business. The remaining 16 per cent pursued multi-product unrelated conglomerate strategies with distribution between businesses, so that no one accounted for more than 70 per cent of sales. The interview programme with CEO/MDs revealed the predominance of this strategic shift to multi-related product businesses and with the advance of globalisation it was an imperative to expand through a multi-products strategy into international markets. The majority of our sample were becoming multinational companies. All organisations over the last two decades had been involved in mergers, takeovers, joint ventures (often with foreign companies) and decentralisation of core activities to subsidiaries to improve product

Table 2.4 Management styles of CEO/MDs leading executive groups[1]

Types of leadership	CEO/MD executive group of PLCs	Main PLC boards
Open partnership	9	7
Open consultative	12	6
Traditional/authoritarian	2	3
Personal	0	2
Reliance on rules	0	3

Source: Questionnaires

Note: 1 Three respondents did not answer this question.

market responsiveness and financial performance. A central feature in their selection to the position of CEO/MDs had been a successful track record in undertaking major initiatives combined with a strong business orientation to improve financial performance in their companies.

We compared the styles of CEO/MDs in the private sector managing their Executive Groups with the styles of chairpersons running main PLC Boards. The results are shown in Table 2.4.

The questionnaire survey asked CEO/MDs to explain their own management style in running their Executive Group meetings. Two questionnaire choices, open participative and consultative styles, were judged to be what Pettigrew and McNulty (1995) called maximilist Boards where leadership maximised information flows and involved other directors fully in the decision-making process on a face-to-face basis. The difference between participative and consultative was the desire of the former either to have unanimous agreement or failing that a majority decision, whereas consultative meant involvement but with the CEO/MD reserving the right to decide unilaterally, if necessary. Several CEO/MDs interviewed made the point that they were not running a democracy. The open team Board style was based on the belief that high director involvement led to better quality decisions and greater commitment to the decisions once they had been made.

The work of Dooley and Fryxell (1999) on the strategic decision process offers a theoretical underpinning to the open management style of executive team working. They argue that strategic decision-making teams improve decision quality during the forming of strategies by encouraging differences of opinion, providing team members exhibit loyalty to the group. In addition, if team members believe the Board to be highly competent then this will encourage commitment to the decisions once made which facilitates implementation of the strategy. Both loyalty and competence are based on shared trustworthiness within the strategic team as decision-makers feel safer in expressing different points of view through the strategy formation phase and consensus and commitment to strategy implementation.

The other three management styles were traditional, high reliance on formal rules and personal. The traditional style assumed the autocratic aggressive leader of a strong personality who believed in the absolute right to manage the Board as he/she thought fit. This type of leadership could be combined with paternalism, a caring image providing the CEO/MD got his/her way. Reliance on formal

Case study 2.1 (Answers)

Your answers to the case study questions should have included some of the following points:

The HR function's contribution to a local business unit's strategic initiative

A. 1 This company had a long history of paternalism going back into the nineteenth century. Eventually the company grew into a multinational leaving the original local company little more than a business unit. The local management recognised that the multinational corporate board of directors possessed the authority and power to route new investment into any location deemed by the corporate board to be the most profitable. All business companies within the corporate group were, to a degree, in competition with each other for access to resources from corporate head office. The subsidiary company needed to secure new investment to improve its performance and to secure its future. The site was vulnerable because of its high costs and in that it exported 40 per cent of its output to northern England. The local business board drew up a strategy to enlarge the product range and to reduce costs significantly through new investment designed to take the company very rapidly from the distant past into the present. The subsidiary company's success relied on initiating a thoroughly worked out business plan and showing the necessary savings that could be achieved. This was done through an effective presentation to the CEO/MD Group of the PLC and by lobbying PLC Board directors. Their motivation owed much to the local management's determination to retain production on the local site.

A. 2 Personnel for many years played an important part in the management of the local company as its three previous personnel directors had become its MD. In addition to securing the funding from corporate headquarters to undertake new investment the main problem in securing success was change management. Working practices at the site required revolutionising shifting from physical skills to knowledge base skills grounded in monitoring technology, diagnostic skills and taking remedial action, should anything go wrong. The aim was not a one step change but to get workers and managers to develop positive attitudes regarding the need for continuous change through a more participative management style. The site had a strong trade union presence which had to be convinced of the need for radical change. The formation and implementation of the plans were driven by the personnel department which had the responsibility to communicate, coordinate and negotiate with trade unions. The personnel director chaired the Brewery Council, a joint management and trade union body.

rules to conduct meetings can be used to establish what Aram and Cowen (1995) have called the statutory Board. Here the CEO/MD minimises executive director and NED involvement, treating them as ornaments conforming only to the requirements of external agencies such as the law, Stock Exchange rules, shareholders' meetings etc. Both these latter two styles of Board management constitute Pettigrew and McNulty's minimalist Board, one of the characteristics of which is little Board discussion. The fifth choice offered by the questionnaire was personal style which assumed the leader to conduct most of the Board's business (making deals) outside of the boardroom. Dealing with individual directors the CEO/MD was able to trade favours and even bully others to secure their support. These latter three management styles were assumed to be individualist in orientation giving a stronger weighting to functional structures whereas the former two were more open leading to team decisions.

The chairs of main PLC Boards and of CEO/MD Executive Groups revealed quite different distributions with the former showing more variation in styles. The different characteristics of both Boards and Executive Groups would seem to bear out these results. Traditional/authoritarian, personal and reliance on rules of main Board styles is explained by meeting less regularly, having a more formal agenda and containing 50 per cent membership in the form of NEDs, all requiring the need for more formal direction, whereas the full-time Executive Group meeting much more regularly, informally and with a flexible agenda is more easily wielded into an effective team. Table 2.4 shows the greater significance of the open participative and consultative styles of management of CEO/MD Executive Groups.

Notwithstanding these structural factors the questionnaire survey revealed that CEO/MDs personal beliefs played a large part in their adoption of an open participative/consultative style of management. The questionnaire survey did not probe what constituted these personal beliefs or the reasons for holding them. Nevertheless they were held in addition to financial reasons. However, the interview programme provided some clues which can be summed up in the idea of stewardship. Here CEO/MDs felt the need to use fruitfully, and to develop, the resources put at their disposal and for which they had ultimate responsibility during their term of office. This means that CEO/MDs not only must achieve good financial results but they must also be competent and capable of balancing the longer-term needs of enterprise success and survival as well as the short-term desire of shareholders for financial results

3   Board of directors and top management teams

The presence of personnel/HR directors

The extent of personnel/HR director representation on boards of directors, CEO/MD Executive Groups and other top management teams

Table 3.1 shows the results from our research of the presence of personnel/HR directors on Boards by organisational level.

A significant finding is the 73 per cent representation of personnel/HR directors on the CEO/MD Executive Groups compared with a 15 per cent presence on main PLC Boards. Given the CEO/MD Executive Group is the engine (power house) driving the business in terms of the business strategy, and its related strategies, this conclusion is in sharp contrast to much of the UK literature which assigns personnel/HR a low presence on Boards and by implication a marginal involvement in strategy formation. In the public sector the trend is the same.

The survey of SMEs showed personnel/HR directors on the Board of Directors at 44 per cent, somewhat lower than the subsidiaries of large corporate organisations. The literature shows (WERS, 1998) employment unit size to be positively correlated with a personnel presence and this was generally the case with the smaller independent SMEs in the study. Although not a like for like comparison in that WERS figures relate to the presence of a personnel specialist, and ours relate to personnel/HR directors, WERS research records personnel presence at 31 per cent for stand-alone workplaces employing between 100 and 199 and 66 per cent for workplaces employing between 200 and 499 employees. This gives a crude average of 48 per cent which is on a par with the 44 per cent recorded by our SME research.

However, our finding is not unsupported in the literature. Torrington and Hall (1998) record personnel's Board presence in Britain at 63 per cent. A 1999 Development Dimensional International survey reported a figure of 72 per cent Board representation for human resource directors compared with 55 per cent for the previous year. Budhwar's (2000) survey of 93 private sector organisations showed personnel/HR Board representation at 55 per cent. In the United States a study by Tsui and Gomez-Mejia (1988) reported 73 per cent of top HR executives, in 900 companies employing more than 2000, served on the enterprise's executive management committee.

The WIRS and CLIRS figures refer to personnel/HR director 'specialist' representation whereas figures for 'any representation' in the same surveys are higher.

Table 3.1 Personnel/HR director representation on boards of directors

Board types and levels	Numbers of boards	Numbers of personnel/ HR directors on boards	Percentage
Main boards of PLCs	26	4	15
CEO/MD Executive Group at PLC level	26	19	73
CEO/MD TMTs at subsidiary/business unit level	159	131	82
SME boards	34	15	44
Public sector boards of directors	7	5	71
CEO/MD Executive Group: public sector	7	7	100
TMTs Executive Group	12	9	75
Not on Executive Group	12	3	25
Total	264	185	70

Source: CEO/MD questionnaires

In this regard WERS (1998) reveals a figure of 64 per cent showing a downward trend from 69 per cent (WIRS, 1992) which itself is a decline from 73 per cent (WIRS, 1984). All this points to the need for researchers to define clearly to what they are referring when using the term Board of Directors. Much of the existing literature on Boards and HRM is lax in this regard.

Most PLCs in our research had adopted Cadbury's recommendations to establish sub-committees chaired and staffed by NEDs. However, our interview programme with CEO/MDs shows they still continued to have an important role on these sub-committees and to influence their deliberations. The importance of the CEO/MD's role in selecting Board members and the Executive Group suggests that the power and influence of personnel/HR directors is dependent on the attitude of the CEO/MD towards personnel/HR. If the CEO/MD holds a favourable attitude then the personnel function is likely to be given authority (i.e. through a formal seat on CEO/MD Group) and thereby the possibility to exercise power and influence. Conversely if the CEO/MD holds a negative attitude towards people management then the likelihood is that personnel/HR function will not secure a seat on the CEO/MD Executive Group and thereby have no opportunity at that level to exercise power and influence.

However, just as the 'star' of the personnel/HR function can rise under a favourably disposed CEO, so it can also decline with a change of CEO/MD who is less favourably disposed than their predecessors (Hall and Torrington, 1998). Purcell (1995) confirms this view when he states, 'The decision of an organisation to have a personnel director is linked to the CEO/MD and unrelated to organisation structure, size and strategy'.

Again Purcell and Ahlstrand (1994) discussing the viability of corporate personnel departments state: 'Much depends on corporate culture and especially the values and beliefs of the chief executive'.

In five of our 60 organisations a change in CEO/MD led the personnel/HR directors to lose director status in one of two ways – early retirement or voluntary resignation but with an appropriate financial package. In the case of a large food processing and distribution company a new CEO considered HR was not capable of adding value to the business and he saw no need for its presence on the CEO/ MD Executive Group. In this case the personnel director took early retirement and was not replaced. In a shipbuilding company, a subsidiary of a foreign multinational, a new MD sought to change the previously established business strategy. This was strongly opposed by three directors including the personnel director, leading to their resignation from the company, but accompanied by a financial compensation package. Again the HR director was not replaced. In both cases the personnel department continued within the company but without a boardroom presence.

As we saw in Chapter 1, in Britain the dominant view of academics drawn from, and supported by the survey data (WIRS and CLIRS), is of a personnel/ HR function poorly represented at main Board level and with little direct involvement in the formulation of major strategic business decisions. The Purcell and Ahlstrand (1994) view that personnel acting as a third order function making downstream decisions, provides a strong and influential exposition to the survey data. They identified the rise of the multi-divisional company which they saw as being finance driven with the corporate centre using financial performance indicators to exercise control over decentralised subsidiaries. Providing subsidiaries meet their financial targets they are given autonomy to grow the business as they saw fit. Decentralisation of organisational structures is essential for sensitivity to different product market segments, customer needs and suppliers. Decentralisation of control from the corporate centre necessitates the decentralisation of personnel/HR decisions to the various subsidiaries and business units. Purcell and Ahlstrand therefore consider the decentralisation of collective bargaining, joint consultation, job evaluation etc., must mean the personnel function is not primarily involved at corporate headquarters where first order business decisions are made. The formulation, and implementation, of HR policies takes place further down the organisation.

Our research revealed many examples of decentralised multi-divisional companies who nevertheless applied corporate policies on a range of issues such as pensions, equal opportunities, health and safety, management development etc., although collective bargaining was normally decentralised. In one subsidiary of a large foreign-owned distilling company, local management had not given sufficient attention to corporate policy on product quality and rising wage costs. Due to an industry recession the company was experiencing a downturn in business whilst the local company's commercial viability was threatened. This necessitated the importation of a senior HR executive from headquarters to tighten up on corporate policies and rein back the power and influence of local management.

In a Scottish textile company, again the subsidiary of a major international oil company, the CEO stated: 'The worst news I can have as CEO is to hear of a lost time accident, our target is zero accidents'. In this case the corporate body had very high health and safety standards partly influenced by its size and importance and the potential to attract adverse media attention.

Management magazines, newspaper articles and academic journals etc., are full of commentaries by academics and consultants decrying personnel's lack of involvement in strategy formation and espousing various solutions to the problem. For example Hunt (2000) says, 'The HR function continues to struggle to get the recognition and influence it deserves' and claims personnel does not have sufficient talent to deal effectively with other managers. To overcome the problem he prescribes the delivery of first class personnel services, the provision of competent HR expertise, the hiring of the best available HR talent and that HR specialists develop their inter-personal skills. A recent Development Dimensional International survey (1999) claimed, 'There is still a perception that the HR function lacks enough business sense or experience'.

The key they suggest is that HR strategy must be debated at Board level. Ulrich (1997, 1998) champions the HR function's involvement in strategy formation and most importantly its implementation and advocates the building of HR capability as a means of business success with a concentration on deliverables rather than roles such as training and pay policies. His view is that HR must measure its output as do other management functions such as marketing and sales, purchasing and supplies, operations, finance etc., to achieve credibility in the eyes of senior executives. Ulrich suggests five key competencies which HR professionals should possess including understanding the business, knowledge of HR practices, ability to manage organisational culture and change, and most important of all personal credibility. The latter means demonstrating business insight, high integrity, appropriate risk taking, 'chemistry' with key players and continuous learning.

The evidence from our work is that in a given set of circumstances personnel/HR has a significant presence where it matters (i.e. Executive Group) and is involved in strategy making. The factors explaining why personnel/HR directors are selected for the CEO/MD Executive Group and why they have influence there is explained in Chapters 4 and 5.

Undoubtedly a presence either on the PLC Board or the CEO/MD Executive Group gives the personnel/HR director a position of authority, provides access to resources and to key players. However, authority has to be based on credibility (Ulrich, 1998) perceived and attributed by colleagues, otherwise it is but an empty shell. The CEO/MD role can be a lonely one and when faced by the uncertainty and ambiguity of business decisions they told us they often seek interactions with others. As a result directors, including the personnel/HR director, who have the chief executive's respect and trust will normally be parties to such interactions which can take a number of forms including being located in close geographical proximity to the CEO/MD office. Purcell and Ahlstrand argue that a good working personal relationship between CEO/MD and personnel director is of the upmost importance. They say, 'Their (personnel) power was more personal than personnel: corridor power was more in evidence than functional authority'.

Our evidence showing identification of a physical proximity and frequent interaction between CEO/MD and the personnel/HR director is important. It means the view that only those on the Board of Directors or the CEO/MD Executive

Group can exercise power and influence in decision-making requires moderation. It is possible for those whose formal executive authority may be subordinate to that of others to nevertheless have easier and more frequent access to the CEO/MD than those in a more formal senior position. In effect 'inner cabinets' can become established, especially where large size Board of Directors exist. The data from our research in this regard is more fully analysed in Chapter 5.

One of the few studies to attempt an explanation of personnel's contribution to strategic decision-making through the exercise of both formal and informal power and influence is that of Brewster *et al.* (2000). They offer a three cell matrix, adapted from the work of Elsik (1992), which contributes to the analysis of the linkage between the personnel function and strategic decision-making. At the most formal level personnel/HR directors participate in strategic planning by having a seat on the Board of Directors. However, not all strategic decisions are arrived at through these formal processes and personnel/HR function can input via informal pressures (the second cell). This is discussed more fully in Chapter 5. The third cell makes the distinction between direct and indirect participation with the possibility of line and operations directors/managers who have spent time in the personnel function taking HR implications into account in strategic decisions. In this case no separate formal office is required for the personnel/HR dimension to exercise influence in the strategy formulation process. These three cells go some way to account for the complexity of strategic decision-making encompassing many of the features outside the formal rationalistic model such as the quality of resources, emergent and incremental strategy, political and informal considerations and bottom up initiatives etc.

An example of Brewster *et al.*'s third cell arising from our research, took place in a Scottish textile company where the personnel/HR director position had been abolished but the Executive Group consisted of CEO and two MDs of constituent businesses, who had been previously personnel directors of the company. The finance directorship was re-titled corporate affairs with responsibility for the HR portfolio. In this case the CEO claimed that good HR management was inherent in the culture of the company and did not in the prevailing circumstance require a separate personnel specialist presence.

Notwithstanding, given the pace and complexity of decision-making in modern organisations, there is no room for complacency or 'yes men', as the demands of the situation require directors who will challenge the status quo and ward off the dangers of what Janis (1983) called 'group think'. CEO/MDs have the difficult task of combining the need for openness with constructive criticism whilst avoiding an overly political board exhibiting inter-personal antagonism and secrecy detrimental to purposeful team working. Successful personnel directors are likely, more than other directors, due to their people management skills and the persuasiveness of their role, to assist the CEO/MD to achieve this goal. At a personal level personnel/HR directors can act as a confidant of the CEO/MD, and at a team working level actively help promote an open, high trust relationship within the Executive Group (Dooley and Fryxell, 1999).

Eighty per cent of the subsidiary companies participating with our research had a personnel/HR director on their top management teams. This finding fits with that of Purcell and Ahlstrand's who also report that personnel/HR had a high presence on subsidiary company boards. However, our research with its finding of a 73 per cent personnel/HR director presence on CEO/MD Executive Groups of PLCs, and providing input to strategy formation is contrary to their view that personnel/HR has a declining presence at the corporate centre.

Our sample of private sector boards was stratified by ownership and industrial sector i.e. manufacturing and services. The literature (CLIRS, 1993) shows ownership to be a major explanatory variable, with foreign-owned firms much more likely to have a personnel director on the Board of Directors compared to British companies. Our results throw no further light on this as all the companies analysed at the PLC Board level were British. There was, however, no difference between foreign-owned subsidiaries and British owned companies with eleven of twelve of the former having a personnel/HR director on the CEO/MD Executive Group whereas ten out of eleven latter had one. Personnel's representation on the CEO/MD Executive Group in the manufacturing sector was slightly lower at five out of seven than in the service sector which recorded nine out of eleven.

The personnel/HR director profile

Our research enabled a profile of a personnel/HR director to be constructed in terms of characteristics such as age, qualifications, length of service on the Board, membership of professional bodies, job title, gender and personnel director remuneration.

Age

Table 3.2 contains the age distribution of the personnel/HR directors surveyed.

The most common age group amongst our sample was 40 to 49 with a mean age of 47. The actual age varied from the youngest at 35 to the eldest at 59. This compares with a mean age for all other directors on PLC boards of 54 and for CEO/MD executive groups of 50. The personnel/HR directors were thus younger than other directors. This can potentially be helpful for personnel/HR directors in terms of influence on the formulation and implementation of strategy since Bantel and Jackson (1989) found that TMTs with younger and more educated members tended to be more innovative in coping with organisational changes.

Table 3.2 Personnel/HR director age distribution

Age groups	Numbers
30 to 39	5
40 to 49	22
50 to 59	15
Total	42

Source: Personnel/HR director questionnaires

Qualifications

As a group in general, personnel/HR directors were qualified to degree level or equivalent with only two possessing no formal qualifications. Twenty-seven possessed more than one qualification, normally a first degree plus a postgraduate diploma in personnel management or management studies. First degrees were mainly in business, arts or social science, although a number had degrees in mathematics, engineering and physics. Personnel, HRM and employee relations qualifications were normally at postgraduate level having completed a first degree. Nineteen had acquired their formal qualifications through part-time study. Our data revealed a positive relationship between the personnel/HR director's age and the qualifications possessed (see Table 3.3).

In percentage terms the younger personnel/HR directors were more likely to be educated to first degree standard and above. Five in the 30 to 39 age category all held degrees whereas 95 per cent of those in the 40 to 49 and 92 per cent in the 50 to 59 age category had degrees. This 95 percentage figure for personnel directors holding higher education qualifications compares with a figure of 42 per cent (Storey *et al.*, 1991) for British management in general. The status of personnel directors as a highly qualified group also receives support from CLIRS (1993) which stated that two thirds of their sample of senior personnel executives held a qualification in personnel or a closely related subject. Hoque and Noon (1999), based on an analysis of WERS findings, identified an increasing trend of personnel specialists becoming better qualified. Although their analysis is for personnel/HR specialists in general and not personnel directors as such, nevertheless they concluded, 'In 1990, 61.3 per cent of personnel specialists had a formal qualification, and this had risen to 72.6 per cent by 1998'.

Length of board service

The mean length of board tenure for personnel directors on CEO/MD Executive Groups was three and a half years which compares with five and a half years for other directors on these groups. The figures for personnel/HR directors on PLC and SMEs boards were six and five years respectively. Only seven personnel/HR directors had held board status previously and their average length of tenure there had been six years. The relative short length of tenure compared to other directors may be the result of a rapid rise in numbers of personnel directors with board representation. This corresponds with the findings of Torrington and Hall (1998)

Table 3.3 Cross-tabulation between personnel/HR director's age and formal qualifications

Age groups	Numbers with formal qualifications	Total in group
30 to 39	5	5
40 to 49	22	23
50 to 59	13	14
Total	40	42

Source: Personnel/HR directors' questionnaires

and those of the Development Dimensional International (1999) who also record a rapid rise in personnel directorships on boards of directors, from 55 per cent to 72 per cent in one year.

Membership of professional bodies

Marginson *et al.* (1993) in discussing the qualifications of corporate personnel managers remark, 'Of the two thirds holding formal qualifications the vast majority were members of the Chartered Institute of Personnel and Development (CIPD)'.

Our own research revealed 27 personnel/HR directors were in membership of CIPD. Of these 15 were Fellows, 10 corporate members and 2 affiliates leaving 15 as non-members. The main reasons given for non-membership included, 'CIPD has a limited perspective ... it has no value to me ... I obtained the position without membership of CIPD'.

However, some of the non-membership is explained in that some of the sample of personnel/HR directors were not professional specialists and had not worked previously in a personnel/HR function (see Chapter 4). Only 16 of the personnel directors had qualified through the CIPD Professional Qualification Scheme, the main means of socialising practitioners into the values, knowledge and skills of the profession. The entry into the occupation remains firmly with the employers. Membership of CIPD is not a necessary qualification to practise the profession. Nevertheless it is important to the power and influence of CIPD that personnel/HR directors become qualified through its Professional Qualifications Scheme or the alternative routes (e.g. work experience and NVQs) to graduate membership. Our survey also revealed that a number of personnel/HR directors had not upgraded from corporate membership to Fellow. This trend, however, has also been noted by Monks (1993) in Ireland.

Fourteen of the personnel directors were in membership of other professional bodies of which six held dual membership of CIPD and another institute. This may have been due to inertia on the part of the personnel directors. However, these professional institutes were in competition with CIPD for the director's loyalty e.g. some directors had started in finance and remained in membership of the appropriate accountancy body.

Job title

Hoque and Noon (1999) have attempted to distinquish between personnel and HRM specialist roles, making the point that the growth in the numbers of specialists between 1990 and 1998 has come from those called HR specialists and not from those titled personnel specialists whose number have remained stable. Grant and Oswick (1998) argue the CIPD has played a large part in bringing about the title HRM. A cross-tabulation between CIPD membership and use of the title HRM by personnel/HR directors is shown in Table 3.4.

Table 3.4 shows younger personnel/HR directors are more likely to be in membership of CIPD and are more likely to use the job title HRM as opposed to

Table 3.4   Personnel/HR director's age, membership of CIPD and use of the job title HRM

Age groups	Numbers	CIPD membership, percentage	Use of HR job title, percentage
30 to 39	5	100	60
40 to 49	23	68	47
50 to 59	14	54	33

Source: Personnel/HR directors' questionnaires

personnel. The authors have argued elsewhere that the debate whether there is a difference between what personnel managers do and what HRM managers do is 'sterile' (Gennard and Kelly, 1994). They conducted a seminar with 28 personnel/ HR directors seeking to establish whether they thought there was any difference between personnel and HRM. They were divided into two groups – those who had thought there was a difference (9 individuals) and those who thought there was no difference (19 individuals). The two groups were then sent away to describe what personnel/HR policies and practices operated in their firms. In the report back session both groups listed the same personnel/HR policies and practices. This led to the question why did they use different titles for the same bundle of activities. Those who said there was no difference worked in well-established personnel departments, normally with a director on the Board or CEO Executive Group. Those directors who had adopted the job title HRM (considered there was a difference) having previously had personnel in their job title, report their organisation following a 'major event' were seeking to give public acknowledgement that senior/executive level management now wanted to give a higher profile to people management. The decision to alter the department's name to HRM was thus to signal to other managers that people management was to be given in the future more power and influence within the organisation than had previously been the case. Adoption of the job title HRM was an acknowledgement of 'discontinuity' between the old order and the new order in which HR was to be given more power in the firm's decision-making processes. The substance of personnel policies has not changed in those organisations who have retained the title personnel, and those that have adopted the title HRM.

Gender

Only two (3.3 per cent) of our sample of personnel/HR directors were women. Both were employed by Health Trusts. This reflects the manufacturing bias of our sample since this sector employs few women at senior management level. The Institute of Management (1999) records that only 4 per cent of directors are women. In the United States women hold only 11 per cent of Board seats of the top Fortune 500 companies. CLIRS (1993) put the figure higher recording 13 per cent females amongst the most senior personnel executives.

Personnel/HR director remuneration

In the market system, *inter alia,* salary level is often seen as symbolising the worth of an occupation and that of its individual members. Table 3.5 shows both the basic and total salaries of personnel directors relative to others in two categories of organisation i.e. smaller organisations with a turnover of less than £35 million and larger organisations with a turnover of more than £40 million.

With the exception of company secretaries in smaller organisations personnel/HR directors are the lowest paid. This suggests personnel/HR directors have relatively low status. However, the salary differentials were not large, especially when tax and other deductions are taken into account. In smaller organisations the basic median pay of personnel directors is close to that of finance and operations directors and in total salaries to those of operations directors. In larger organisations the differences are more marked, especially when personnel/HR directors are compared with finance directors. The latest Reward Group survey (for 2000), however, shows personnel directors to have closed the gap with an average salary of £56,752 compared to an average for all the directors of £55,000.

The work of personnel/HR directors on the board of directors

Business strategies

The questionnaire survey of personnel/HR directors on PLC Boards and CEO/MD Executive Groups showed personnel/HR directors spent 47 per cent of their time dealing with Board tasks rather than functional responsibilities. Non-personnel work included involvement in mergers and joint venture decisions, capital expenditure, membership of acquisitions and disposal teams, organisational restructuring, product development, commercial contracts and business planning. At the subsidiary company level, personnel/HR directors were involved in TMT work

Table 3.5 Median salary levels of directors in membership of the Institute of Directors

Occupation	Large firms: turnover +£40m		Small firms: turnover −£35m	
	Basic salary	Total salary	Basic salary	Total salary[1]
General director	£65,000	£75,000	£50,559	£55,000
Finance director	70,000	77,000	46,933	53,645
Marketing director	56,000	59,718	50,000	52,000
Operations director	64,000	69,000	47,500	49,099
Personnel director	52,500	57,250	46,650	48,301
Company secretary	–	–	36,002	40,000

Source: Reward Group, 1999

Note: 1 Total salary included additional cash supplements such as bonuses but not non-monetary remuneration.

activities for 30 per cent of their time. At this level non-personnel work ranged over issues like customer care, production problems, acquisitions and quality assurance. The questionnaires to CEO/MDs of Britain's top 200 companies and SMEs probed the extent of the personnel/HR directors involvement in the making of business strategies. The results are shown in Table 3.6.

The results showed PLC corporate personnel/HR director involvement towards the high end of the distribution. Indeed a summation of highly and moderately involved categories provides a percentage of 84 compared to 17 per cent for little or not involved. It is interesting that the involvement percentage is higher than the 73 per cent established for personnel/HR membership of CEO/MD Executive Groups and 15 per cent for the main PLC Boards. This gap is explained by Torrington and Hall's (1998) view that personnel directors are sometimes involved in strategy formation on an issue-by-issue basis which in turn reflects the Mintzberg and Waters (1985) view that strategy can be a stream of decisions rather than a process of long-term rational planning.

The SME distribution is more even when compared with that for PLCs. The summation of the top two categories gives 62 per cent compared to 83 per cent for PLCs. Again the personnel/HR directors involvement in business strategy at 62 per cent is higher than their 44 per cent presence on Boards of Directors, although compared with the PLCs the gap between involvement in strategy and board presence is wider. This suggests a fluid and changing situation within SMEs where personnel/HR directors are involved with their CEO/MDs and Boards but, as yet, they are not as well established as directors on CEO/MD Executive Groups of top PLCs. Table 3.7 attempts to refine the aggregated responses of Table 3.6 by asking CEO/MDs of top PLCs and SMEs to prioritise the personnel/HR directors involvement in business decisions.

It shows for PLCs a slightly skewed distribution towards business planning, budgets and resource allocation, mergers and acquisitions and disposals. Marketing/ sales and capital expenditure come last in the list with business planning being at the top. Although no direct comparison is possible the results appear to question the CLIRS (1993) and Hunt and Boxall's (1998) findings that personnel/HR directors are not heavily involved in the formation of non- personnel decisions but mainly in their implementation. However our findings are consistent with those of Budhwar's (2000) research which shows 87 per cent of the 93 firms surveyed had corporate strategies and that 77 per cent included the personnel function either at the outset or early in the consultation process.

The participation of personnel/HR directors in SMEs in making business decisions differs from the PLC sector. Business planning, budgets, mergers/ acquisitions and disposals/divestment come top of the PLC sector whereas, mergers/acquisitions and disposal/divestments come towards the bottom of the SME sector. In the SME sector operations, marketing/sales and quality/customer care are more highly prioritised. This is not unexpected as large PLCs are increasingly involved in buying and selling companies.

Our research supports the view that personnel/HR directors are seriously concerned with business decisions and that their professional personnel expertise

Table 3.6 Involvement of PLC CEO/MD Executive Group and SME board of directors personnel/HR directors in the formation of business strategies

Categories	Number		Percentage	
	PLCs[1]	SMEs	PLCs	SMEs
Highly involved	8	13	33	38
Moderately involved	12	8	50	24
Little involved	3	10	13	29
Not involved	1	3	4	9

Source: CEO/MD PLCs and SMEs questionnaires

Note: 1 Two CEO/MDs did not respond to this question.

Table 3.7 Relative involvement of personnel/HR directors in various business decisions

Business decisions	Weighted response distribution[1]		Percentages	
	PLCs	SMEs	PLCs	SMEs
Business planning	70	84	13	12
Budget/resource allocation	67	72	12	10
Mergers/acquisitions	67	73	12	10
Disposals/divestment	65	66	12	9
Operations	64	99	11	14
Quality/customer care	63	81	11	12
Information technology	58	74	10	11
Marketing/sales	54	74	10	11
Capital expenditure	50	73	9	10

Source: CEO/MDs PLC and SMEs questionnaires

Note: 1 The Likert type scale was used with 'highly involved' weighted 4 through to 'not involved' weighted 1. These scores are aggregated for each column to establish a total score.

must fit and facilitate business strategy (Tyson and Fell, 1986, Tyson, 1995). Their role on the CEO/MD Executive Group is to lead on personnel matters and to configure the function's expertise and policies to the business requirements of the enterprise. This can mean tempering their HR policy aspirations to the cost and timing of business expenditures. At the same time their business orientation puts them into a stronger position to challenge and to argue for HR's contribution to improving business effectiveness.

Personnel/HR strategies

Our questionnaire to personnel/HR directors sought to establish and prioritise the type of personnel/HR activities in which they were engaged. Table 3.8 shows their open unprompted responses. Table 3.8 provides a ranking which reveals the importance of training and development, recruitment and employee relations with over three quarters of personnel/HR directors participating in these activities. The interview programme confirmed the importance of management development, especially in the top PLCs, to achieving changes in attitudes in a

Table 3.8 Personnel/HR directors' HR job responsibilities

Job responsibilities	Numbers of responses
Training and development	37
Recruitment	36
Employee relations	33
HR planning	29
Personnel policies	29
Personnel/HR strategies	27
Rewards and benefits	26
Occupational health	19
Discipline and dismissal including redundancy	13

Source: Personnel/HR directors questionnaire

turbulent corporate environment. Other activities such as formation of personnel policies, personnel/HR strategies and rewards and benefits are activities for between one half and three quarters of personnel directors.

Another contribution personnel/HR directors make at corporate PLC board level is through their interaction with the NEDs on main Board sub-committees. Our research revealed that CEO/MDs continue to be active in audit, remuneration and nominations committees despite Cadbury's recommendation that they be staffed and chaired by NEDs. The research revealed these committees are highly dependent on personnel/HR directors to conduct research and to offer advice on salaries and benefits and the recruitment process. This access of personnel/HR directors to NEDs, including chairpersons, is an important avenue for enhancing their power and influence within organisations. It enables personnel/HR directors to establish relationships with NEDs, whilst not themselves being members of such committees. They are able to exercise what Pettigrew and McNulty (1995) have called 'relationship influence'. In some PLCs project teams had a mixed membership of executive and NED directors including the personnel director who chaired the committee, sometimes on non-HR problems.

Three examples from our case studies illustrate the point. In an engineering company the personnel director worked closely with the MD in selecting people to chair project teams. In addition to informal knowledge of the person, personnel techniques including the psychometric Belbin group test and development appraisals were used as to whether or not they would make a suitable leader. At the ship repair company the HR director led a multi-disciplinary project group investigating the personnel implications of future business strategy, as the yard stood to lose a major submarine contract in 2001. Highly developed multi-disciplinary project groups (called transition groups) were initiated and chaired by the HR director of a large private utility company. In addition to working with NEDs, sub-committees of the board, membership of the CEO/MD Executive Group, and ad hoc project teams, the research revealed at least two additional ways in which the integration between HR activities and business strategy is delivered. These are through personnel/HR directors broadening their portfolios by taking non-personnel tasks and second by participation in multi-disciplinary management projects.

Of the 41 private sector organisations 16 had personnel/HR directors who had broadened their portfolio to encompass both personnel and specific non-personnel responsibilities. Even in the 19 public sector organisations nine personnel/HR directors had wider portfolios. In one case the personnel/HR director had taken over responsibility for the hotel operations at a Health Trust, whilst in a large local authority a personnel/HR director also had responsibility for corporate resources. A larger proportion of personnel/HR directors at subsidiary level (48 per cent) than at corporate level (28 per cent) had taken on wider responsibilities. This is explained by the more generic involvement of corporate level personnel/HR directors in business strategies (Table 3.5) whereas at subsidiary level relatively more junior personnel directors sought to broaden their work experience with a view to future promotion. The types of non-personnel responsibilities held by personnel/HR directors included corporate affairs, information technology, quality management and executive management responsibilities for a subsidiary of the company. At a large brewers and leisure group the corporate personnel director held responsibility for information technology and security and at a large aero manufacturer had responsibilities for property/real estate, legal, information technology and corporate affairs. At an engineering group the personnel director held responsibility for buying and for contracts including legal aspects. In this case he had a thorough understanding of the business having been previously the MD at a subsidiary business unit.

Personnel/HR directors were also engaged with the broader business decision-making process through their membership of project teams. As we have seen the modern Board of Directors and CEO/MD Executive Group have changed to being more open and participative and have moved away from being rigidly functional and operational. Such are the pressures on Executive Groups today that delegation to project teams and sub-committees are commonplace (Katzenbach, 1998). Ulrich (1997) illustrates the involvement of HR specialists in multi-functional task force teams in merger situations. Chase Manhattan Bank established an acquisition task force to audit and integrate mergers that included experts in finance, information technology facilities, as well as HR. Personnel/HR directors in some of our case study companies had been asked to lead such project groups on non-personnel aspects and/or to be members. In the large brewer and leisure group referred to above the personnel director led the executive team to ward off a hostile take over by a foreign brewer (Kelly and Gennard, 1996).

Some critics of personnel might argue that the foregoing illustrates that personnel/HR is not important enough to justify a full-time position on the board. However, this was not the view of the CEO/MDs interviewed who said they had deliberately, as part of their management development, deployed their personnel/HR directors in this way. They reinforced the view that personnel/HR directors, unlike many finance directors, are more active in the general business of the board as team players. This finding puts a different complexion on the WIRS/WERS survey findings that 'any personnel representation' as opposed to 'specialist representation' on main Boards is much higher.

The 'T'-shaped manager

Our research findings thus suggest personnel/HR directors undertake a combination of both business and HR roles. On this basis the successful personnel/HR directors can be described as a T-shaped manager. The large majority of our personnel/HR directors had been trained in HR technical knowledge and understanding acquired through both work experience and by gaining higher education qualifications in personnel/HR. This was their core competency and stem of the T. In addition they have acquired and developed a general understanding of the business as a whole by operating successfully in other management functions, by developing inter-personal and team working skills in project teams interacting with representatives from other management functions and by self learning and development. This is the bar (general skills and business understanding) of the T. This understanding of the business also enabled them to enhance their credibility with other directors or members of the CEO/MD Executive Group in that their personnel/HR input is argued for in terms of a business case rather than a sectional management interest perspective. The strength of the T stem is reinforced by training and previous HR work experience in the personnel/HR function including membership of CIPD. Moreover the combination of wider business awareness (the bar of the T) with specialist personnel/HR expertise (the stem of the T) in our view moderates Purcell and Ahlstrand's argument that personnel/HR directors personal power is more significant then their personnel power.

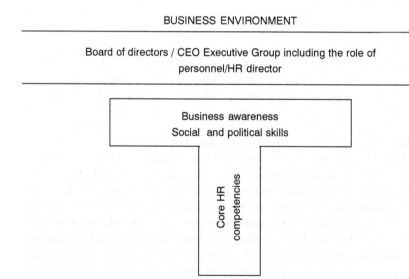

Figure 3.1 The 'T'-shaped personnel/HR director

Storey (1992) and Tyson (1995) argue the personnel/HR director business manager orientation is likely to subsume personnel/HR within the demands of the business. Both imply the adoption of a business orientation downgrades the power and influence of the HR specialist contribution. Our research findings are on par with Tyson's original point (1985) that personnel directors can be, and often are, business managers. In general the personnel/HR directors we surveyed and interviewed did adopt such an approach to their work and colleagues. However, our findings do not support the implied idea that these roles are separate and may even be mutually exclusive.

Storey (1992) identifies four roles illustrated on a matrix containing two dimensions, the tactical to strategic and interventionary to non-interventionary. Tactical/interventionaries are 'regulators' who possess a strong industrial relations orientation and are immersed in collective agreements and procedures. The 'handmaidens' are tactical/non-interventionaries reacting to line managers' requests for information on personal records, minutes of meetings, statistics etc. The 'advisory' role is strategic/non-interventionary, offering senior management strategic advice about new ideas and future plans but leaving executive management with responsibility to action it. The 'changemaker' role is strategic/interventionary, therefore, personnel/HR directors are proactive in making things happen. The changemaker role, the most appropriate for the personnel/HR director, has two variations, namely the human resource specialist who is concerned to apply high professional standards and the personnel/HR director whose business orientation is so strong he/she is fully integrated into the Board or top management team. Storey acknowledges the difficulty in striking a balance between these two with the result the personnel presence is likely to be subsumed within the business culture of the enterprise. Of the 15 companies studied in detail by Storey only two had personnel directors who were changemakers and both fitted the latter subtype. Indeed in most of the companies the newer HR initiatives came from general and/or line management and not from the personnel department which remained tied to the regulator role.

Tyson, and Tyson and Fell, using a construction industry analogy, identify three roles played by the personnel function, namely 'clerk of works', 'contracts' and 'architect'. The clerk of works is not unlike Storey's handmaiden providing a reactive routine administrative service to line management. The contracts manager like Storey's regulator is heavily involved with trade unions and the making and implementing of collective agreements including the administration of disputes, grievances, redundancies, disciplinary procedures etc. In the architect role the personnel/HR director is engaged in strategic long-term planning and more fully integrated into the Board of Director's business decision-making process. As with Storey, Tyson and Fell's architect has two subtypes, the change agent and the business manager. The change agent is employed to assist in bringing about large-scale organisational change seen as necessary due to the increasing uncertainty in the enterprise's external environment. The business architect is concerned primarily with the integration between HR and business strategies. This latter type gives the advantage for personnel of credibility with other directors as they are seen to be adding value to the enterprise. Tyson (1995) says, 'The business role can be and is performed well by non-personnel specialists'.

Our results indicate a high to moderate involvement of personnel/HR directors in the formation and implementation of business strategies. In the case of strategy formation CEO/MDs reported an 84 per cent involvement for PLCs and for SMEs 62 per cent. The typical personnel/HR director in our study is similar to Storey's changemaker and Tyson's architect in so far as they are key players in the management of the business. With regard to employee relations (Storey's regulator and Tyson's contracts manager) our research shows this still to be an important role for personnel/HR directors but not as important as their roles of managing employee development and resourcing. HR policies were principally configured to fit business strategies, although at times it was necessary to amend them. However, our research does not support the views of Storey and Tyson that the integration of personnel/HR into business strategy down grades the power and influence of the personnel function at the CEO/MD Executive Group level. The T-shaped manager (explained above) who combines personnel/HR expertise with a wider business experience meant that our personnel/HR directors were to integrate at the same time both these requirements.

Marginson *et al.* (1993) sought to establish the degree of involvement of senior personnel executives in the making of business strategies by asking them whether they contributed or not to a range of decisions concerned with corporate change. These included merger and acquisition, investment in new locations, expanding existing sites, divestment of existing sites, closure of existing sites, run down of sites and joint ventures. According to the respondents their involvement ranged from 71 per cent in merger and acquisition decisions through to 93 per cent in decisions to run down a site. The presence of a personnel director on the main board increased the probability of the function's involvement further (Purcell, 1994; Guest and Hoque, 1994). This is a fairly optimistic picture. However, Marginson *et al.* cross-checked the survey findings by seeking the perceptions of finance respondents as to personnel's involvement and influence in these decisions. They concluded:

> In general, our finance respondents saw the personnel function to be somewhat less involved than our personnel respondents. The discrepancy was most marked in the case of personnel involvement in drawing up proposals ... as opposed to their implementation.

Why they should have given greater weight to the finance respondents is not explained. We believe our method to be more robust, as it relies on the responses of CEO/MDs who as a group are most likely to be neutral between functions as they are responsible for the successful operation of the enterprise. This means they have a non-sectional interest approach. Hunt and Boxall (1998) conducted a similar study in New Zealand using 14 large multinational companies. They asked about personnel's involvement in strategic decisions including the introduction of new technology, the development of quality initiatives, plant openings and acquisitions. Hunt and Boxall found, that with the exception of total quality management, the majority of personnel/HR directors were neither greatly involved in formulating strategies on new technologies nor in plant openings and acquisitions. Notwithstanding, they argue that their personnel/HR directors were focused on the business as a whole and were fully involved in strategy implementation. Our research partly supports the work of Hunt and Boxall as we found that personnel/HR directors play a significant role in strategy formation.

Another perspective on the role of personnel/HR directors at Board of Director level is provided by Purcell and Ahlstrand (1994) who offer nine roles for corporate personnel/HR directors and their departments. These are: espousing corporate culture and communications, helping formulate and monitor corporate policy, providing HR planning for strategic management, offering 'cabinet office' services, helping to identify and develop senior management talent including career planning, advocating the organisation's cause to external agencies, providing a corporate coordination role on HR issues, acting as internal consultant, offering mediation services where tensions between divisions are hindering progress and providing corporate personnel services to small business units. An important point arising out of their analysis from the standpoint of our own research is illustrated by the following quote:

> Much of the activity identified in the list of nine possible functions places a premium on political and inter-personal skills and 'corridor power'. In this situation the authority of corporate staff comes more from their own expertise and style than from a clearly defined role and function.

Our research confirms their argument on this point except, as shown in the next chapter, the CEO/MDs interviewed placed significant importance on the personnel director's professional HR competence.

Case study 3.1

This case study of a large privatised utility providing services in electricity generation and distribution, telecommunications and water illustrates some of the points made in this chapter.

Organisation mission, structure and culture transformation at a large privatised multi-utility

Privatised in 1991 this Scottish company has grown from a regional producer and distributor of electricity to a multi-utility offering water, gas and telecommunications services. It was the mission of the company to be a highly profitable major player in the multi-utility market both domestically and internationally. In 1991 the company had 1.8 million customers, an annual turnover of £1.2 billion and a market capitalisation of £1.8 billion. By 1999 it had five million customers, an annual turnover of £3 billion and a

Case study 3.1 *continued*

capitalisation of £6 billion. In the world it is ranked in the top 25 electricity companies.

The company grew by taking over companies in the UK and in the north-west of the United States. The global market provides an outlet from anti-competition regulations in Britain and allows it to improve profits by reducing costs in less efficient performers. Within Britain the major electricity company's business strategy has witnessed successful takeovers of another major electricity provider in England in 1995 and in 1996 a water supplier reducing the cost base in the former by 55 per cent and saving £25 million in the latter company. In 1993 the company entered the telecommunications market taking over small existing suppliers but thereafter has grown rapidly employing 2,500 across Britain with sales by 1998 of £300 million per year. Domestically the whole Group (excluding the North American acquisition) employs 15,000 a reduction of 50 per cent since privatisation in 1991.

Organisationally the UK company structure consists of three divisions, namely generation, power systems and retail plus three semi-autonomous businesses in telecommunications, water supply and electricity. The emphasis is on decentralisation with co-ordination achieved through a small staffed headquarters. The main Board of Directors consists of eleven directors, a part-time chairperson, five NEDs and five executive directors including the CEO, finance and three MDs of the above businesses. The Board has an audit sub-committee and a joint remuneration and appointments committee. The main PLC Board is concerned with corporate governance to meet 'city' requirements, the company's share values, dealings with shareholders, taking reports from the CEO Group on proposed mergers/takeovers, and discus-sions on director remuneration, appointments and management succession. The main PLC Board exercised its authority to hear CEO Group strategic and policy proposals, to ask probing questions of them and to amend and/or send proposals back for further consideration.

The CEO Group was larger with 12 members, five executive directors who ran the divisions and businesses and seven functional directors including personnel/HR. The CEO Executive Group was the 'heart beat' of the business initiating and making strategies for approval by the main Board and ensuring their implementation. Given the decentralised structure of the organisation, the Executive Group required extensive lateral communications and accordingly met every two weeks. The CEO kept continuous contact with the chairperson and NEDs of the main PLC Board keeping them informed of developments within the Executive Group. Although the organi-sational strategy was one of a small corporate office within a decentralised company the power and control of headquarters should not be underestima-ted as shown by the departure in 2000 of the MD of the successful telecom-munications business owing to a dispute with the corporate centre.

Case study 3.1 *continued*

The transformation required a major shift in organisational culture, employee attitudes and behaviour. As a previously nationalised company, decisions were highly centralised with activities closely regulated. Modelled on civil service policies and practices, equity of treatment were highly valued rather than cost efficient performance. The company had been run by professional engineers whose primary concern was continuity of service irrespective of cost. The culture was rule driven, formal and rigid. This formal system was reinforced by high levels of trade union membership, throughout all grades including management, with centralised collective bargaining leading to formal and rigid agreements, systems and procedures.

The HR contribution to this transformation was to engage proactively in the formation of business strategy to improve performance. Important here was the original HR director (he moved on in 1998) who had been recruited to the main PLC Board and CEO Executive Group. His replacement was a member of the CEO Executive Group at the time of writing. The original HR director had the vision to see that the major changes planned through the business strategy caused important people management problems which would have to be overcome to be successful. One important HR initiative was to establish transition teams to smooth the integration of acquired companies into the parent company's commercial policies and culture, as these organisations too, with the exception of telecommunications, had been in the public sector with similar problems. These multi-disciplinary teams had an HR presence providing an opportunity for HR specialists to broaden their business experience.

The HR director developed quickly from a purely HR role to become CEO and chairperson of two of the three decentralised businesses whilst still retaining the HR portfolio on the main PLC Board. The HR director was central to strategic business decisions working out the costs and savings of each project from personnel's perspective. In this way HR's input was quantified similar to that of production, finance, sales, supplies etc. In addition the HR function was heavily involved in the considerable down sizing of employment going on throughout the company and in recruitment at senior management level. Recruitment policy was important to achieving culture change as was the need for business managers with skills in change management and not engineers who dominated senior management throughout the group. Collective bargaining was decentralised to the divisions to tailor the terms and conditions to their financial circumstances. This was made acceptable to the trade unions through policies on employability and training. Moreover, despite losing its original HR director with main PLC Board representation, the headquarters HR department under its present HR director, is occupied with the transition of the United States acquisition into the parent company's commercial policies and culture.

Case study 3.1 *continued*

Questions

Q. 1   Identify the significant differences between the main PLC and CEO Boards.

Q. 2   Explain the multi-utility's mission and the non-HR changes required to achieve it.

Q. 3   What role did the HR director adopt to facilitate the management of change to achieve the business mission?

Case study 3.1 (Answers)

Organisation mission, structure and culture transformation at a large privatised multi-utility

Your answers to these questions should have contained most of the following points:

A. 1   Differences were largely functional with the main PLC Board, meeting once per month, concentrating on corporate governance including monitoring the effectiveness of executive management via financial performance, the company's share values and dealings with the stockholders and taking reports from the CEO Group on proposed takeovers/mergers and discussions on director remuneration, appointments and management succession. The main PLC Board from time to time exercised its authority to ask probing questions, seeking more information, amending a CEO Group proposal or sending it back for further work.

The CEO Group, meeting fortnightly, was the epi-centre of power, the heart beat of the business, generating ideas to progress the business mission, seeking opportunities to grow the business either by organic growth or take over, reconfiguring organisational structure and ways of securing change management. All factors relating to new products, mergers/takeovers, cost structures, management development and employee relations were discussed by this Group before becoming policy. Major policy changes incurring significant funding would be sent to the main PLC Board for approval. In this way the main PLC Board remained the recognised font of authority within the enterprise, although power to make things happen lay with the CEO Executive Group. However, it would be misleading to view these two Boards as existing in isolation linked only by minimal formal relationships. This was not the case as the CEO Group fostered extensive formal and informal relationships with main Board members so that no major problem or proposed change arrived there without the prior knowledge of the chairperson and other appropriate NEDs.

Case study 3.1 (Answers) *(continued)*

A. 2 For 40 years this company was a nationalised producer and supplier of electricity confined to a geographical area of Scotland. At privatisation, as a new commercial company, it established the mission to become a multi-utility supplying a range of products/services. As a result it has diversified into gas supply, water and telecommunications and penetrated the electricity market in Northern England and overseas in the north-west of the United States. To achieve this mission the enterprise has decentralised the organisation, creating three divisions from the original Scottish based electricity company and three businesses from those taken over and merged into it. All divisions/businesses have Boards of their own exercising a degree of autonomy, but with direct representation through their MDs on both the main PLC Board and CEO Executive Groups.

A. 3 The HR director played a major role in the development and implementation of business and HR strategies at this company. Given the company mission to be a multi-utility the management of change was to be a major priority presenting personnel with an opportunity to meet these new demands. This opportunity was grasped by the personnel/HR director who established multi-disciplinary transition teams to facilitate the take over of firms and to bring them into the commercial culture of the parent company. Additionally the centralised collective bargaining and pay structures of the old nationalised company were devolved to the divisions and businesses thereby bringing congruence between their labour costs and their market conditions. Third, the HR director made a major contribution to stripping out labour costs with a 50 per cent down sizing in employment whilst expanding services. Indeed the success of the HR function's contribution can partially be put down to measuring continually and quantifying its contribution to business performance as do other operational directors.

4 Getting to the top

The career pathways of personnel/HR directors

We now turn to how personnel/HR directors achieve Board of Director status. The chapter analyses their pathways to the top. Three such pathways are examined. The first involves vertical occupational mobility within the personnel/HR function. The second entails vertical and horizontal occupational movement between, and within, management functions, including entry, exit and return to personnel. The third is the 'parachuting' into a personnel/HR directorship individuals who have no previous experience of work in that function. In addition we identify the factors which explain the career progression of personnel/HR directors.

As shown in Chapter 1, over the last twenty years organisations have faced more complex, uncertain and rapidly changing environments than in the preceding twenty years. This stemmed from increasing international competition, deregulation of markets, privatisation of nationalised industries, the exposure of local authorities to market pressures (e.g. compulsory competitive tendering) and a rapid rate of implementation of new technologies of production and service provision. Within this more uncertain business environment, management functions moved closer to their external and internal customers by becoming leaner and fitter. They decentralised their operations, delayered their management and reduced their workforces (Arnold, 1997; Herriot and Pemberton, 1995; Purcell and Ahlstrand, 1994). Organic, flexible and lean organisations were seen as the key to competitive advantage. The employees who remained in employment became more flexible in the job tasks they performed. Managers also found themselves having to undertake a wider range of duties rather than a limited range of specialist ones. To advance their careers managers needed to become generalists, with a core specialism, rather than specialists.

These occupational changes have implications for manager's career paths. In the past managers normally followed established career paths within management and operational structures (Arnold, 1997; Tyson, 1995). The contemporary organisation requires the vertical and horizontal integration of previously demarcated management functions and job tasks. Relatively rigid vertical career paths within management functions are no longer the dominant route of career advancement. In the contemporary labour market this is more likely to entail movement between functions. There will be more than one route of career progression. There is no reason to believe personnel/HR specialists have been isolated from these trends.

The 'downsized' organisation means shortened career paths, increased functional flexibility, increased management turnover and more external market recruitment. Managers are more likely to move frequently, into and out of organisations. Career progression through several jobs either within, or between, organisations and management functions has been facilitated by increased training and development opportunities. However, frequent job moves are not necessarily a bad thing. Herriot and Pemberton (1995) and Kakabadse (1991) argue that those who undertake frequent job changes have the highest probability of entering senior management. Nevertheless most organisations still require 'core' managers to provide continuity.

The contemporary business environment leads to the prediction that personnel/ HR directors are more likely to graduate to Board membership by more than one career pathway. Some will remain in their 'core function' progressing by vertical movement into jobs of greater seniority. Others will gain director status by a pathway characterised by vertical and horizontal job movement within, and between, management functions and organisations. The horizontal and vertical integration of tasks means personnel directors, regardless of their career progression are likely to be HR generalists, and not specialists. This is supported by an Institute of Management report of 1992 which remarked:

> Forty-five per cent of corporate respondents to a previous IM survey expected their middle managers to become more generalist over the next five years: only 13 per cent thought they would become more specialist.

The broadening of a manager's role enhances the organisation's competitiveness and the manager's future employability.

The career pathways

The personnel/HR directors had progressed to director status by more than one pathway. Twenty-one had progressed by upward vertical movement within the personnel/HR function. Thirty-four had acquired Board or Executive Group status by horizontal and vertical movements within, and between, the personnel/HR functions and other functions. Of these, eight commenced work within the personnel function and then made a horizontal movement to a management position outside personnel followed by a further horizontal movement back into personnel and then a vertical movement within that function. A further twenty-six had commenced work outside the personnel/HR function, then transferred into it, whence some moved back out again, then back into it, before becoming personnel/HR director. Beardwell's (1998) study of CIPD membership upgrades also identified, albeit for younger personnel practitioners, this zig zag pattern (which he labelled 'wanderers'). Five directors exhibited a third pathway to the post of personnel/HR director. They had been 'parachuted' by the CEO/MD to become personnel/HR director having had no previous work experience in the personnel function. These personnel/HR directors are the equivalent of Tyson's (1995) business manager but they constituted only five of the 60 personnel directors covered by this study. Table 4.1 details the distribution by both pathways and industrial sector.

The vertical pathway

The directors following this route commenced work in a junior personnel/HR position and then moved upwards into jobs of increasing seniority and responsibility. Two personnel/HR directors in engineering, three in drink and food, and two in electronics had followed the vertical pathway. In local authorities and in the Health Trusts three personnel directors followed the vertical route. Although these directors had not worked outside the personnel/HR function, they had experience of, and had gained a knowledge and understanding of, wider business issues as members of management committees, integrated management teams considering the HR implications of various business decisions, e.g. regarding takeovers/mergers, and from a widening of their portfolio to include non-HR tasks. They had not been cocooned in a functional box.

At an engineering company, a subsidiary of an American owned multinational, the HR director was a member of the Quality Council consisting of the directors

Table 4.1 Distribution of pathways by industry of personnel/HR directors

Industry/sector[1]	Vertical	Zig Zag	Parachute	Distribution
Engineering	2	4	1	7
Drink and food	3	3	0	6
Electronics	2	0	2	4
Textiles	0	3	0	3
Printing	1	1	0	2
Shipbuilding and ship repair	0	3	0	3
Steel	0	1	0	1
Chemicals	1	1	0	2
Total manufacturing	**9**	**16**	**3**	**28**
Financial sector	1	2	1	4
Retail distribution	0	2	0	2
Transport	1	1	1	3
Utilities	1	3	0	4
Local authorities	3	6	0	9
Health Trusts	3	2	0	5
Other public sector	0	1	0	1
Construction	2	0	0	2
Universities	1	1	0	2
Grand total	**21**	**34**	**5**	**60**

Source: Personnel/HR directors interviews and questionnaires

Note: 1 Most of the private sector organisations are multi-business. They have been classified by their dominant activity.

of manufacturing, finance, human resources, three directors of business units and the quality manager. The chair of the Quality Council rotated between the functions. To quote the HR director, 'HR is involved closely with the business and participates in projects some of which are non-personnel, but led by an HR manager'. Another example from a large British printing company shows the corporate personnel director appointed by the CEO to the Boards of subsidiary companies as a means of widening his business experience.

The range of personnel activities undertaken on their route to a directorship is shown in Table 4.2. It shows the generalist personnel professional, rather than the specialist, is more likely to reach the top.

Amongst those reaching director level the dominant specialism was industrial relations which they claimed provided an understanding of the key levers and drivers of the business, since as part of management's bargaining team they had to assess the likely impact of concessions to the employees on the business as a whole and not just its component parts. Training and development and health and safety were the least significant specialist routes to a seat on the board of directors. The low rating of training and development is interesting as Table 3.8 in Chapter 3 shows personnel/HR directors to be most occupied in this activity. This is probably explained by a time lag between the directors formative years when industrial relations was a high priority on the management agenda. The successful introduction of change for organisations to remain competitive has been a high priority in the last 20 years. The successful implementation of change requires a change in employee attitude and culture which in turn can be achieved by the training and development of staff. Hence today's personnel/HR directors are highly likely to be more involved in this activity than industrial relations.

The vertical pathway was most common in the public sector where seven of nineteen personnel/HR directors reached the top by this route. Table 4.3 shows the route to the top for personnel/HR directors by type of board. One third of personnel directors on the PLC Board and subsidiary company Boards had arrived there by the vertical pathway. These industrial sector and Board levels differences are not significant but show even in the public sector, with its high percentage of professions, the vertical pathway is the minority route.

Table 4.2 Vertical career pathway: range of personnel/HR activities

Activity	Number
Generalist	26
Industrial relations	21
Resourcing	16
Pay and rewards	14
Training and development	6
Health and safety	3

Source: Personnel/HR director interview programme and questionnaires

Note: Personnel/HR directors were asked to tick from a list of activities which best represented their career. Respondents often ticked more than one box.

Table 4.3 Distribution of personnel/HR directors' pathways by level of boards

Board level	Vertical	Zig Zag	Parachute	Number of boards/Executive Groups
PLC, parent board	2	4	0	6
CEO/MD Executive Group	5	9	0	14
Personnel directors not members of either parent board/ CEO/MD Group	1	2	1	4
Total	**8**	**15**	**1**	**24**[1]
Subsidiary companies and business unit TMTs	7	11	3	21
Personnel directors not members of subsidiary TMTs	1	1	0	2
Total	**8**	**12**	**3**	**23**
Public sector boards/ Executive Groups	5	10	1	16
Personnel directors not on boards/ Executive Groups	3	0	0	3
Total	**8**	**10**	**1**	**19**

Source: Interview programme and questionnaires

Note: 1 Personnel directors on PLC parent boards were also members of Executive Groups, therefore, the parent board figure has been excluded from the total to avoid double counting.

The vertical and horizontal (zig zag) pathway

Those becoming directors via the zig zag route also possessed an all round training in the different aspects of personnel/HR work. The greater flexibility of internal and external labour markets plus organisational restructuring facilitated their movement into, and out of, and back into personnel and other management functions. Those taking this zig zag pathway, especially in electronics and engineering, had rotated between management functions and spent time in line management roles. The career movements of these personnel/HR directors were mapped by identifying the first management function in which they were employed, and then tracking their subsequent job changes. Bain (1995) suggests that it is rare for a personnel executive to be elevated to general management, although he provides such an example. However, the evidence from our research shows the zig zag career pathway to be common and typically to involve an average of three functional moves, ranging from a low of one to a high of six. Not all moves equate with those of separate functions as the zig zag pathway often took managers into personnel for a period, out of it, and back again. This finding is contrary to that of Hall (2000) who states, 'Personnel managers tend to join the HR department at

Table 4.4 The zig zag pathway: distribution of functional moves

Number of functional moves (N=34)	1	2	3	4	5	6
Numbers of personnel directors	4	8	12	7	2	1

Source: Personnel/HR director questionnaires

the bottom and rise through it ... this is the main reason why there are not more HR management specialists in the Boardroom'. The distribution of moves between functions is shown in Table 4.4

The distribution of the personnel/HR directors reaching the top by the zig zag route between different types of Boards shows nine of the fourteen personnel/ HR directors on CEO/MD Executive Groups had followed this pathway. The corresponding figures for subsidiary Boards and public sector organisations was eleven and ten respectively. The most functional moves were recorded at subsidiary company level where on average personnel/HR directors had undertaken 3.3 moves compared to 2.9 at PLC level and 2.5 in the public sector. The zig zag pathway was dominant in engineering, textiles, shipbuilding and repair, privatised utilities and local authorities.

CEO/MDs had preferences for developing, promoting or recruiting personnel/ HR people who had work experience outside the personnel/HR function. However, the choice between the two routes was not stark, as the vertical route personnel/ HR directors took as they progressed their career, had all broadened their business experience through membership of multi-disciplinary project teams and taking on non-personnel tasks whilst remaining within the personnel function. Nevertheless, the duality in personnel/HR director work highlighted by Storey (1992) and Tyson (1995) is best understood through the zig zag career pathway culminating in the T-shaped manager who is able to ride both horses by combining business and HR activities. Other factors significant to the CEO/MDs choice between personnel/HR directors who had zig zagged and those coming via the vertical route included, as a causal sequence, circumstances facing the organisation, the composition of the existing board, personal qualities and the availability of individuals.

The parachute pathway

Five personnel/HR directors had had no previous work experience in the personnel/HR function. Three were located at a subsidiary company level, one at PLC, CEO/MD Executive Group level and the other in a public sector transport company about to be privatised. These 'parachute' personnel/HR directors divided into two types. Two worked for American owned electronics manufacturers who, as part of company management policy, rotated managers with engineering and production backgrounds into and out of personnel. The other three directors were appointed by CEO/MDs who felt the current problems of the organisation required a personnel/HR director with personal qualities to solve them. The CEO/MDs concerned reported that in different circumstances they would have selected a personnel/HR director who had a different set of talents. The situation was illustrated by the following quote from a CEO/MD who had 'parachuted' in a personnel/HR director.

> His (i.e. personnel director) personal contribution and interpersonal skills are very important to the interactions of the Board. I would say they are more important than professional competence, although in different circumstances my view on this might be different.

The circumstances to which the chief executive referred was reorganisation, following privatisation, and a need for cost reduction and flexible work patterns. These associated changes were expected to be opposed by the trade unions and the CEO wanted a personnel/HR director who knew the business and had line management experience with a record of taking unpopular and tough decisions. These skills could only be found in an existing commercial manager.

In a life insurance company special circumstances arose when an individual who had accepted, but not taken up the position of personnel/HR director, decided not to take up the post. However, after a prolonged period without a personnel/HR director and to avoid another prolonged recruitment delay, the CEO decided a personnel/HR director be appointed immediately. The CEO offered the position to a senior manager with an information systems background but who, through previous job rotation, was networked within the whole organisation, and had a thorough understanding of the business. In the third case, the existing personnel director retired unexpectedly due to illness. Given severe financial difficulties the manufacturing director was asked to combine the personnel director portfolio with his existing one for manufacturing operations.

All three of these 'parachute' personnel/HR directors had a strong understanding of the wider business, possessed the political skills of operating at senior level and were well networked both within and outside the firm. These directors were akin to Purcell and Ahlstrand's directors' view that personal power is often more significant than personnel power. They did not possess the technical HR expertise. However, this was available to them within their own personnel departments and could be drawn on as and when appropriate. In addition, all three learned fast by consultation with their 'network' in management clubs and by attending HR seminars. By these methods the parachute personnel/HR director were able to ensure they suffered no disadvantage in boardroom influence than those gaining Board status by other routes.

Factors explaining the career progression of personnel/HR directors

Our research revealed four principal factors which explain the elevation of personnel/HR directors to the Board of Directors:

• The attributes the CEO/MD looks for in directors (demand side);

- Personnel/HR director's perception of what CEO/MDs require of directors (supply side);
- Company policy on management development and succession;
- The individual's interpersonal, team working and networking skills.

Attributes CEO/MDs require of directors

Given CEO/MDs are the key players in the appointment of directors it is unlikely a personnel/HR specialist will acquire Board or Executive Group status unless the organisation's CEO/MD has a positive attitude towards people management. They must believe people management can 'add value' to the organisation. Hall and Torrington (1998) have called this the CEO/MD 'mind set'. If the CEO/MD has a negative attitude towards the contribution of personnel/HR to business success then the probability of personnel/HR representation on a top decision-making body will be low. All personnel/HR directors in the study worked in organisations whose CEO/MD had a positive attitude towards personnel/HR's contribution to the achievement of business success. All the CEO/MDs interviewed stated they selected a personnel/HR specialist to serve on their Board or Executive Group partly because they recognised people management competence was one of their lesser strengths but appreciated 'getting the people equation right' was crucial to business success. They thus had invited a personnel/HR person to join the Board (or Executive Group) to provide to that body the necessary skills lacking in themselves. However, some CEO/MDs possessed, or thought they possessed, the necessary skills, but nevertheless thought an HR director was necessary to promote and remind the board of its people responsibilities.

Irrespective of sector (i.e. manufacturing, finance, transport) we found CEO/MDs signalled to managers the qualities they sought in personnel/HR directors. These were then 'signalled' through the organisation to aspiring directors by rewarding individuals who displayed these qualities. For example by delivering assigned tasks, displaying a strong customer focus, working effectively in teams and showing vision and creativity in managing organisational change. Performance appraisal was another instrument through which chief executives signalled to other managers the organisation's values and criteria for judging successful performance and career advancement. Appraisal was linked to management development programmes designed to groom future directors. The attributes, values of a newly appointed director were a further 'signal' providing aspiring directors the opportunity to benchmark their personal qualities against those of the new director and thus to identify their own development needs (i.e. the gap to be filled) if they were to achieve director status. All these signals indicate proactive individuals are required (Tyson, 1995; Wilkinson and Marchington, 1994; Storey, 1992) and not someone merely to implement policies, systems and procedures.

Spence (1973) argues individuals make decisions to invest in education and training if they believe the knowledge and skills acquired will be purchased by employers. He suggests the basis upon which employers' distinquish between their employees is their ability to recognise signals from senior managers as to which human capital decisions are likely to improve organisational competitiveness. Amongst such signals he includes the level of education, specialised technical training and job experiences. However the values captured in these signals are often derived from social interaction and networking between people (Kotter, 1982) rather than economic objectivity.

Spence's work would predict the purchasers of personnel/HR directors' services radiate signals as to the characteristics, attributes etc they expect of directors. Individual managers pick up these signals and to gain director status undertake the investment to acquire and develop the attributes. If personnel/HR managers perceive top management to value broader business experience combined with functional specialisation, then they will acquire broader business experience by, for instance, self-development or participating in management development programmes.

The interviews with CEO/MDs demonstrated clearly CEO/MDs sought three main skills from personnel/HR directors – professional/technical competence in the personnel/HR function, the ability to make business focused decisions, and interpersonal skills including the ability to be a team player. CEO/MDs required personnel/HR professionals who could make business focused decisions via an understanding of business strategy, marketing, financial analysis and the processes whereby the company's products or services were delivered to its customers.

Table 4.5 shows CEO/MDs gave the highest priority, in the selection of directors, to individuals with effective interpersonal and team working skills. They saw personnel/HR people having diffused and persuasive understanding of the whole organisation, whereas other functions were perceived as more sectionally based. Finance directors are also in this position, although there was a dominant view amongst CEO/MDs that such directors were more likely to retreat into the safety of their specialistion. CEO/MDs expect their personnel/HR director to develop trust relationships with themselves and other executives and not to alienate them. A Hospital Trust chief executive cited an example of a personnel director appointed from private industry to instil into senior executives a more private sector commercial culture. However, the individual only succeeded in alienating the other directors, thereby defeating the purpose of the appointment. The Trust replaced him with a personnel/HR director with very different attitudes. These findings are similar to those of Hall and Torrington (1998) who identify the key skills of personnel/HR directors as functional expertise, business awareness and influencing and political skills. We probed more deeply into the social skills sought by CEO/MDs in personnel/HR directors and the results are shown in Table 4.6.

It shows our work confirms that of Purcell and Ahlstrand (1994) in that the most influential personnel directors were those with a close personal working relationship with the CEO. Moreover even a disaggregation of the data between PLCs and SMEs shows 'trust relationships' continues to be first in both sectors. However, tuned to 'political sensitivities' obtains a much higher ranking in PLCs than in SMEs. This supports the view that the greater political complexity of larger organisations increases the requirement of personnel/HR directors to possess such skills.

Table 4.5 Skills sought by CEO/MDs in personnel/HR directors

Skills	Most important (3)	Medium importance (2)	Least important (1)	Total
Professional/technical competence in core management function	9×3=27	7×2=14	10×1=10	51
Make decisions in interests of overall business	3×3=9	11×2=22	11×1=11	42
Team player (inter-personal and group skills)	13×3=39	7×2=14	4×1=4	57

Source: Interviews with CEO/MDs

Note: The different category of responses are weighted to distinguish the strength of response. 'Least important' is weighted 1, 'medium importance' weighted 2 and 'most important' weighted 3. The responses for each skill are multiplied by the weighting to provide the rank order. Six CEOs preferred not to make this distinction.

Table 4.6 Social skills sought by CEO/MDs in personnel/HR directors

Social skills (N=47)	Weighted responses	Percentages
High trust relationship between CEO/MD and personnel/HR director	169	17
Facilitates communications	144	14
Offers constructive criticism	136	13
Tuned into political sensitivities	123	12
Courage and persistence	118	12
Group networking	114	11
Team builder	112	11
Defuser of conflicts	107	10

Source: CEO/MD questionnaires

Note: This data was subsequently (later than the data in Table 4.3) obtained from the PLC and SME CEO/MD questionnaire surveys. Sixty CEO/MDs completed the questionnaire but 13 did not respond to this question. The weighting is derived from scoring 4 as the most important response through to 1 the least important response on a Likert type scale.

CEO/MDs also regarded as crucial that in the building of a successful management team members of their Executive Group accept management values. However, CEO/MDs stressed the unimportance of an Executive Group comprised of 'like minded people' who never differed over how 'things should happen'. They preferred personnel/HR specialists, wishing to become directors, to make crucial interventions in decision-making forums by, when justified, challenging the proposed solutions of senior managers – hence the importance of 'constructive criticism' combined with high trust in Table 4.6. These results lend support to Dooley and Fryxell's (1999) argument that high trustworthiness in the executive team accommodates, through loyalty, differences of opinion in the formation of strategies, leading to effective decision-making.

In their selection of the most important qualities to be possessed by personnel/ HR directors CEO/MDs ranked professional/technical competence second. The importance in the selection of an HR director of these qualities with a proven track record is illustrated by the following comment from a chief executive of a multinational, multi-utility supplier.

> There were a number of factors in his favour: he was an engineer, had an MBA, understood business, had private sector know how, had a strong background in HR and had a proven track record having successfully put in a similar change at a major car manufacturer, albeit of a smaller scale.

Again we probed more deeply what was meant by the contribution of the personnel/HR function to Board of Director/Executive Group discussions. Table 4.7 contains a breakdown of the HR competencies sought by CEO/MDs in personnel/HR directors.

This ranking favours on the part of the personnel/HR director a 'rounded knowledge of people' management problems and 'proactivity' with the other three items commonly associated with the professional personnel/HR function coming lowest. These responses show CEO/MDs seeking a commonsense, pragmatic and involved problem-solving approach rather than a stand-offish theoretical stance by personnel/HR directors. Expertise in law and HR processes, prolonged experience in the HR function and CIPD membership might be linked in the CEO/MD mind to an isolationist position confirmed by the use of professional language, although as shown above this does need not apply to those who have taken the vertical pathway.

What CEO/MDs meant by business acumen as a quality they expected personnel/HR directors to possess is shown by the results contained in Table 4.8. Time spent in a 'line management' job is the most favoured followed by a 'willing-ness to take on non-HR responsibilities'. In both these ways personnel/HR directors are seen to have a better grasp of business problems and be more rounded. A willingness to take on non-HR responsibilities was also seen as a desirable quality reflecting business acumen values. Experience of international business and of takeover/mergers were seen as lesser priorities by CEO/MDs when assessing whether potential personnel/HR directors had business acumen.

What then does this evidence say about the contribution of personnel/HR as a specialist function on the Board of Directors or CEO/MD Executive Group? First it is important to note that in the view of CEO/MDs personnel/HR competence is rated second to social skills with business awareness third in the three main competencies sought by CEO/MDs.

Second, it is clear that the contribution sought is more general and dynamic as befits a director operating at this level of management. As one PLC main Board personnel/HR director put it,

> HR professionals can be too keen to be involved in HR language and not the deliverables of the business. This HR orientation makes the function less

Table 4.7 Professional/technical skills sought by CEO/MDs of personnel/HR directors

HR competences	Weighted responses	Percentage
Rounded knowledge of people problems	221	27
Proactive in HR policies	180	22
Expertise in law and HR processes	169	21
Prolonged experience in the HR function	156	19
CIPD membership	78	10

Source: CEO/MD questionnaires

Note: This data was subsequently (later than the data in Table 4.5) obtained from PLC and SME CEO/MD questionnaire surveys. Sixty CEO/MDs completed the questionnaires but seven did not respond to this question. The weighting is derived from scoring 5 as most important through to 1 as least important on a Likert type scale.

Table 4.8 Business acumen sought by CEO/MDs in personnel/HR directors

Business competencies	Weighted responses	Percentage
Experience of line/general management	172	35
Willingness to take on non-HR responsibilities	132	27
Experience of international business	91	19
Experience of mergers/ takeovers	90	19

Source: CEO/MD questionnaires

Note: This data was subsequently (later than the data in Table 4.5) obtained from PLC and SME CEO/MDs questionnaire surveys. Sixty CEO/MDs completed the questionnaire but 13 did not respond to this questionnaire. The weighting is derived from scoring 4 as most important through to 1 as least important on a Likert type scale.

creditable in the eyes of other directors. Use of HR language encourages personnel professionals to be policemen and to think in boxes when modern business is too dynamic to require it.

As shown previously many commentators (Hall and Torrington, 1998; Ulrich, 1997; Tyson, 1995; Purcell and Ahlstrand, 1994 ; Storey, 1992) have contributed to this discussion each offering their own solutions to the problem. Storey subdivides his 'changemaker' into business and HR specialist; Tyson his 'architect' into business and change agent; Purcell and Ahlstrand give emphasis to personal and political skills and Hall and Torrington to partnership between personnel/ HR and line management. Our own evidence avoids a dichotomy between HR, business and other roles in favour of a generic integrated role as revealed in the T-shaped manager (see Chapter 3). The majority of personnel/HR directors who get to the top of organisations have followed the zig zag pathway having obtained work experience in various management functions, especially in line management. We relate the significance of these required competencies to the changing circumstances facing Boards of Directors with the shift to a more open team based commercial style of management. Hall and Torrington (1998) say, 'The idea of functional strategy is nearing its sell by date'.

Personnel/HR directors' perceptions of what CEO/MDs require of directors

Our survey also sought to establish the perceptions of personnel/HR directors as to the skills sought by CEO/MDs for effective operation at Board of Director and Executive Group levels. In other words had the personnel/HR directors picked up the signals given out by the CEO/MD and the Board? The results are shown in Table 4.9.

Their perceptions generally matched those of CEO/MDs, but there were differences in priorities. CEO/MDs regarded interpersonal and team working skills as the most important attribute required of a director, but personnel/HR directors perceived CEO/MDs gave the highest priority to a wider understanding of the business. This evidence confirms that all three competencies are important to both CEO/MDs and personnel/HR directors. However, it is clear that CEO/MDs seek in personnel/HR directors effective social skills and HR competencies both embedded within a framework of wider business understanding and contribution. Wider business experience can be developed as personnel/HR directors make upward progress within their careers. Hence many personnel/HR directors who progressed through the vertical pathway became involved in multi-disciplinary

Table 4.9   Personnel/HR directors' perceptions of skills sought by CEO/MDs in personnel/HR directors

Skills	Most important (3)	Medium importance (2)	Least important (1)	Total
Professional/technical competence in core management function	10×3=30	11×2=22	24×1=24	76
Make decisions in interests of overall business	21×3=63	17×2=34	7×1=7	104
Team player (in-personal and group skills)	14×3=42	17×2=34	14×1=14	90

Source: Interviews with personnel/HR directors

Note: The different category of responses are weighted to distinguish the strength of responses. Least important is weighted 1, medium importance weighted 2 and most important weighted 3. The responses for each skill are multiplied by the weighting to provide the total rank order. One personnel director preferred not to make the distinction.

management committees, both standing and ad hoc, or were moved out of the personnel function into an MD role for a period normally at a subsidiary company.

Other factors helping to explain the career progression of personnel/HR directors include their individual interests and motivations. Schein's (1978) concept of career anchors provides insights as to why managers gain director status. Such anchors include interests, values and competencies possessed by individuals. He identified technical competence as an anchor for those valuing professional expertise who had no wish to enter higher general management levels. General management competence is an anchor for those possessing analytical, interpersonal group skills, emotional resilience and technical knowledge and who wish to become senior managers. Schein's (1993) study found technical functional and general management anchors still relevant and that managers' anchors remain consistent throughout their careers. Derr's (1986) work based on similar anchors suggested career orientations do change with age and external influences. Yarnall (1998) testing Shein and Derr's work, found no significant relationship between biographical variables (age, gender, length of service and location) and particular anchors, but that those in higher grades were more likely to possess general management anchors which had changed with age and broader work experience. The work of Schein, Derr and Yarnall suggests personnel/HR directors will have a proven record of technical competence, success in their management specialism and general management skills.

Levinson *et al.* (1978) postulated managers experience a series of career phases. In the 'stable' phase they gained job satisfaction from task achievement. However, subsequently job satisfaction wanes, at which stage the manager enters the 'transitional' phase during which they reflect and decide whether to stay in their present position or move to a more challenging job. Levinson's work suggests some personnel/HR directors may have graduated to Board status via a number of job moves where the motivation was, after a period of reflection, a more challenging position having successfully performed in their present situation which no longer stretched them. A more challenging job is likely to mean an upward movement within the personnel/HR function and/or a horizontal movement out of personnel into another management function or a move from another management function into the personnel/HR function. This career stages thesis is consistent with the expectation there may be more than one career pathway to the post of personnel/HR director.

The importance of this work by occupational psychologists is their emphasis on the choice exercised by the individual personnel/HR directors themselves. For our sample of personnel/HR directors a host of contextual factors such as increasing labour market flexibility, changes in organisational culture, new job opportunities and company management development programmes all influenced their personal career choice. Nevertheless within these constraints they made rational decisions regarding career progression. Schein's and Derr's career anchors and Levinson *et al.*'s stable and transition phases were all relevant to the career paths of our personnel/HR directors regardless of their route to the top. Required to take the next step in their career ladder the majority of personnel/HR directors worked in and out of the personnel function and changed the organisation with which they worked. However, it is not clear from the research how long term a view individuals took regarding getting to the top. For many it was a mixture of circumstances and a willingness to take advantage of opportunities as they arose. However, for the zig zag careerist it was sequential development, albeit with no long-term plan, mastering their present job, and seeking new challenges at a more senior level by either applying to another organisation or by negotiating elevation to the Board with the CEO/MD. In Derr's terms these personnel/HR directors career anchors changed as they became more senior and the external signals of CEO/MDs became more powerful irrespective of the pathway taken in getting to the top.

We provide two examples dealing with the career motivations of personnel/HR directors. The HR director of a large food processing and distribution company said,

> I never set out to be an HR director – there was no long term plan. I found people more interesting as my experience of management increased shifting away from engineering to personnel problems. To me challenge is important, I am an innovator getting bored with the status quo.

The personnel director of a large steel manufacture who had previously been an MD of a subsidiary company said,

> Personnel directors have to be seeking challenges regarding improvements in the business. We have a big problem in steel regarding employee attitudes as it is a very traditional industry. It is necessary to exercise power and influence and use what levers are available to achieve change. I remain personally ambitious. My next move is to get on the Executive Board, possibly with a wider portfolio than personnel.

According to Schein's theory (1978; 1993), general management competence is an anchor for those who possess analytical interpersonal group competencies and emotional resilience as well as technical knowledge. The personnel/HR directors had demonstrated in previous employment situations their comfort with exercising high levels of responsibility, influence and power. Our research indicates that if personnel/HR people are to become directors then both technical and general management competencies need to become integrated anchors. Derr (1986) and Yarnall (1998) suggest this is possible. The career progression of the majority of multi-functional personnel/HR directors illustrate Levinson *et al.*'s (1978) stable and transition phases as they sought to broaden their business experience.

Management development and company policy

Arnold (1997) argued that delayering management combined with increased fluidity of occupations, shifted the balance in management training from development directed by the organisation to individual self-development. On the other hand,

Guest and Mackenzie Davey (1996) argue organisations, after a transitional phase, return to traditional management development forms. Arnold also argued self-development does not mean organisations don't provide support for managers but they seek greater value from training expenditures.

The majority of personnel/HR directors had shunned a purely technical route and demonstrated an ability to apply technical knowledge and understanding to solve broad problems of organisational and behavioural change. Those becoming personnel/HR directors by the zig zag route had, in general, worked for organisations which had formal management development policies covering senior executives, or potential senior executives, for different management functions. The importance of rotation between jobs was summed up by one personnel/HR director as follows:

> I did a 15 month stint as a general business manager. This took me into line management which proved very helpful in my career to becoming an HR director as it improved your understanding of and credibility with line managers. It also broadened my knowledge and skills giving me a better all round understanding of a business.

Other personnel/HR directors had worked for companies that had placed them into general management positions, such as CEO/MD of a subsidiary company, before transferring them back to senior personnel/HR positions.

These formal management development programmes were mainly directed at those regarded by senior executives as 'high flyers'. Potential senior managers were identified at an early stage in their careers, often recruited to a talent pool, and encouraged to pursue, often on a part-time basis, higher educational qualifications. Their management potential was tested by setting them specific tasks and/or projects which usually entailed facilitating team working. If they succeeded with these tasks than senior management gave them further tasks which, again if completed successfully, would lead to further career progression. However, should they fail to deliver the assigned tasks further promotion was unlikely.

Self-development was more common amongst those personnel/HR directors displaying the vertical pathway to the top. This included study in an educational institution to gain a business degree qualification and the building of a network of contacts inside (e.g. managers in other functions) and outside (e.g. participation in organisations such as employers' associations and Chambers of Commerce) the organisation to be accessed for information and advice about business as a whole. However, the dominant way by which vertical route personnel/HR directors acquired wider business understanding was by working with other managers, from outside the personnel function, on team based projects for a specific purpose or by providing personnel/HR support to integrated production teams. For some personnel/HR directors gaining a greater business awareness was achieved as members of the corporate team, charged with securing the acquisition of another organisation, and then achieving a smooth harmonisation of the different processes, systems and cultures of the two organisations.

In general, personnel/HR directors who had taken the zig zag route to the top acquired their business orientation more through company sponsored management development programmes rather than by self-development initiative designed to widen their knowledge and skills to improve their employability (Handy *et al.*, 1995) for senior management positions. The reverse was true for those taking the vertical route. However, it was clear all personnel/HR directors had read in their earlier careers 'market signals' (Spence, 1973) and had engaged in 'social interaction and network building between people' (Kotter, 1982). The self-development undertaken by those getting to the top by the zig zag path included building networks within and outside the organisation, gaining academic qualifications, and resignation from their existing job to move to a more challenging one (Levinson *et al.* thesis, 1978) resulting in a deepening and widening of their competencies and experiences.

Another career facilitator important to all personnel/HR directors, regardless of the route to the top, is their formal qualifications. Spence (1973) argued that individual's investment in their human capital only becomes effective if congruent with certain signals from employers as to what they value. Higher education and formal professional qualifications, as a necessity for career advancement, had been signalled as showing commitment on the part of the manager to make progress.

Self-development of the zig zag personnel/HR directors also included a willingness to widen their work experience. Rapid organisational change linked to high levels of senior executive turnover resulted in frequent job opportunities. Many of the 34 zig zag personnel/HR directors moved companies to seek the challenges of new and more responsible jobs. Eighteen were recruited from outside the organisation and five promoted from within. This compares with 60 personnel directors of which 28 were externally recruited and 32 promoted from within. All those parachuted into a directorship were internal promotions. Those personnel/HR directors gaining Board status via the vertical route gained a new challenge by their portfolio being extended to cover issues outside personnel. For example one director was given responsibility for finance, another for information technology and yet another for contracts with suppliers. In many cases personnel/HR directors volunteered to be members of project teams and to take on extra non-HR responsibilities. In this way they secured career advancement by taking on tasks important to the CEO/MD and their Executive Group.

Interpersonal, team working and networking skills

Irrespective of the career pathway pursued, personnel/HR directors' effectiveness depended on congruence with CEO/MD requirements. Management literature ranks personal ambition and confidence in the exercise of power as critically important in a successful manager. Personality traits are relevant, although which are the key to success is difficult to isolate. In our study effective personnel directors possessed courage and confidence to engage in debate with CEO/MDs and other directors over a wide range of business issues other than HR. They were tuned into the political sensitivities of small team working, offering both support and constructive criticism of strategic proposals. Pettigrew and McNulty (1995) referring to NEDs relate many of these attributes to their 'will' and 'skill' in making use of sources of power in and around the boardroom. Our research on open team-based Boards and Executive Groups suggests it is no different for personnel/HR directors. However the relationship between CEO/MD and personnel/HR director is not one of mutual admiration but of dependency, each getting from the relationship what they want. The personnel/HR director showed loyalty and commitment in the best interests of the organisation and its chief executive. This does not mean blind allegiance but a willingness to be constructive in helping the board to operate positively by suggesting solutions free from negative attitudes.

In the contemporary corporate environment team working is important to the successful functioning of an organisation. The CEO/MDs interviewed argued that, assisted by the Board/Executive Group, it was their role to create an environment which allowed policy initiatives to develop, and if worthy, be agreed and implemented. These interviews confirmed personnel/HR directors were all responsible for devising and implementing in conjunction with other directors the HR strategy and policies to achieve the business plan which they had participated in devising. As in Kotter's (1982) study of successful general managers they knew many hundreds of people both within and outside the organisation. To be influential with the CEO/MDs and others, personnel directors need to be widely known and this is done by establishing networks of contacts both internal and external to the organisation.

Case study 4.1

This case study relates to the career progression of a personnel/HR director in an engineering company.

A pathway to the top

The personnel director is a member of the CEO Executive Group with the official job title of Director of Personnel and Commercial Operations. The company operates in a highly technical sector of engineering. Since 1990 the company has gone through major organisational changes. Prior to 1990 the company produced military products for the Ministry of Defence and charged for them on a cost plus profit basis. In the 1990s this was replaced by commercial pricing. The government change of policy required the company to compete for orders and once contracted any run over on costs had to be borne by the company. This led to a massive reversal in fortunes with the company experiencing a change from a profit of £6 million to a loss of £5 million on a turnover of £50 million in one year. The CEO decided that from then on the name of the game was survival.

The human resource implications have been considerable with a down-sizing of the labour force from 2400 in 1988 to less than 580 in 1998. As a

Case study 4.1 (*continued*)

technical company priority in the past had been given to the promotion of engineers into management positions irrespective of whether they had flair for managerial jobs. If they had been good engineers they got promoted to management jobs regardless of their managerial skills. They had no training in setting job targets, planning work, standard costing and certainly not in leadership skills. The personnel department was expected to handle all HR problems in this heavily unionised company, usually on the basis of crisis management. As reported elsewhere (Kelly and Gennard, 1996) the new HR strategy included devising a new career structure to encourage technical people with modest management skills, promoted when cost pressures were not so acute, to leave managerial posts in favour of those with more commercial competence. The management hierarchy was reduced from eleven reporting levels to four, while supervisors were replaced by team leaders with different responsibilities. This resulted over a period of three to four years in a 60 per cent change in management personnel. During this change period the unions were fully consulted and despite the reduction in head count their acceptance and commitment to the strategy was gained.

In terms of career background the personnel director left school at 15 years of age with no formal qualifications. He commenced work in another engineering company in their finance department attending night school and obtaining a Certificate in Office Studies. During this period in clerical work he became a shop steward with the clerical trade union picking up negotiating skills. In his mid-twenties management appointed him to the position of personnel officer, specialising in remuneration and benefits. At this point he successfully studied for graduate membership of CIPD at a then local technical college. Management then appointed him to a line management job in charge of assembly, promising that the move would be temporary as he wished to remain in personnel. Nevertheless, he acknowledged that this move turned out to be good for him as he saw personnel work from the line manager's standpoint. Subsequently he decided to leave the company to join the case company, as it wished that he remain in line management, whereas he wanted to return to personnel.

Our subject joined the case company as industrial relations manager at the time when it was experiencing business trauma and commencing on its change programme. He was later promoted to personnel manager immersed in the role of change agent with responsibility for training and development as well as remuneration and union negotiations. In 1992 he was appointed to the position of personnel director when the incumbent left the company to take up a personnel/HR director position elsewhere. Subsequently he was transferred for a spell as MD of a subsidiary plant in North Wales before returning to Glasgow to take on wider job responsibilities as director of personnel and commercial operations.

Case study 4.1 *(continued)*

Questions

Q. 1   Explain the career moves made by this personnel/director and how he developed his HR knowledge and skills to facilitate promotion to the top.

Q. 2   Discuss the extent to which his career progression was a combination of circumstance, deliberate choice and management development policy.

Case study 4.1 (Answers)

A pathway to the top

Your answers to the case study questions should have included most of the following points

A. 1   This personnel/HR director made six career moves. He started in finance, moved to personnel, then to a line job, returning to personnel, albeit with another company, then into general management as an MD of a subsidiary company before returning to the top job of personnel/HR director. The change of company was critical to him getting back into the personnel/HR function as the former company had planned that he remain within a line role. Although clearly following the zig zag route to the top, he became a generalist personnel manager acquiring knowledge and skills in industrial relations, remuneration, training and development and as an organisational change agent. This time spent as an MD prepared him for a senior directorship on the CEO/MD Executive Group by widening his Executive Group portfolio to include personnel/HR and commercial operations.

A. 2   It is clear from tracing the personnel/HR director's career history that all three items (i.e. circumstance, deliberate choice and company management development policy) played their part in his career progression. The most important changes of circumstances include the business trauma experienced by the company providing personnel with the opportunity to change direction and come to the fore of the change programme. Second the incumbent personnel director left the company resulting in a vacancy at the Executive Group level. Of course our subject had to convince the CEO he was the person best fitted to fill the role as the Executive Group could have decided to recruit externally or not to have filled the vacancy. Deliberate choice is important in getting to the top as our personnel director, although having

---

Case study 4.1 (Answers) (*continued*)

left school at 15 years of age without formal qualifications, decided to improve his career by studying for graduate membership of CIPD. In addition the decision to change employer was critical in getting back into his preferred career from line management, although his stint in line management turned out to be very important in his subsequent career development. Finally, there is evidence of company management development policy at work in shaping his career, as when the former company took him out of the personnel department into line management and when the case company transferred him out of personnel/HR to be MD at a subsidiary company. This prepared him to return to the top personnel job but with a broadened portfolio at CEO Executive Group level.

5   The power and influence of personnel/HR directors on key business decisions

The concept of authority, power and influence

In both the private and public sectors the CEO/MD is the most influential person on a Board of Directors/CEO/MD Executive Group. However, this power and influence is exercised within the constraints of the politics of organisations and the interrelationship between Board and/or Executive Group members. A distinction needs to be made between authority on the one hand and power and influence on the other. Authority is a relationship of dependency between two or more individuals/or groups (Frooman, 1999; Pfeffer, 1992; Anthony, 1986; Fox, 1971; Dalton, 1959 and Weber, 1964) holding offices or positions legitimised by the legal owners. Such legal owners can be institutional and/or in the case of private sector PLCs, individual shareholders and in public sector organisations (e.g. a local authority) on behalf of individuals collectively. In employing organisations authority is usually structured in a hierarchical format with those in top positions delegating some of their authority to those in lower positions. The ability to reward, and impose sanctions, necessitates the exercise of power by having command over resources. Most staff in any organisation experience authority as something imposed externally upon them by higher management, who have legitimised the use of power to reward and punish in accordance with their subordinates conformity or otherwise to the formal rules of the organisation.

Power can be wielded outside formal authority. Sources of power, such as money, information, equipment, people etc., possessed by one actor, and sought by another, allow the first actor to reward or punish the second and thereby to influence the second actor to behave in a manner, which they would not otherwise have done, if free to decide for themselves. Actors can measure approximately the consequences of their action or inaction. However, in the sphere of social relations objective power is insufficient to explain the complexity of dependency relations. The concept of subjective power becomes relevant. If one actor believes, or perceives, another to possess the power to reward or punish, even though it does not, then the actor wishing to share that perceived resource will allow its behaviour to be influenced, and if that is the outcome, then it is an objective reality (Watson, 1977). Subjective power is normally deployed through processes of managing information, by bluff and persuasion and by negotiation to establish or amend outcomes.

Importantly power, as opposed to authority, can be 'initiated and taken' by an actor who may use it for adverse reasons as happens when a gunman commits a robbery or for good reasons for example when a group challenges a legally constituted but bad law as in the case of British Community Charge (commonly known as the Poll Tax). A minority of the personnel/HR directors in our study were located outside both their company's main PLC Boards and CEO/MD Executive Groups, yet still exercised considerable influence over key business decisions. Others were able to use their influencing skills to persuade their CEO/MDs to elevate them to a seat on the Board or the Executive Group. Formal positional authority is normally important but not sufficient in itself. As Legge (1978) says:

> It is with regard to how decisions on policy and strategy are formed, developed, approved and implemented that takes us to the heart of power within organisations.

Notwithstanding this distributive approach, the exercise of power does not deny the sharing of power by collaboration, participation, team working and joint gain between actors in the achievement of organisational goals.

The relationships of dependency between actors are not static. They are likely to change over time. Watson's (1977) analysis of material and formal rationalities provides an explanation of the dynamics of interrelationships of dependency at work. Based on social action theory the assumption is of key actors interacting with one another to establish structural arrangements for the achievement of some purpose. Material rationality consists of the values, beliefs and economic interests of the actor or group and formal rationality, the means by which these values and interests are pursued. Organisational authority structures are not neutral as they are established by powerful actors in accordance with their own values and interests. Another aspect of Watson's model is that of unintended consequences where subordinates, subject to the organisation's control system (formal rationality), find their own material rationality constrained for example, to enhance their own pay or protect their employment security. Hence the potential for conflict arises, calling forth the need for personnel management coping strategies such as employee involvement to promote common interests and/or disputes procedures to resolve conflicting economic interests. The pattern of causation is two way with people establishing or amending formal structures which in turn influence the behaviour of those subject to its authority. However, the situation is potentially unstable with the widespread multiplicity of values and interests causing a continuous stream of new ideas, inventions and reorganisations to challenge established authority.

Factors influencing power and influence within organisations

Legge (1978), influenced by the work of Hickson *et al.* (1971), identifies contingent factors affecting the distribution of power within organisations between management functions. These factors included the degree of 'uncertainty' experienced by the organisation or its sub-units in achieving their objectives, the function's 'centrality' regarding organisational values, and the degree to which a function's level of expertise can be easily 'substituted' from an alternative source. Kamochie (1994) argues that within management, various departments compete for status and control and that any one function's power is partly derived from the dependency of other departments to have its assistance in achieving the organisational imperatives of profit, added value and cost reduction.

First, in the 1990s Boards of Directors/Executive Groups experienced heightened uncertainty as the complexity and pace of change, from both external and internal environments, increased. If the personnel/HR director can assist the CEO/MD and other directors to find solutions to such problems, then it is more likely the personnel director, and the function represented, will have influence in the decision-making process.

Second, the personnel/HR function's centrality regarding the PLCs dominant value system can be problematic in a market economy with its emphasis on profit, value added and stock market valuation. Traditionally personnel management with its origins in welfare, but more recently equity of treatment of employees, and collective bargaining has been defined as distant from core values of business in capitalist societies compared to other management functions such as finance and marketing.

Third, the authority and power of the personnel/HR director is based on the function's possession of expertise in people management knowledge and skills. Legge discussed the ambiguity of this expertise compared to other management functions highlighting its boundary problems, and the threat to the function's role from line managers (Storey, 1992) or accountants (Armstrong, 1995). In our view successful people management does require a degree of expertise. The competent personnel/HR director who combines high functional expertise with a wider business orientation and effective interpersonal and political skills brings something extra to boardroom deliberations (Hunt and Boxall, 1998; Hall and Torrington, 1998).

Pfeffer's (1992) work on power within organisations provides several insights that may help an understanding of the personnel/HR director's power and influence. He argues that a manager wishing access to sources of power must build credibility with other key actors by satisfying their salient needs and thereby the dependence upon his/her contribution. It is important therefore for personnel/HR directors to establish a reputation for competency in their own field and for getting things done in a successful manner. In this way alliances are established to provide support which can be called on when the personnel/HR director requires the support of others for an HR initiative (Kotter, 1982). Within the boardroom a preparedness to meet the needs of other directors by a willingness to widen their portfolio beyond the personnel/HR function will increase the CEO/MD and others' dependence upon the personnel/HR director.

Pettigrew and McNulty (1995) in their study of NEDs on main boards of directors argue that power is a relational phenomenon as it is generated, maintained and lost in the context of relationships with others. Although NEDs do not have

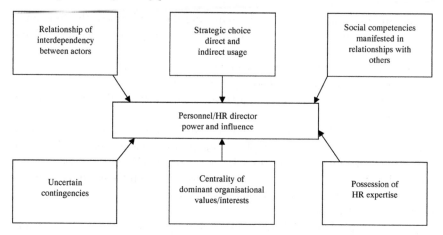

Figure 5.1 Factors influencing the personnel/HR directors' relationships of dependency

the power and influence of executive directors they can enhance their own by making use of the chairperson or CEO/MD as a resource, by networking within the company, by matching their expertise to company context and by the authority provided by formal office such as chairs of audit, remuneration and appointment committees. Pettigrew and McNulty argue individuals have different abilities, skills and willingness to act. Therefore their influence is partly dependent on their 'will' and 'skill' in mobilising the limited power resources available to them. Within this context the important relationships for personnel are the orientation of the CEO/MD to people management, business awareness, the personnel/HR director's effectiveness in interpersonal and team working and professional/technical competence (Kelly and Gennard, 1998).

Pfeffer (1992) and Kamochie (1994) challenge the rationalist imperative of the goals model of organisations. They argue organisations strive for rationality in decisions even if they are made for other reasons. Organisations may restructure for political reasons but claim it to be for the benefit of cost reduction and profit. The goals model requires evaluation of feedback information to judge, if plans are on track and, if not, to take corrective action. However, there is a dearth of such assessment, especially of HR activities such as training and recruitment. Pfeffer also argues there is always room for the use of alternative criteria to challenge established criteria if the latter is showing poor results. Finally, complex multi-dimensional decisions are unlikely to be totally derived from a pure process of analysis. Blame can usually be dispersed due to the multiple of factors influencing decisions, the long time lag involved and shared responsibility. These political considerations can be used to amend or replace targets, standards and assessment criteria within organisations more suitable to an actor's interests and values.

Frooman (1999) takes the work of Pfeffer and Salanick (1978) further by introducing a typology of relationships based on resource exchange between actors i.e. firms and stakeholders. Frooman identifies four relationships of dependency between actors, namely low interdependence where both actors derive limited benefit from the relationship, and high interdependence where they both maximise benefit, and firm, and stakeholder power. Firm and stakeholder power mean an asymmetrical exchange relationship where one or the other actors has a power advantage over the other. A symmetrical exchange relationship exists in both low and high interdependency categories where the actors are either little dependent on one another or alternatively are highly dependent on one another. Frooman introduces to these categories the idea of strategic choice by which an actor decides the means to influence the relationship between them.

We adapt Frooman's categories by substituting CEO/MD power for the 'firm' and personnel/HR director for 'stakeholder's' within the model (see Table 5.1). Matrix cells 1 and 2 are withholding strategies. In cell 1 (no/no) the CEO/MD does not rate personnel/HR as adding value to the business and personnel/HR function does not seek a place on the Board or Executive Group. Cell 2 (no/yes) sees the CEO/MD dependent on the personnel/HR function causing the personnel/HR director to resort to a direct withholding strategy, for example when disagreeing with a particular policy. Such an example from our research was a new MD whose arrival at the shipbuilding company saw a change in its business direction. This led to disagreement within the directors' group, a withholding of cooperation, ending, in time, with the departure of four directors including the personnel director. Cell 3 (yes/yes) covers high interdependence between the actors with the personnel/HR director using a direct usage strategy. Both actors recognise mutual benefit causing the personnel/HR director to emphasise a professional HR style but ensuring integration between business and HR strategies. In this case personnel/HR will have a Board or Executive Group presence. Finally, cell 4 (yes/no) is where the CEO/MD has power over, but is indifferent to personnel/HR, causing the personnel/HR director to resort to an indirect usage strategy to secure influence. Indirect usage strategies used by personnel/HR directors are likely to involve the use of third parties such as NEDs and/or increasing saliency with the CEO/MD and other directors by taking on a broader portfolio and membership of multi-functional project teams.

Table 5.1 Relationships of interdependence between CEO/MDs and personnel/HR directors

		Personnel/HR director dependent on CEO/MD	
		No	Yes
CEO/MD dependent on personnel/HR director	No	1 Indirect withholding (low interdependence)	4 Indirect usage (CEO/MD power)
	Yes	2 Direct withholding (personnel/HR director power)	3 Direct usage (high interdependence)

Source: Adapted from Frooman (1999)

Factors explaining the power and influence of personnel/HR directors

The orientation of CEO/MD to people management

CEO/MDs are the most important actors regarding personnel's presence on any Board including the CEO/MD Executive Group which is the epi-centre for the formulation and implementation of strategy. Within the context of Board structures, history and culture, the CEO/MD in consultation with the chairperson and other directors decides the Board composition and new appointments. Most of the CEO/MDs participating in our research had a positive orientation to the personnel/HR function convinced by experience of its value of the HR contribution to successful business performance. In a minority of cases CEO/MDs did not feel they were highly competent in people management skills, but recognised the importance of such skills for the successful functioning of the Board, and their Executive Group and the company. This point is emphasised by the following quote from a CEO/MD:

> A personnel director who is well networked and has the confidence of his MD and other directors can be very influential. The personnel function of XYZ company has probably been the driving force to a large extent for change in the organisation. For the personnel director it is a question of confidence, getting to know the business and being brave enough to speak his/her mind.

In the case of a major Scottish bank, the personnel/HR director, although not a member of the PLC Board or CEO Executive Group, was on the Board of the largest subsidiary responsible for generating two thirds of the Group's revenue. Other subsidiary companies also had personnel/HR directors. The group CEO was a member of this subsidiary Board. When interviewed he stressed the importance of not over emphasising personnel's formal position in the management hierarchy pointing out:

> We all know and work with each other and much of what we do goes on informally. There are few surprises as any specific proposal will be widely discussed within the executive structure before coming to the main Board. The HR director may not be a formal member of the CEO Management Board but he is not excluded, and if required will be asked to join in the discussion regarding a particular issue.

In this organisation the personnel/HR director was a member of the Group's largest subsidiary bank which often discussed issues of wider implication affecting the Group, and therefore in this forum he was a party to discussions with the CEO and deputy CEO who were also members. The company exhibited characteristics similar to those described by Purcell and Ahlstrand's financially driven decentralised multi-divisional company. It illustrates, however, the influence of personnel at the corporate centre.

The CEO/MDs interviewed were convinced of the business case for personnel/ HR management on three grounds. First, the quality of strategic business decisions was improved if account were taken of their HR implications. In one case a private engineering company entered into a joint venture with a French multinational to improve its competitiveness and to gain access to wider international markets. The new venture required a stronger commercial approach, reorganisation and considerable downsizing of the workforce. The new partner insisted the HR strategy be achieved without major industrial strife. If this happened it was thought it would be damaging to the company's image and delay its ability to deliver in new markets.

Second, even in the turbulent and fiercely competitive markets of the early twenty-first century firms take a longer-term strategic view of their future. Much has been written (Storey and Sisson, 1993) about short-term financial pressures on companies, causing them to reject longer-term HR considerations, placing a premium on behaviours and investments which have an immediate payback. Many HR initiatives fall into this long-term category with management unable to invest in training and development and methods of employee commitment. Our sample suggests some change in direction with more time and effort being put into longer-term HR activities, especially regarding management development, recruitment and employee relations. Boards of Directors and CEO/MD Executive Groups have to balance the competing pressures of short-term financial viability with long-term survival of the organisation.

Third, the involvement of personnel/HR directors obtained a better fit between business and HR strategies leading to better implementation of policies and strategies once decided. Dooley and Fryxell (1999) argue the importance of openness and trustworthiness based on consensus, competence and commitment to improve strategy formation and the successful implementation of strategy to cope with turbulence and complexity arising in the firm's environment. It was argued previously that the implementation of strategy grounded in resource capability theory is as important as its formation (Hunt and Boxall, 1998). These authors take the view that the balancing of the strategy formation and implementation debate provides a more significant role for the HR function.

However, the questionnaire revealed nine out of sixty CEO/MDs did not value the personnel/HR function sufficiently highly to appoint a personnel director to the Board or CEO/MD Executive Group. Some CEO/MDs failed to see how personnel/HR could add value to the business at a strategic level whereas others saw personnel has having a contribution to make, but, with the need to keep Board sizes down to a manageable number, personnel was squeezed out. In these cases the personnel/HR director would report to the Board through an Executive Group member, although the personnel/HR director would be called into Board meetings as and when required. Most important, however, to the exercise of power and influence by personnel/HR directors in an informal way was via frequent interactions with CEO/MDs, as in the steel company case described in a later section of this chapter. Eventually they often gained a seat on the Executive Group as they earned their spurs through, as judged by the CEO/MD and other directors, worthy and creditable contributions.

Finally just as CEO/MDs can establish the personnel/HR function at Board and/or Executive Group levels so they can also unmake it. Since contemporary organisations change rapidly it requires only a change in business direction or the retirement of an established personnel director or the replacement of a people-oriented CEO/MD to alter dramatically the organisational status and influence of personnel management including the position of the personnel/HR director. In our research seven out of sixty personnel/HR directors had at one time lost their jobs due to reorganisation and to a change of CEO/MD. One of our case studies was a conglomerate company de-merged into two businesses as this was judged to be of greater value to shareholders. In one of the resulting companies the new CEO caused the removal of the personnel director from the Executive Group of the PLC. In this case the CEO was convinced personnel/HR had little to contribute at the top strategy level of decision-making. At a Hospital Trust cost reduction considerations required the introduction of performance indicators and the need for senior management to bring about a change of employee attitudes. This caused the CEO to bring in a new director who was from the private sector. However, the new HR director proved too abrasive and upset health service management. The CEO then brought in a new HR director with different qualities. At another company a people centred managing director was replaced by a non-people centred one. The new MD, against the board's wishes, changed the business strategy. This, together with an anti-people management attitude, led to deterioration in relations with the personnel director who subsequently left the company.

Notwithstanding the general argument that a position on the PLC Board or the CEO/MD Executive Group will accord authority, power and influence to the personnel/HR director, it does not follow that the opportunity provided by a seat on the Board will be effectively used. Such examples, however, are difficult to come by. The authors are aware of one case where a personnel director on the main board of directors did not influence the direction of a major change in HR strategy. British Shipbuilders decided in 1979 to centralise collective bargaining at corporate headquarters to facilitate their business strategy to rationalise and reduce numbers working in the industry. This major policy was driven by the executive industrial relations director in conjunction with the CEO at the Executive Group level without one paper on the strategic change going to the main corporate Board. The main Board personnel director was not involved in the formation of the most important employee relations strategy initiated by the company because the CEO did not want his involvement. This example demonstrates the importance of the CEO/MD Group *vis-à-vis* the main Board on such matters.

The business centredness of personnel/HR directors

Our research demonstrated the importance to personnel/HR directors having influence and power by sharing the business values of the other directors and particularly the CEO/MD. Too heavy an emphasis on professional personnel values and standards, is likely to be regarded by CEO/MDs and others as placing too rigid a constraint on the dynamism of modern business, leading to unnecessary tensions within the Board. This may explain Table 4.7 which recorded low rankings (fourth and fifth in a ranking of five) given by CEO/MDs to personnel/HR directors having 'prolonged experience in the HR function' and 'CIPD membership'. CEO/MDs gave the highest priority to a 'rounded knowledge of people problems' and 'proactivity in espousing and implementing HR policies'. Moreover CEO/MDs prefer personnel/HR directors with practical ideas who, as Table 4.6 shows, can offer 'constructive criticism' of policy proposals without becoming intransigent in their opposition and thereby generating conflict within the Executive Group. As Legge (1978) has argued by sharing business values the personnel function had become more central to the dominant value system of a market economy enterprise.

Table 4.9 provides evidence of the pro business attitudes held by the forty-five personnel/HR directors interviewed. They believed their CEO/MDs sought in them as a top priority business competencies i.e. they could make decisions in the 'interests of the whole business' and not just their specialist function. In fact, although CEO/MDs considered business awareness important, they rated it last in a ranking of three. Many personnel directors responded to this question saying that expertise in personnel/HR was taken as a given beyond which you had to contribute more. On the other hand many CEO/MDs took the view that it was openness and a willingness to learn and improve business competency that mattered most in personnel/HR directors. As shown in Chapter 4 business competency was developed by the majority of our sample of personnel directors by moving between management functions, transferring into line management and then back again into the personnel function. In terms of business acumen sought in personnel/HR directors, CEO/MDs preferred them to have had experience in general/line management and/or a willingness to take on non-HR responsibilities as a means of broadening their experience (Table 4.8). The personnel/HR directors' participation in multi-project teams and/or strategic secondments were also excellent methods of broadening their general management experience, even for those who had not worked outside the personnel function.

This sharing of business values by personnel/HR directors has caused several commentators (Tyson, 1995; Storey, 1992) including the authors (1996, 1998) to state that successful personnel directors are businessmen first and personnel specialists second. A more detailed consideration of this question has caused us to shift our position to a more balanced view. Our findings confirm the view that personnel/HR does not rule or dominate private and public sector organisation strategies and can only secure power and influence if HR strategy is seen to contribute to improving business performance. Nevertheless HR is an important ingredient contributing a distinctive competency (knowledge, skill and attitude) to business decision-making. The authors have illustrated this through the concept of the T-shaped manager (Chapter 3) with the stem of the T representing functional expertise combined with the bar of the T representing wider business competency. Successful personnel/HR directors ride both horses, finding a synthesis between them. In our empirical study only five out of sixty personnel/HR directors had been parachuted into the position without any previous work experience in the personnel/HR function. These personnel/HR directors by their own admission were heavily dependent upon the personnel departments within their organisation to supply professional expertise.

The personnel/HR directors' record of success in personnel matters

Although personnel/HR directors contributed to business discussions as members of the Board or CEO/MD Executive Group, they were expected to lead on HR items, to research problems, to provide judgements and to be proactive, not just with regard to ideas, but in delivering policy decisions for the Group. As the personnel director of one large private multi-utility said, 'The CEO is hot on milestones, measurement etc., he wants things to happen once decided'.

Previous chapters have highlighted the importance of the changing external environment faced by contemporary organisations requiring cost reduction and organisational and culture changes in both the public and private sectors. Personnel's ability to deliver for the CEO/MD and the Executive Group can be explained by their social competencies in areas of interpersonal skills, team working, political acumen and networking with others both inside and outside the boardroom (Pfeffer, 1992).

Boards of Directors and Executive Groups are a mixture of knowledge, technical skill and personal talent which have to be brought together to achieve effective performance (Smith, 1995). In sport, team games offer many case histories of highly skilled individuals who under perform as a collective because they fail to work for one another. Team working in business is no different. In a world of increased competition and a quickening pace of change the need in business for collective team and project working has never been greater. Projects and problems requiring new ideas and solutions come ever faster to the fore. No one CEO/MD, personnel/HR or other director is likely to have a monopoly on ideas. There has been a demise of both the functional and finance driven operational Boards in favour of Boards requiring greater openness and collective awareness as a team. As Aram and Cowen (1995) put it, 'The key towards a value creating board lies in the development of a more open attitude on the part of the CEO'.

Kakabadse (1991) argued there has been a shift from 'reactor roles' with Boards containing executives who value their functional expertise to 'thinkers' who reflect on and integrate the work of the Board. Today Executive Groups spend more time anticipating the business's future. This is in contrast to the past when functional directors made reports to their Boards based mainly on what happened in a past period.

Kakabadse (1991) asked executives what skills they needed to perform their jobs effectively. Interpersonal social skills obtained the highest scores. Pettigrew and McNulty (1995) highlight the social skills of persuasion, assertiveness, collaboration, diplomacy, logical argument, trust and respect to improve NEDs' influence in decision-making. Kotter (1982) identified three critical activities, one of which was networking and lobbying through others, that made general managers effective. In Kotter's study the senior general managers knew hundreds of people from whom they could obtain information to help them overcome obstacles to improved performance.

The personnel/HR directors in our research had built up an extensive network of personal relationships as a source of information which was available to assist them in formulating and implementing policy. They were widely known in industry and management, via networks of established contacts with superiors and subordinates; with managers in other functions; with members of cross-functional project teams; with attending general management and personnel conferences; and with links to the wider, academic and consultancy communities. This network of resources could be called upon at the appropriate time to help implement difficult policies. One MD made the following remarks regarding his personnel director:

> The HR director is very important because of a number of factors: he has long service, is thoroughly networked and has street credibility. He is also a skilled negotiator who can be tough when required. His networking includes chairmanship of the Employers' Association of which I am a council member. In this way we interact both in and out of the company keeping each other informed.

In this instance there was a relationship of dependency with both managing director and personnel director working closely together exchanging information, not only about what was happening in their company, but in the wider industry. This early access to information increased both their networking and team playing influence.

The proactivity of personnel/HR directors in achieving board status

Our evidence supports the view that for personnel directors to have significant influence on key business decision-making they require effective relationships with key players, which are more important to the former than their formal position in the organisation. As shown before, personnel/HR directors who do not have a seat on the main PLC Board and CEO/MD Executive Group can nevertheless wield considerable influence on business decisions. Table 4.5 reveals that CEO/MDs require their personnel/HR directors to be team players (i.e. interpersonal and group skills) with professional skills and business acumen. Moreover in a ranking of eight social skills (Table 4.6) high trust relations between CEO/MD and personnel/HR director came top (Dooley and Fryxell, 1999). Our research supports the hypothesis that in organisations where CEO/MDs are favourably disposed to people management, the personnel/HR director has the opportunity to achieve high status and influence. This is Frooman's matrix cell 3 showing high inter-dependence providing mutual benefit to both actors, with personnel making use of a direct usage strategy. When this position is achieved greater integration between business strategy and HR policies is possible.

On the other hand, where CEO/MDs are not so favourably disposed, the road is more difficult. Several of the personnel/HR directors studied had CEO/MDs whose business priorities lay in areas other than people management. However, some personnel/HR people had persuaded the CEO/MDs of the significance of personnel/HR in contributing to, and achieving, business success. In this way personnel/HR directors had initiated and taken power and influence into their own hands. At the shipbuilding company the MD, the first MD after privatisation, had to be persuaded, by the then personnel manager, to appoint a personnel director and to recognise the part personnel/HR strategy could play in business success. In other organisations including an ex-public utility, NHS Trust and a local authority, CEOs had come to recognise the need for strong personnel/HR directors to complement Board activities having initially been sceptical of the public sector administrative role of personnel. In these circumstances Frooman's matrix cell 4 offers a viable explanation with personnel/HR directors resorting to indirect usage strategies to increase the CEO/MDs dependency upon personnel. In this way they had built the dependency of the CEO/MD upon their contribution by satisfying their salient needs (Pfeffer, 1992).

Indirect usage strategies used by personnel/HR directors included most importantly the taking on of a wider portfolio to encompass non-personnel responsibilities. Case study 5.1 illustrates how a proactive personnel/HR director gained promotion to the main board of a Hospital Trust. However, in other cases personnel/HR directors were able to integrate themselves better with the CEO/ MD and other directors by taking over responsibility for an activity of critical importance to the Board. A second indirect usage strategy was for personnel/HR directors to develop their relationships with NEDs, who as chairs of remuneration and appointments committees were dependent on personnel/HR directors for information and advice. Here there was normally a triangular relationship between CEO/MDs, NEDs and the personnel/HR director. It is up to the personnel/HR director to make the most of this opportunity. Third, the credibility of personnel/ HR directors with CEO/MDs and other directors was enhanced when the personnel/HR director had gained non-HR experience through career development by having spent time in a general/line management role. This improved their business credibility in the eyes of other directors.

The power and influence of personnel/HR directors

We judged the influence of personnel/HR directors in making strategic business decisions against four criteria. First, their involvement in the formation and implementation of business and of HR strategies; second, the presence of personnel/ HR directors on the Board of Directors as a means of integrating business strategies and HR; third, informal criteria like close proximity and free access to the CEO/ MD and, finally, multi-directional organisational influence in that the levers of power in contemporary organisation are horizontal, diagonal, and upward.

Strategy formation and implementation

Mintzberg and Waters (1985) warn of the dangers of a dichotomy between strategy formation and implementation. These include an overly static process with one following the other which fails to recognise the artificialness of the separation and to encompass the dynamic effects of continuous feedback between implementation and formulation. Yet many academics have used this division espousing the former to be more important than the latter (Marginson *et al.*, 1993). In the CLIRS survey the personnel/HR function was shown to be more involved in the implementation than in the formation of business strategy, therefore according to its authors less influential. Other commentators notably Sisson (1994) have argued that for the personnel/HR function to be influential it needs to be involved directly in strategy formation as well as its implementation. Although not explicitly addressing power and influence Budhwar (2000) used the involvement of personnel in the formation of strategy as a measure of integration between HR and business strategies. There is a sense in which involvement at the outset in working up a policy (e.g. through membership of a project group) increases the participant's expertise, command over the resource, and therefore influence with others who adopt the strategy and to secure its implementation.

The research data showed CEO/MDs rating personnel/HR directors as highly to moderately involved in the formulation of business strategies. Eighty-three per cent in the case of PLCs and 62 per cent in the case of SMEs. This finding receives support from Budhwar who shows that 87 per cent of 93 firms covered by his study had corporate strategies and that 77 per cent involved the personnel function either at the outset or early in the consultation process. In terms of Legge's (1978) 'centrality' category, personnel/HR directors were involved at the centre of decision-making by working up new strategies as members of the CEO/MD Executive Group. There would appear to be no conflict of values for personnel/HR directors who might otherwise have been constrained by welfare and equity considerations. Our argument, reinforced by the findings in Chapter 4, is that personnel mangers are likely to pick up a rounded business experience. Personnel/HR directors when asked (Table 4.9) what skills they thought CEO/MDs sought from them ranked 'make decisions in the interests of the overall business' at the top.

According to Legge's second category, the personnel/HR director's power and influence relates to the dependency of the CEO/MD Executive Group's on personnel's strategic input. In Frooman (1999) matrix cell 3 records high interdependency of mutual benefit between the actors with the personnel/HR director making use of a direct usage strategy to influence the CEO/MD. Direct usage strategy is defined as offering a professional HR service which fits and facilitates achievement of the company's business strategy. In this regard our research revealed a high trust relationship between CEO/MDs and personnel/HR directors (Table 4.6) through which chief executives' preferences were for HR directors who offer constructive criticism, communicate well, are tuned to the political sensitivities of the Board, and are proactive in helping to solve business problems. It was beneficial to the personnel/HR director's influence if he/she had a rounded career experience in line/general management as well as personnel. The importance our work gives to the trustworthiness between strategic actors in improving the quality of decisions through encouraging dissent at the formulation stage has also been highlighted by Dooley and Fryxell (1999).

Legge also highlighted the role of the professional expertise of the personnel/ HR function. The more HR expertise is in demand by clients, the more powerful will be the personnel/HR function's input to strategy formulation. Our research shows that personnel/HR directors on CEO/MD Executive Groups of PLCs spent 47 per cent of their time on general Board business. At the level of the subsidiary business unit the time devoted to business strategies was 30 per cent. Over three quarters of our personnel/HR directors were involved in the management of training and development, employee relations and recruitment. Other activities such as the formation of personnel policies, personnel/HR strategies, rewards and benefits took between one half and three quarters of their time.

The personnel/HR directors played a significant role, through relationships with NEDs, on strategic conditions covering the recruitment, promotions and remuneration of top executives. However, NEDs are part-time, meet infrequently and possess limited expertise regarding the business itself. They are dependent on the full-time executive directors, including the personnel director/HR, for advice and technical data such as pay norms etc. This provides an opportunity to personnel/HR directors to develop relationships with NEDs who are in Frooman's sense, a third stakeholder. This opens up the possibility for the personnel/HR director to exercise influence on the CEO/MD through an indirect usage strategy promoting the salience of the personnel/HR function (Pfeffer, 1992). Finally CEO/ MDs were not looking for overly professional personnel/HR directors (as reflected in their low ranking of 'prolonged experience in the personnel function' and 'CIPD membership', Table 4.7) but for directors possessing a well 'rounded knowledge of people problems' who were 'proactive in initiating HR policies' appropriate to securing, and then delivering the company business strategies.

The presence of personnel / HR directors on the board of directors

The personnel/HR function's presence on Board of Directors has been taken by some academics as a proxy for the function's authority, power and influence. A position on the Board *a priori* suggests high status, the function is adequately resourced and has command over and access to information, budgets and criteria for judging successful performance (Purcell, 1994). The work of Pfeffer (1992) shows the importance of being in a position to influence the formal criteria set up for judging successful performance as these are often politically determined. According to Tyson and Fell (1986) the work of management cannot be wholly scientifically determined.

Much of the variance in results of the extent of personnel/HR directors on Boards of Directors is due to differences in sample sizes and the methods of obtaining the data. In addition the authors also consider that the definition of the

Board of Directors itself has not been dealt with adequately in the academic literature in that the type and level of Board being referred to is not clear. Our questionnaire surveys and interview programme with CEO/MDs and personnel/HR directors, for example, revealed this existence not only of the main PLC Board but also the CEO/MD Executive Group whose role and function has been virtually ignored by previous research into the power and influence of personnel/HR directors. The latter was the point at which the detailed work on the formulation on business strategy was conducted.

The CEO/MD Executive Group was responsible for formulating and implementing business and HR strategies, therefore, any analysis of the real influence of the personnel/HR function in the contemporary corporation must include CEO/MD Executive Groups. As Legge (1978) has argued, 'It is with regard to how decisions are formed, developed and implemented that takes us to the heart of power within organisations'.

PLC Boards are the ultimate authority for monitoring and approving the work of the Executive Group, but it is the CEO/MD Group where decisions regarding strategic direction and expenditures are initiated, discussed and worked up into firm proposals for submission to the main Board, for approval. Evidence relating to the existence of the CEO/MD Executive Group was last recorded in the HRM literature over 20 years ago (Brannon *et al.*, 1979; Pahl and Winkler, 1974). In recent years its existence has not even been mentioned and certainly not in academic debates concerning the extent of the power and influence of the personnel/HR director on key organisational decisions.

Informal power and influence

The Brewster *et al.* (2000) model highlights the significance of informal influences on the formulation of strategic decisions. Tables 3.5 and 3.7 (Chapter 3) show that personnel/HR directors participate more in the making of business strategies than their formal position on the main PLC Board and CEO/MD Executive Groups would on the surface indicate. Personnel's representation on CEO/MD Executive Groups was 73 per cent, but their involvement in making business strategies according to evidence from CEO/MDs interviews and surveys was 83 per cent. For SMEs the respective figures were 44 per cent presence on boards but with a 62 per cent involvement in strategy formation.

Our research revealed a number of situations where a personnel/HR director was neither a member of the PLC Board nor the CEO/MD Executive Group but had established high credibility with the chairperson/CEO and other executive directors and was influential on strategy formulation. One of these was in the steel industry where the CEO had issued an instruction that no HR issue should arrive at the CEO Executive Group without having been routed through the personnel director's office. In this way the personnel director offered advice and undertook the necessary research to provide the appropriate information for boardroom discussion. Although not a member of the Executive Group the personnel director, through his network of informal relations with the CEO and others, was frequently called to attend Board meetings to discuss the HR implications of the decisions they were being asked to take.

There thus existed in some of our case study organisations an informal, dynamic and fluid situation (Watson, 1977) where personnel/HR directors interacted with their CEO/MDs and the Board/Executive Groups in the formulation of strategy, but were not formally members of the Board or the Executive Group. Given the pace and complexity of changes facing contemporary businesses the reality of actor relationships is ahead of formal institutional arrangements. Personnel/HR directors are involved in meeting new challenges but their contribution in this regard has not yet been formally recognised by the Board or Executive Group. Our research also uncovered evidence of newly appointed personnel/HR directors not gaining formal Board representation until such times has they had proven themselves to the CEO/MD and other members of the Executive Group. They were being required to earn their spurs before being invited into the 'inner cabinet'.

In one major utility the main Board HR director left and was replaced by an individual who was given the title HR director and who was appointed to the CEO Executive Group but not the main Board. At another company the CEO said, 'To get onto the main Board the HR director must show that he/she can contribute to the whole business and not just personnel. Our own HR director will be judged by his performance on the Executive Group'. Hall and Torrington (1998) make a similar point when they say, 'The most senior personnel person had been a Board member, but when they left the new appointee to head the personnel function was not automatically given a place on the Board – they had to earn their spurs'.

In Frooman's terms, as a strategy, matrix cell 4 seems the most appropriate in this regard as it would emphasise high CEO/MD power causing personnel/HR directors to choose an indirect usage strategy to enhance their influence. Progressive personnel/HR directors make extensive use of informal relations with chairpersons and other NEDs. In this regard our research shows personnel/HR directors in subsidiaries/business units are more likely than those at PLC level to widen their job portfolio to include non-personnel tasks. Hence a proactive orientation by personnel/HR directors based on an effective relationship of influence and social skills (Pettigrew and McNulty, 1995) is important in the context of informal power and influence.

Multi-directional organisational influences on strategy

Informal criteria recognises that power and influence in formulating business and HR strategies is not totally top down from the corporate centre to the peripheral sub-units of organisations. Modern multinational companies generally comprise decentralised business units exercising a degree of autonomy to ensure closer relationships with customers, suppliers, domestic laws and governments of various countries etc. Subsidiaries are capable of initiating and developing new policies in production, marketing and employee relations etc., contributing savings to the corporate centre and ensuring their own survival. Communications can be exercised in upward, horizontal and diagonal directions. We have pointed out previously the strategic initiative of a subsidiary company in the brewing industry through which the local company persuaded the corporate centre to invest in new technology and its employee relations implications. Moreover many of the manufacturing business units researched had initiated cellular team working arrangements to accommodate changes in production technologies thereby becoming the leading edge or corporate group experts in this area. These changes were frequently reported back to the corporate centre and subsequently adopted as Group strategies to be rolled out to other subsidiaries within the Group (Ferner and Varul, 2000a).

Case study 5.1

This case is drawn from a Hospital Trust. Questions are posed at the end of the case study to which indicative answers are provided at the end of the chapter.

An HR director negotiates a place onto the board of directors

In 1993 the Conservative government reformed the National Health Service introducing competition between hospitals. The National Health Service Trusts became the employers of staff. This Hospital Trust located in Scotland employed 1800 people. The Trust contracted with the Area Health Board securing 82 per cent of its income from that source. Other sources included 3 per cent from other Health Authorities, 2 per cent from GP fund holders and the remainder from private and miscellaneous sources. The Trust's business strategy was heavily influenced by the Area Health Authority which was known to be considering the establishment for the area of one main supplier for acute surgery. The Trust was in direct competition with another major surgical Trust in the area. The health authority had a number of reasons for this strategy. First, the population norm for an acute Hospital Trust carrying out specialist medical procedures was 300,000, whereas its area population was 270,000. Second, the drive for economy in the health service meant it made sense to concentrate the cost of high tech equipment in one centre. Third, there was a national shortage of consultants, junior doctors and specialist nurses. This problem was exacerbated by the government's agreement with the British Medical Association (BMA) to reduce the working hours of junior doctors. The Trust's Board was determined to win this competitive race by reducing its cost base and improving its performance indicators. The Trust, as a new employer, was required to establish contracts of employment, an appropriate salary structure, and to decide whether or not to recognise trade unions and if so the scope of collective bargaining and joint consultation.

Case study 5.1 (*continued*)

When established in 1993 the Trust Board consisted of a part-time chairperson, five NEDs and five executive directors consisting of the CEO and directors of medicine, nursing, finance and contracts. The HR director did not have membership of the Trust Board of Directors but did have a presence on the CEO Executive Group. Moreover the CEO attitude to the personnel function, based on his pre-1993 employment experience, was not positive. He regarded it as administrative and rule bound. The HR director had been appointed in 1994 and by 1996 he had secured membership of the main Trust Board. To secure this elevation the HR director worked on a number of levers. First, he identified the critical nature of HR strategy to the success of the Trust's business strategy of becoming the sole supplier of acute services within the area. A hospital's reputation amongst medical peers depends on the quality of its consultants who in turn attract quality junior doctors to train under them. Given the national shortage of consultants, junior doctors and specialist nurses, he persuaded the chief executive that the Trust's recruitment and retention and training and development policies for junior doctors would thus be crucial.

Second, the HR director had close interaction with the Trust chairperson and NEDs who staffed the appointments and remuneration sub-committees of the Trust Board. NEDs were formally responsible for the appointment of executive directors but relied on the advice and technical data provided by the CEO and HR director. These tri-angular inter-personal interactions and their need for team working gave the HR director the opportunity to show his abilities. Third, the HR director took on responsibility for management of the Trust's hotel operations. The Trust held strategic discussions on whether or not to put hotel operations out to private contractors. The HR director was opposed to this strategy arguing that to do so would allow for a one off cost improvement after which the Board would no longer be in direct control of the means of achieving continuous improvements in this area. In addition to retain the hotel operations 'in house' the HR director argued, meant the trade unions would be more willing to support future efficiency measures designed to keep the service in house. The HR director won the argument and the Board gave him responsibility for management of hotel operations.

The HR director had used an indirect usage strategy (Frooman, 1999) to bring his influence to bear on the CEO, despite the latter's initial negative views on the contribution of personnel/HR to adding value to the business.

Questions

Q. 1   Explain the threats and opportunities facing the hospital Trust in the case study.

Q. 2   Using Frooman's usage strategies of interdependence explain how the HR director secured elevation to the Trust's Board of Directors.

Case study 5.1 (Answers)

An HR director negotiates a place in the boardroom

Your answers to these questions should have included most of the following points:

A. 1 The principal idea of the government's reform of the National Health Service was to inject competition into it by a separation of purchasers (the health Boards) and suppliers (the Trusts) with the latter competing for business within and outside its geographical areas. Providing the Trust could improve costs, establish a reputation for quality and timely delivery of services, it had the opportunity to expand its business and reputation with the health Board, patients and the professional world of medicine. Here the quality of staff was critical to the Trust's mission, and therefore the key role for the personnel/ HR department in reducing employment costs was its policy implementation for attracting, developing and retraining consultants, junior doctors and specialist nurses.

The greatest threat arose from the Area Health Board's strategy to have one major provider for the area for acute surgery services. This strategy was based on its limited population of 270,000 when the established view of the medical profession was that the optimum provision of acute medical proce- dures by one Trust required a population of 300,000. Second, given the drive for economy in the health service it made sense to concentrate the high cost of expensive technical equipment into one centre and then increase its use. Third, there was a national shortage of consultants, junior doctors and specialist nurses, exacerbated by the government's agreement with the BMA to reduce junior doctors' working hours. This threat sharpened the competitive edge of the Trust which attempted to win the race with the other Trust, in the area, for the acute surgery services by reducing costs and improving its performance.

A. 2 Frooman's usage strategies of interdependence between two or more actors have both direct and indirect elements. A direct usage strategy is most appropriate where both actors perceive a relationship of high dependence and mutual benefit, whereas an indirect usage strategy is appropriate where the power distribution is asymmetrical with one actor having dominance over the other. In the latter case the weaker actor will choose to influence the stronger by involving a third actor or valued event. In the case of the Trust the HR director was not a member of the main Trust Board of Directors but was a member of the CEO Executive Group. Moreover the CEO held negative views on the value of personnel management based on past experience when personnel services were provided by the Area Health Board. How then did the HR director achieve elevation to the main Trust Board two years after joining the Trust?

Case study 5.1 (Answers) (*continued*)

First, he identified the critical nature of HR strategy to the success of the Trust's business strategy to become the sole supplier of acute surgical services. A Trust's reputation amongst medical peers depends on the quality of its consultants who in turn can attract quality junior doctors to train under them. Given the national shortage of consultants, junior doctors and specialist nurses the Trust's recruitment and retention policies and training and development of junior doctors became critical to its mission. In Frooman's terms this was a direct usage strategy.

Second, the HR director had close interactions with the Trust chairperson and NEDs who staffed the appointments and remuneration sub-committees of the Trust Board. NEDs were formally responsible for the appointment of executive directors and relied on the advice and technical support provided by the CEO and HR director. These inter-personal interactions and contributions to team working gave the HR director the opportunity to show his abilities. Third, the HR director demonstrated the 'will' to take on responsibility for the hospital's hotel operations. The Trust Board held strategic discussions on whether on not to put hotel operations out to private contractors. The HR director argued against this development as sub-contracting the service would deliver a one off cost improvement but the Trust would lose control for the opportunity for continuous improvement year on year. In Frooman's terms this was an indirect usage strategy.

Frooman's direct and indirect usage strategies can thus be combined to explain the elevation of the HR director to the main Trust Board. He enhanced his influence both directly and through a third party (the NEDs) and by a willingness to take on a non-HR activity important to the business strategy of the Trust.

6 Personnel/HR directors in small and medium enterprises

We turn now to examine the role of the personnel/HR director in the small and medium-sized enterprise (SME) in both the manufacturing and service sectors. A continuous theme is the comparison of the personnel/HR director role in these sectors with that of the personnel/HR director on the corporate PLC Board and/ or the Chief Executive Group. The focus of analysis remains the power and influence which personnel/HR directors exert in the strategic decision-making processes in SMEs.

The context of SMEs

In the 1970s the typical employing unit was the large centralised organisation with standardised policies managed by formal rules (and collective agreements with trade unions). In the UK almost one third of the labour force was employed in the public sector (see Chapter 8). Many of these large organisations were often over staffed and inefficient. Personnel and industrial relations research in the 1960s and 1970s focused on these organisations to the almost exclusion of SMEs. All this began to change, however, over the last two decades of the twentieth century, as large organisations downsized workforces, and divisionalised, decentralised and devolved decision-making to smaller business units. Redundancies, higher unemployment and the gradual awareness that large organisations would not necessarily be the source of new employment opportunities, motivated individuals becoming redundant from such organisations, encouraged also by central government incentives to do so, began to establish their own small enterprises. The Conservative governments of the 1980s established agencies such as the DTI's Small Business Advisory Unit, Scottish Enterprise, and local enterprise companies to provide advice to new, and potential, entrepreneurs to draw up business plans. It was envisaged small firms would grow into medium size and subsequently larger firms to provide the new employment opportunities of the future. In 1980 the number of SMEs was estimated at 2.4m but by 1998 had risen to 3.7m. In 1993 the SME share of employment was 50 per cent but had increased to 56 per cent by 1998 (DTI, Statistical Bulletin, 1994; 1999).

In 1999 the DTI estimated there were 3.7m SMEs in the UK of which 2.3m were single owners or partnerships without employees. These constitute 64 per cent of businesses, 13 per cent of total employment in the economy and 5 per cent of turnover UK wide. Table 6.1 provides a further breakdown of these figures.

In terms of distribution by industry the highest percentage of SMEs were found in agriculture, forestry and fishing, construction, education and personal services. The lowest presence of SMEs was in utilities such as electricity, gas and water supply, mining/quarrying and financial services. The geographical distribution of SMEs centred around Northern Ireland and Wales, with the least concentration in London and the East Midlands.

The Workplace Employee Relations Survey (Cully *et al.*, 1999) investigated both small stand-alone businesses and small multiples (i.e. small establishments owned by larger firms) finding the former were more likely to be found in manufacturing, health and business services. Some 40 per cent of small stand-alone businesses were family-owned and controlled. This compares with small multiples which were characterised by no individual or family having a controlling interest, and many of which were to be found in the wholesale and retail trades.

Conventional models of employment relations in SMEs

The HRM literature on SMEs identifies two main employment relations models – the 'harmonious' and the 'bleak house' (Sisson, 1993). The 'harmonious' model pictures the SME owned and controlled by a family and in which the level of professional management is unlikely to be high. The owner devotes most of their time to the technical, production and sales aspects of the business. Communications are open and informal with the owner manager engaging with employees, albeit in an informal manner, on the job. The small numbers employed, together with the absence of formal procedures, encourage good human relations and increased task flexibility as employees turn their hand to what is required. Family friendly work arrangements are more easily established to meet the needs of individuals where circumstances justify it.

The history of the 'bleak house' scenario can be traced back to the nineteenth-century small sweated trades/companies paying low wages in highly competitive industries. In 1909 these conditions necessitated the introduction of Trade Boards (renamed Wages Councils in the Wages Council Act of 1945) offering some minimum protection to workers against the worst conditions (*Industrial Relations*

Table 6.1 Numbers employed in SMEs including percentages of total businesses, employment and turnover

Company size	Total employment	Percentage of businesses	Percentage of employment	Percentage of turnover
Less than 10	4 million	31	18	18
10–99	4 million	5	19	22
100–249	3 million	0.3	12	16

Source: DTI *Statistical Bulletin*, 1999

Handbook, 1961). The 'bleak house' is characterised by poorer working conditions and lower pay compared to those pertaining to larger organisations. Indeed according to Cully *et al.* (1999) many firms paying below the national minimum wage are found in the small firm sector. According to the Low Pay Commission Second Report (1999) the introduction of the national minimum wage in April 1999 at £3.60 per hour affected mostly small businesses in terms of having to raise pay rates to the minimum wage level. The Commission surveyed 1000 firms with less than 50 employees and compared them with a sample of larger firms employing more than 50 employees. This showed the pay distribution of the smaller firms to be at the lower end of the scale compared to that of the larger firms. The Commission nevertheless concluded that the majority had managed successfully to adjust to the new minimum wage.

In smaller organisations there is an absence of formalisation and sometimes a disregarding of employee rights and protection. The characteristics of the 'bleak house' model mean there is little demand on the part of owners to employ specialist personnel/HR expertise.

According to Cully *et al.* (1999) trade union recognition is practically non-existent in smaller firms (i.e. those employing between 10 and 99), but it is estimated at 12 per cent for all stand-alone businesses, and 7 per cent for those SMEs with a full-time working owner (Rainnie, 1989). Although organised collective conflict is virtually non-existent, interpersonal tensions are to the fore as demonstrated by the higher number of resignations and dismissals in stand-alone relative to larger businesses and small multiples (Cully *et al.*, 1999). This is reinforced in that the rate of applications to Employment Tribunals over a breach of employment rights is higher in SMEs generally than in small multiples but slightly lower than in larger businesses (Cully *et al.*, 1999).

Notwithstanding these caveats employees are said to derive greater job satisfaction than their colleagues in larger organisations. The Bolton Report (1971) and Schumacher (1973) record the benefits of working for the smaller firm include employee self-selecting by trading off higher financial rewards for more satisfactory human relations. In the circumstances of family ownership, of the absence of a professional management orientation, of low unionism and policy informality, Cully *et al.* (1999) argue there is little need for professional personnel/HR expertise.

More sophisticated models of HR in SMEs

The 'harmonious' and 'bleak house' models do not capture the complexity of the SME sector. For example many SMEs in the graphical (where the average size of enterprise is nine employees), engineering and construction industries are active members of their respective employers' associations taking advice from those bodies on modern HR practice including disciplinary procedures, trade union recognition and entering into and abiding by industry-wide collective agreements. The press-rooms of the graphical industry have over 90 per cent trade union membership. The industry is a small firm sector with a high degree of union membership, relatively good employment conditions and effective collective bargaining institutions and procedures which establish minimum employment pay and conditions standards. Curran and Stanworth (1981 cited in Bacon *et al.*, 1996) argue that employees do not self-select their workplaces, that the pattern of social relations varies, and that small organisations have higher instability and labour turnover. On the other hand Hornsby and Kuratko (1990) conluded on the basis of a study of 247 SMEs in the USA that by adopting leading edge management practices the personnel policies of smaller firms are more sophisticated than the academic literature conveys.

An interesting study on HRM in SMEs is the Leicestershire 'new management' survey undertaken by Bacon *et al.* (1996). Their survey covered 229 SMEs each employing under 200 workers. Selecting eleven new management policies covering such items as job flexibility, team working and performance appraisals they scored the firms on HR initiatives they had introduced over the last five years regarding whether the initiative had been sustained and/ or whether it contributed to the objectives of the business. The scoring on the adoption of five or more of the initiatives was surprisingly high. Team-work and increased job flexibility reported adoption rates of around 75 per cent. Other highly scored management initiatives included devolved management and harmonised conditions of employment. To quote the authors, 'It suggests that the new management agenda has penetrated deep into the UK and that innovative and progressive employee relations practices are no longer restricted to large main stream companies'.

Bacon *et al.* sought to verify their findings by conducting interviews in 13 case study organisations which they had surveyed by postal questionnaire. Unfortunately they were not borne out. For example, 12 organisations claimed in the survey to have team working but in the interview programme only seven could confirm such a practice actually existed. Eight claimed in the questionnaire survey to conduct performance appraisals for non-management staff but only four could produce evidence in the interview programme to confirm this. Ten claimed to have harmonised terms and conditions of employment, but in the interview programme only two could produce documentary evidence of this. Bacon *et al.* concluded that these new employment policies had achieved their objectives and contributed significantly to the attainment of the firms' business objectives. Notwithstanding, the reduced number of new management agenda polices actually adopted as opposed to claimed, the results show considerable sophistication and variance exists in the management styles and policies of SMEs thereby exposing the superficiality of both the 'harmony' and 'bleak house' models.

The Workplace Employee Relations Survey (1998) confirmed, but to a less optimistic degree, the Leicestershire survey findings. Its sample contained 250 independent private workplaces employing less than 100 employees. Regarding the adoption of new management policies such as employee involvement, performance appraisal, performance related pay etc., the WERS showed that 28 per cent of SMEs had initiated five or more such practices. However, Marlow (1997) proffers caution in her study of 28 SMEs arguing, due to cost pressures, they have no strategic approach, little professional management and are major contributors to poor employee relations. Marlow's work receives support from WERS (Cully *et al.*,

1999) which shows the number of dismissals from work to be higher at an average of 2.3 per 100 employees compared to an average of 1.5 per 100 employees for larger organisations. Small stand-alone businesses had more individual employee complaints against them (average of 1.5 per 1000 employees) to Employment Tribunals than small multiples (average 0.6 per 1000 employees). The existing research literature on the adoption of new management policies in SMEs suggests a trend towards formalisation and the requirement for more professional management, including personnel expertise.

Pressures of the external supply chain

Kinnie *et al.* (1999) have shown the importance of external relationships between the SME and its customers, suppliers and competitors as an influence on internal HR policies and processes. Boon and Ram (1998) outline the importance of pressures from large firms to get SMEs to adopt quality standards. The supply chain is important to understanding management decision-making in SMEs. To quote Kinnie *et al.*:

> Critically, most SMEs do not face product markets made up of hundreds or thousands of customers, but instead have relatively few customers with whom they do regular business. Commonly these customers are much larger organisations who potentially have a great deal of power over suppliers.

The management of SMEs can decide either to establish an actively networked institutional relationship with a large customer to reduce the vagaries of competitive market pressures or to live with short-term uncertainty. If they choose the former, the SME becomes highly dependent on the big organisation to take a large share of its output and this large, almost sole customer, may therefore require as a condition of continuing to do business, the SME adopt certain HR policies and practices. Beaumont *et al.* (1996) distinguished between direct and indirect influences. In the former case the customer, through an audit process, establishes if the supplier has achieved specific standards in employee relations whereas in the latter, the most common method – customer performance demands – will indirectly require the supplier to change its arrangements for human resources.

Two examples of such customer pressure were witnessed during our research. A meat manufacturer in central Scotland with 240 employees supplied meat to the retail outlets of a large supermarket. This customer accounted for 90 per cent of the company's revenue stream. Competitive pressures in retail resulted in the supermarket seeking lower prices from its suppliers. The small meat manufacturer in order to keep the contract had to supply at the same quality, lower prices and absorb any extra costs. It responded by seeking improved efficiencies by introducing 12-hour shifts and reducing employee tea breaks from four to two per shift. Management argued that tea breaks increased down time, because of the need to clean tools and equipment before departure to the canteen and the work location. The employees initially resisted the changes in working patterns on the grounds that the severe cold temperatures in meat preparation and packaging required employees to have more frequent breaks to stay warm than was the case in a normal workplace. However, the employees accepted the proposed changes in working patterns recognising that not to do so was likely to result in the loss of the supermarket contract and thereby the possible closure of the factory or significant redundancies.

Our second example features a company in distribution (employing 240) which also held a contract to supply the retail outlets of one of the top four retail grocery supermarkets chains in Britain. Such an agreement between the SME and the supermarket is known in the industry as an 'open book' contract under which the SME's employment and equipment charges are reimbursed by the supermarket subject to the quality of product and service provision. The supermarket paid a fixed management fee to the SME for these services. The supermarket insisted that as a condition of a continuing commercial relationship the SME insert a clause in the disputes procedure, jointly signed with the trade union representing its employees, that in the event of their pay negotiations breaking down the two parties would invoke pendulum arbitration to resolve their differences. The 1999 pay and conditions negotiations did break down with the union rejecting management's final offer which was only half of one per cent lower than the union's final claim. However, the supermarket refused to fund this difference so the dispute went to arbitration with the arbitrator awarding in favour of the company. The customer (i.e. the supermarket chain) thus had a more direct influence on the employment relationship within the SME and its employees than the SME itself.

Human resource processes in SMEs

Recruitment and selection

Recruitment and selection concerns the means by which employers attract candidates to apply for vacancies and assuming a greater number of job applicants to vacancies the screening out process leads to a valid and reliable job offer to the successful candidate(s). Given the characteristics of SMEs one might expect cost minimisation, and a personal and informal style to be adopted in the recruitment and selection of candidates. The research evidence of Carroll *et al.* (1999) covering 40 SMEs (employing between 7 and 207 employees) showed the most important recruitment methods to be recommendations by existing staff and former employees, registers kept on interested applicants and former employees, casual callers, job centres and the local press. Word of month was a major method of selecting employees and although job analysis and person specifications were virtually non-existent, 60 per cent did make use of job descriptions (Cully *et al.*, 1999). Stronger employer preferences for more formal recruitment methods was found in the high-technology sector and in recruiting clerical and technical employees as opposed to managers and manual workers.

Selection methods utilised the informal one-to-one interview with the sole criterion being the degree of fit between the job applicant and the others in the organisation. In other words social integration is what matters with little attempt made to assess technical capabilities. An Australian SME study by McDonald and Wiesner (1998) indicates greater formalisation with formal one to one interviews and application pro forma most popular at 48 and 31 per cent respectively. In the Leicestershire survey (Bacon *et al.*, 1996) only 3 per cent of firms employing 15 to 24 employees used psychometric tests rising to 5 per cent for firms employing 25 to 199 employees. The WERS (1998) estimate that overall a figure of 22 per cent use of attitudinal tests in selection, but this covers the whole sample of small to large companies. McDonald and Wiesner record a 2 per cent use of psychometric tests in SMEs in Australia.

Carroll *et al.* found little existence of formal and systemised procedures which required specialist expertise in personnel/HR to design and implement. Nevertheless, there were some indicators supportive of increasing sophistication in HR policies arising from promotions in a larger than expected internal labour market, the significant use of formalised means such as job centres, education establishments and local advertising media.

Training and development

Training and development is another area seen as pertinent to the success of SMEs. Both the 'harmony' and 'bleak house' models suggest formal training programmes are too costly and unnecessary. What training, if any, carried out is likely to be at an informal level with training needs identified on the basis of personal perceptions and expectations. Performance appraisal, a formal means of identifying training needs, may be regarded too bureaucratic and time consuming for SMEs. However, Bacon *et al.* (1996) and McDonald and Wiesner's Australian studies record significant formal performance appraisal policies in SMEs. Formal education and training courses supplied by external agencies and tertiary education institutions are often said not to meet the customised requirements of SMEs. Moreover, small firms are generally more reluctant than larger enterprises to assist employees to obtain formal qualifications thereby increasing their employability but also the probability of leaving the organisation. SMEs generally suffer higher turnover rates relative to larger firms (Cully *et al.*, 1999). As Matlay (1999) says, 'Employees question the validity and relevance of formal, off the job training programmes, which in their opinion, take them away from the very job they are supposed to learn how to do more efficiently'.

SME expenditure on training and development is thought to be low. A study by Barclay's Bank (1994) records only 23 per cent of small businesses made any form of investment in training and development for any employee category.

A 1999 Scottish survey of SMEs conducted by the Department of Human Resource Management at the University of Strathclyde showed informal on-the-job training and development to be the most common method, followed by external consultants and tertiary education providers some way behind in third place. Training programmes for managers preferred by SMEs on the basis of this survey included skills in employee counselling, employment selection, absenteeism, grievance handling, negotiating and team building.

Loan-Clarke *et al.* (1999) identified a number of factors explaining the minimalist informal approach to training and development in SMEs. These factors included family ownership. Organisations without a founding member of the family in its current management invested significantly more money and time in management development than businesses where the family still had a significant influence. In Ireland Cromie *et al.* (1995) reported a similar finding. This has been put down to a strong preference by the family owner/manager for technical as opposed to management training. It is most unlikely the owner would have had such training, and does not perceive the need for training of other managers. More cynically some have suggested owners way not wish other managers to be more knowledgeable and/or competent than themselves.

As SMEs grow from very small organisations to medium-sized ones the degree of formalisation, specialisation and delegation in decision-making increases (McDonald and Wiesner, 1998). Newton and Hunt's study (1997) into general practice in the health sector of 474 SMEs, showed delegation to increase from 24 to 35 per cent between small and medium-sized organisations; specialisation increased from 18 to 21 per cent and formalisation from 21 to 25 per cent for the same organisations. The corresponding figures for larger general practices were delegation 44 per cent, specialisation 31 per cent and formalisation 30 per cent. Larger employment size also correlates with a greater number of managers allowing larger organisations economies of scale whereby the work of the manager away on an external training course can be covered by other employees, a luxury the smallest enterprises cannot afford. The larger the organisation the more difficult it is for the owner manager to deal with all managerial issues, hence training investment will increase with organisational size.

Notwithstanding these factors the Loan-Clarke *et al.* (1999) study provides evidence of a change in direction with conditions favourable to the development of formal HR policies. SMEs are more likely than previously thought to operate an internal market. Promotion and career development is more prevalent with SMEs more committed to expenditure on management qualifications and not just short courses. Other evidence to support this systematic approach comes from the Bacon *et al.* (1996) study which shows performance appraisal policy initiatives at 44 per cent of SMEs employing between 15 and 24 employees rising to 46 per cent for firms with between 25 and 199 employees. McDonald and Wiesner (1998) show 75 per cent of SMEs encouraged formal objective setting between line managers and their subordinates. This compares with 56 per cent reported in the 1998 Workplace Employee Relations Survey.

Australian research data generally reveals a more optimistic picture than that for Britian. It defines SMEs as firms employing between 20 and 200 employees categorised into small businesses employing 99 or fewer employees and medium-sized firms as employing between 100 and 199. Table 6.2 shows training and development practices in Australian SMEs.

The Australian data therefore shows that medium-sized organisations, compared to smaller SMEs, are more likely to have a formal training budget, management development training programmes, to provide formal in-house training by their

Table 6.2 Training and development practices in Australian SMEs

Practices	Percentage of SMEs	Numbers
Technical or vocational training	76	414
Management development training	76	408
Informal mentoring	77	398
Formal mentoring	38	393

Source: McDonald and Wiesner, 1998

own staff and/or by consultants, and to provide external training by the tertiary education sector.

Employee relations

Employment size is a factor in trade union recognition (Cully *et al.*, 1999) with 39 per cent of the smallest category of firm (25 to 49 employees) recognising unions compared to 57 per cent of workplaces in the medium category (100 to 199 employees) and 78 per cent in the largest category (500+ employees). However, these categories are based on workplaces many of which are sub-units of larger organisations where it may be corporate policy to recognise trade unions for collective bargaining purposes. In stand-alone businesses employing less than 100 employees trade union recognition is at 12 per cent, although union density (i.e. the proportion employees holding union membership) is higher at 22 per cent. In Italy average union density is reported at 24 per cent in companies employing between 10 and 99 employees and 35 per cent for companies employing between 100 and 499 employees (Negrelli, 1998). In their Australian study McDonald and Wiesner estimate 25 per cent of SMEs have entered into formal agreements with trade unions.

According to some commentators (Cully *et al.*, 1999; Gennard and Judge, 1999) it is not SMEs or workplace size which is the most important determinant of trade union recognition but management attitudes towards trade unions. To quote Cully *et al.*:

> The high correlation between union presence and recognition is not related to employment size, but is associated with management attitudes and is substantially lower in workplaces where management are not in favour of union membership.

This finding is not new having been a theme in the 1960s' industrial relations literature, particularly by Bain in his submission to the Royal Commission on Trade Unions and Employers' Associations (1968) and in his work on the growth of white collar trade unionism (1970). However, our research into personnel/HR influence in SMEs provides support for our main hypothesis, namely it is the CEO/MD, assisted by an Executive Group or Board, who determines the status, power and influence of people management within the organisation. The CEO/MD who rates HR management, as an important ingredient in the success of a business enterprise, is more likely to appoint a personnel/HR director with whom they will decide whether trade union recognition is in the best interest of the business.

One of our SME case study organisations was a local newspaper in the Kent area where the personnel director proposed to the board they prepare for trade union recognition in the light of the statutory trade union recognition provisions of the Employment Relations Act (1999). Its journalists were well organised but the company had resisted recognising the National Union of Journalists. The CEO disagreed with the personnel director's proposal remaining totally against trade union recognition. This fundamental disagreement over employee relations strategy led the personnel director to resign. However, the CEO of another firm in the same industry made contact with him and offered him the position of HR director, with a seat on his Executive Group, to formulate a strategy for trade union recognition in the light of the 1999 Act. The CEO in the second firm took the view that it was better to take the initiative and influence the recognition process rather than wait and have recognition forced upon the firm on terms over which it would have no influence.

In SMEs, nevertheless, non-unionism and management prerogative dominate employee relations. In many family-owned SMEs, unions are often seen as an intrusion into what is otherwise regarded as a private business. Matlay (1999) argues, in the absence of trade unions, management make unilateral decisions to award across the board pay rises to their employees. Individual bargaining usually takes place over piecework, the introduction of a new job, and with workers who possess a highly sought after technical skill. Employee grievances are normally dealt with on an individual and personal basis keeping the relationship as informal as possible, especially with more senior staff. In contrast, dismissals involving manual workers are dealt with more formally by supervisors with the appeal against their decision being to the owner/manager, whose decision is then final.

On the surface Matlay's research paints a picture of little involvement of personnel/HR specialists in employee relations in SMEs. His research covered 5,383 micro firms (employing less than 10 employees), 457 small firms (employing between 10 and 48 employees) and 129 medium-sized firms (employing between 50 and 250 employees), giving a strong bias to the smallest firms. Matlay's research shows 100 per cent owner/manager control in micro firms, but with a shift from owner manager to personnel manager in small firms (11per cent personnel manager) and a significant shift in medium-sized organisations (66 per cent personnel manager). This implies greater delegation and specialisation as the size of SME increases (Newton and Hunt, 1997).

The presence and function of personnel/HR specialists in SMEs

The dominant view from the HRM literature is that smaller SMEs allow little scope for the presence of personnel/HR specialists. Personnel specialists are considered unnecessary due, *inter alia*, to a lack of financial resources while people management is not viewed as a technical matter requiring specialists. Some literature, however, as we have seen, then implies there is a personnel/HR presence in SMEs whilst in industries such as printing, construction and engineering many small employers rely on the employee relations services they receive from membership of employers' associations. Research nevertheless by Hoque and Noon (1999), based on Workplace Industrial Relations Surveys, suggests the employment of personnel/HR specialists correlates positively with increasing size of organisation (see Table 6.3).

In the period 1980 to 1998 in SMEs employing between 25 and 499 employees the personnel specialist/HR presence averages 6 per cent for the smallest firms (25 to 49 employees) and 60 per cent for the medium-sized firms (200 to 499 employees). More importantly every size category between 1980 and 1998 shows an upward trend in personnel's presence. Even the smallest size category in the 1998 WERS (10 to 24 employees) records a 3 per cent presence. These figures point to an increase in the presence of professional personnel/HR management in the SME sector. Supporting evidence for this trend comes from the work of Matlay (1999) who shows that as SMEs grow in size, an increase in delegation in decision-making from owner/managers to personnel specialists takes place.

The increasing degree of formalisation of HR in the SME sector is also a factor explaining the growth of personnel specialist presence. The adoption of HR policies such as team working, performance appraisal and job flexibility requires a degree of specialist knowledge and expertise to design, establish and implement such practices. Increased formalisation of policies and procedures is contrary to the benefits claimed for SMEs (i.e. flexibility, informality, effective communications, good personal relations, high job satisfaction etc.) compared to larger organisations where the aim has been to reduce the degree of rigidity. This contradiction is perhaps resolved in the following quote from Bacon *et al.* (1996), 'The challenge of introducing change in the small organisation was managing the introduction of the formalisation necessary to retain management control while not destroying the informality and culture of the small business'.

Although the increase in formalisation is likely to enhance the need for personnel/HR specialists the autonomous introduction of personnel specialists, into SMEs can also result in greater formalisation of policy. Professional manage-

Table 6.3 Personnel/HR specialists by size of establishment 1980–98 (figures in percentages)

| Date | Number of employees | | | | | |
	25–49	50–99	100–199	200–499	500–999	1000+
1980	5	12	25	52	74	88
1984	4	12	29	54	68	88
1990	6	12	34	64	81	87
1998	10	18	40	71	84	89
Total average	6	14	32	60	77	88

Source: Adapted from Hoque and Noon, 1999

ment standards and skills can increase in SMEs as a result of the changing industrial context of downsizing of large organisations. HR managers made redundant from these larger more professionally run organisations find their next employment in smaller organisations. Moreover downsizing of organisations during the last twenty years has taken some larger organisations, in terms of employment size, into the upper end of the SME size category at less than 500 employees. Market pressures on SMEs to obtain externally assessed kite marks such as authorised quality and training standards has also encouraged them to adopt professional standards requiring a greater personnel presence.

In this respect agencies such as Investors in People (IIP), Local Enterprise Councils and Training and Enterprise Councils in England and Wales have played a significant part in encouraging SMEs to adopt a more formal and professional approach to management. According to IIPUK (1998) 8,379 small businesses had attained accredited status with another 21,466 committed to the process, covering 10 per cent and 21 per cent respectively of the UK workforce. Nevertheless despite government encouragement commentators (Ram, 1999; Hill and Stewart, 1999) have shown the adoption of IIP within SMEs to be limited, although growing. Another factor has been the increase in the number of students (both full-time and part-time) in higher education institutions reading business and management studies. Many of these students' first management position has been in SMEs into which they have brought professional management standards acquired and developed during their studies. Several commentators (Clarke-Loan *et al.*, 1999; Bacon *et al.*, 1996) have argued it is the small family dominated firms which have been most resistant to the adoption of formal management policies. A study by consultants Grant Thornton (1999) found that more than half of Scottish SMEs employing between 250 and 350 staff expected a change of ownership over the next five years. Only eight per cent of owners of Scottish SMEs were planning to pass on the firm to the future generation of family members.

The presence of personnel/HR specialists

Small SMEs tend not to employ personnel specialists and do not have a personnel department. Generally the owner/manager performs the people management role making the final decisions on recruitment, training, rewards, discipline and termination of employment. The Workplace Employment Relations Survey (1998) reported that nine out of ten workplace managers interviewed said they were the person responsible for employee relations at their workplace. It is clear from this survey (see Table 6.3) that as organisational size increases so also does the probability of the presence of a personnel specialist. Even with the independent stand-alone SMEs the trend between increasing organisation size and personnel specialist presence still holds (see Table 6.4).

All our sample firms (see Chapter 1) employed a personnel/HR specialist, although not necessarily a personnel/HR director as a member of the Board or CEO/MD Executive Group. More typically, the SME employed a single personnel specialist with secretarial support. As firms grew in size, more personnel professionals were employed and there was a tendency towards a limited degree of

Table 6.4 Presence of personnel specialists in stand-alone workplaces

Workplace size[1]	Percentage of workplaces
25 to 49 employees	11
50 to 99 employees	25
100 to 199 employees	31
200 to 499 employees	66
500 or more employees	82

Source: Cully *et al.* (1999), *Britain at Work*, Routledge

Note: 1 Figures are based on 1190 owner-managers.

specialisation within the personnel function in that job designations featured titles such as training, recruitment and employee relations. Notwithstanding these distinctive job titles the generalist personnel/HR specialist was the most common job designation (Hoque and Noon, 1999; Kelly and Gennard, 2000). Moreover, given the small size of SMEs, job specialisation was not rigid with those employed in resourcing and training jobs expected to help out and to rotate throughout the general personnel/HR function.

In our SME research the majority of personnel managers reported directly to their CEO/MD even when not Board members. In a minority of larger SMEs personnel managers reported to an operations or finance director. A major distinction between personnel managers in SMEs and their counterparts in large multi-divisional companies concerned who they managed. In the latter, personnel/HR directors had managers reporting to them both directly and indirectly. At corporate PLC headquarters, the personnel director frequently held direct respon-sibilities for headquarters staff and the remuneration and development of the top 200 or so executives. In addition non-HR managers such as quality, corporate affairs, pensions, information technology, security etc., usually reported to the personnel/HR director. Additionally personnel directors of the company's various divisions and business units had an indirect functional relationship with the corporate personnel/HR director in regard to the implementation of corporate personnel policies. Functional responsibility in this sense did not normally apply in our single establishment SMEs where numbers employed were small. Moreover in larger multi-site SMEs it was unusual for the smaller sites to have a dedicated personnel specialist as the function was managed from the main company workplace or head office. In the larger SMEs the personnel director/manager often held responsibilities for non-HR activities such as facilities management, security, pensions and quality.

Personnel/HR's presence and composition of SME boards of directors

No distinction was made between Boards of Directors and CEO/MD Executive Groups. Forty four per cent of SMEs in our survey (i.e. 15 out of 34) had, as reported by their CEO/MDs, personnel/HR directors on their Boards/Executive Groups. This compares with 15 per cent for main PLC Boards and 73 per cent for

CEO/MD Executive Groups at corporate level. In addition to the CEO/MD the most common directorships in terms of frequency of ranking were finance, operations, marketing/sales, company secretary, personnel/HR, information technology and quality. Personnel/HR was fifth of eight in terms of frequency. The numbers of directors (not just personnel directors) on SME Boards/Executive Groups including their age and length of tenure is shown in Tables 6.5 and 6.6.

These figures conform to expectations with the smaller numbers on SME Boards explained by small company size, plus limited financial resources, whilst the larger corporate Boards exhibit a higher average age than the SME Boards. With respect to length of service main PLC Boards have longer serving directors but there is no significant difference between corporate CEO/MD and SME Board/Executive Groups. Another characteristic of SME Board/Executive Groups is the absence of non-executive directors (NEDs). The majority of our sample (20 out of 34) were private limited SMEs registered under the Companies Acts. SMEs can decide voluntarily to appoint NEDs to their boards of directors and a number of our survey companies had NEDs. Mileham (1996) argues many SMEs are not professionally managed and the engagement of good independent NEDs has the advantage of bringing to their boardroom professional business expertise which offers the opportunity to improve the SMEs business long-term planning and networking with the wider business community. This finding receives support from the *Sunday Times* Enterprise Network survey (2000) discussed in Chapter 2.

What personnel/HR directors actually do on SME Boards

Our research also examined the role of personnel/HR directors on their SME Board/Executive Groups to see if it differed from those at corporate PLC level and within subsidiary Boards of multi-divisional companies. The principal job of

Table 6.5 Numbers of directors on boards/executive groups of SMEs

Types of board	Mean	Range
SMEs boards/executive groups	7	3 to 14
Main corporate PLCs boards	10	8 to 20
CEO/MD PLC executive groups	9	3 to 16

Source: SME and PLC CEO/MD questionnaires

Table 6.6 Age and tenure of directors on SME board/executive groups

Types of board	Age		Tenure	
	Mean	Range	Mean	Range
SMEs board/executive groups	44	32 to 55	5	3 to 14
Main corporate PLCs boards	54	48 to 58	6	3 to 15
CEO/MD executive groups	50	42 to 53	5	2 to 20

Source: SME CEO/MD questionnaires

all personnel directors in different types of organisation is to lead on HR activities to facilitate the achievement of enterprise goals.

Table 6.7 shows personnel/HR directors to be extensively involved in making business decisions on SME Board/Executive Groups but less involved than those on PLC CEO/MD Executive Groups. Table 6.8 outlines the competencies valued most by CEO/MDs in personnel/HR directors employed in SMEs and PLCs. It shows a very similar scoring between the two groups with social skills put at the top followed by HR competencies and business acumen. This similarity in CEO requirements is taken further in Table 6.9 where, with the exception of expertise in law and HR processes, both SME and PLC scoring is remarkably similar.

In both cases rounded experience of people problems and proactiveness in HR policy making and implementation are preferred to prolonged experience in the personnel function. The greater weighting given to employment law and expertise in HR processes in SMEs suggests that these responsibilities are more easily delegated by personnel/HR directors at the corporate level compared to the SME level. Given the smaller numbers employed by SMEs and the existence of fewer financial resources there is less scope for specialisation and delegation between business and personnel work and within HR work itself. Much of the relationships in and around the recruitment, training and employee relations

Table 6.7 Personnel/HR directors involvement in SME business and PLC executive group corporate strategies

Degree of involvement	SME numbers	Percentage	PLC numbers[1]	Percentage
Highly involved	13	38	8	33
Moderately involved	8	24[2] (62)	12	50 (83)
Little involved	10	29	3	13
Not involved	3	9 (38)	1	4 (17)

Source: CEO/MD questionnaires

Notes: 1 Two CEO/MDs did not reply to this question.
2 The bracketed figure is a summation of high and moderate involvement in business strategy formation to distinguish their involvement from little and not involved.

Table 6.8 CEO/MDs ranking of what competencies they value most in personnel/HR directors

Competencies	SME weighted responses*	Percentage	PLC weighted responses[1]	Percentage
Social and team work skills	144	44	124	44
HR competence	120	36	92	33
Make decisions in interests of whole business	67	20	63	23

Source: CEO/MD questionnaires

Note: 1 Weighted responses are based on 4 most important through to 1 least important.

Table 6.9 HR competencies SME CEO/MDs seek in personnel/HR directors

HR competencies	SME weighted responses[1]	Percentage	PLC weighted responses[1]	Percentage
Rounded knowledge of people problems	125	26	96	30
Expertise in law and HR processes	114	24	55	17
Proactive in HR policies	103	21	62	20
Prolonged experience in the HR function	94	19	77	24
CIPD membership	50	10	28	9

Source: CEO/MD questionnaires

Note: 1 Weighted responses are based on 5 most important through to 1 least important.

processes are informal and flexible, to facilitate adoption to the uncertain environment experienced by SME Boards of Directors. This compares with the similar sized subsidiary business units of larger companies where a large part of the personnel director's job is to adhere, interpret and implement formal corporate policies.

Power and influence of personnel/HR directors in SMEs

Our research established the formal presence of personnel/HR directors on SME Board/Groups at 44 per cent compared to 73 per cent presence on CEO/MD Executive Groups of PLCs. In terms of Frooman's (1999) categories a relationship of high interdependency is expressed by providing personnel with formal recognition through positional authority on the top decision-making body of the firm. Where personnel/HR has a Board presence CEO/MDs clearly recognise the importance of people management to the successful operation of the business. What then is the role, background and management style of CEOs in SMEs?

CEO/MD background, work experience and management style

Investigation of the work/functional background experience of the 34 CEO/MDs showed the importance of general management experience which accounted for 50 per cent of the total. This was less than for those CEO/MDs with general management experience running corporate Executive Groups (recorded at 54 per cent). SMEs are more likely to have been started up by functional specialists such as engineers, information technology, personnel/HR or market/sales people some of whom continue to perceive themselves within their management functions. On the other hand the larger PLC is more likely to have a well rounded generalist as CEO/MD. The SME sample revealed a higher proportion of CEO/MDs with a finance and legal background. However, some of this is explained by the inclusion in the sample of a number of professional accountancy and law firms.

Table 6.10 Comparison of CEO/MD leadership styles between SMEs and corporate
PLCs

Types of leadership	SMEs board of directors		CEO/MD PLC executive groups	
	Numbers	Percentage	Numbers[1]	Percentage
Open partnership	21	62	9	39
Open consultative	9	26	12	52
Traditional/authoritarian	2	6	2	9
Personal	2	6	0	0
Reliance on formal rules	0	0	0	0

Source: CEO/MD questionnaires

Note: 1 Three respondents did not answer this question.

The management styles dominant on both PLC main Boards and CEO/MD
Executive Groups was examined in Chapter 2. Table 6.10 shows the same information for SME Board/Executive Groups. Given their smaller size, family ownership
and informality SMEs could be expected to reveal a strong emphasis on the personal
qualities of the leader, who may have started it up. Even if personal ownership
had been diluted, due to the inception of other shareholders, then one would still
expect to find a strong family and personal style presence. Table 6.10 shows this
not to be the case.

Surprisingly the results emphasise the significance of the more open participative
and consultative styles of management on SME Board/Executive Groups and
not the dominance of personal or autocratic CEO/MD styles as reported in some
of the literature (Bacon *et al.*, 1996). This result is similar to that recorded for
Executive Groups at PLC level. Indeed if the two categories, participative and
consultative, are added they score 88 per cent for SMEs and 91 per cent for PLCs.
Although personal and authoritative management styles at 6 per cent are much
lower than expected, they are higher than the zero recorded for the corporate
Executive Groups of CEO/MDs. The popularity of participative and consultative
management styles is explained by contemporary external environmental pressures
on top management teams (Dooley and Fryxell, 1999 and Katzenbach, 1998). At
PLC level, team working and delegation in coping with the complexities and
turbulence of rapid environmental changes are important. Our own results show
for SMEs increasing complexity of organisation with the strategic shift to multi-
product businesses discussed below. Moreover the current literature shows a
management agenda is taking root within SMEs (WERS, 1998; Bacon *et al.*, 1996)
by their adoption of HR policies and increased specialisation and delegation in
the form of more personnel specialists. This is confirmed by Tables 6.3 and 6.10
which show increased professional personnel management combined with more
open management style of team working to cope with the demands of an
increasingly turbulent business environment. As a result new more generalist CEO/
MDs are appointed as private limited companies dominate and the family influence
declines (Grant Thornton, 1999).

CEO/MDs personal beliefs and values also play a part in shaping the management style adopted at Board of Director or Executive Group level. Our CEO/MDs of SMEs were provided with three choices to answer the question, 'what factors influence Board/Executive Group management styles'. The choices were personal beliefs/values, need to improve profit/productivity and turbulence arising from product market competition and technological innovation. The raw scores in terms of ranking these three, from the most to the least important, showed profit/productivity improvement as the top followed by personal beliefs/values and uncertainty from product market competition and technological innovation.

Changes in the strategic direction of SMEs

The SME questionnaire asked CEO/MDs if since taking office they had changed the direction of their enterprise from a single to a multi-product strategy. Seventy six per cent claimed to have done so. As shown above new CEO/MDs are frequently brought in to introduce strategic change as financial stakeholders demand improved performance. As White *et al.* (1997) argue these new CEO/MDs often possess different functional backgrounds from their predecessors. In our sample of SMEs, the significance of the private limited company and insignificance of the family firm possibly explains the response of the SMEs change in strategic direction. Although registered limited companies can be controlled through majority family share ownership the questionnaire allowed respondents (Table 1.5) to chose between family and private limited company categories. It is reasonable to assume that limited companies in our sample had broader share ownership and therefore diluted family influence. According to Bacon *et al.* (1996) in the HR sphere a change in ownership had been the key dynamic for change. Moreover, small family-owned firms are likely to be conservative and adopt fewer new management policies and undertake less investment in management development (Loan-Clarke *et al.*, 1999; Bacon *et al.*, 1996). However, in some instances this conservatism can be offset by customer pressure, as when larger organisations who are key customers require SMEs to adopt more radical strategies both in operations and HR as shown by our case studies above and by pressures from public agencies such as IIPUK.

The questionnaire also asked CEO/MDs in SMEs to identify their dominant type of business strategy on a classification adopted from the work of Smith and White (1987). The results are shown in Table 6.11.

Table 6.11 Dominant business strategies in SMEs and corporate PLCs

Types of strategy	SMEs	Percentage	PLCs[1]	Percentage
Single product	11	32	5	20
Multi-product (related)	20	59	16	64
Multi-product (conglomerate)	3	9	4	16

Source: CEO/MD questionnaires

Note: 1 One respondent did not answer this question.

As expected SMEs have a larger proportion of their activities devoted to single product strategies than their PLC counterparts and a smaller proportion in multi-product/conglomerate activities than PLCs. Nevertheless, the proportion of SMEs pursuing a multi-product strategy is high at 68 per cent. The complex and turbulent environment faced by SMEs probably helps explain the high proportion of CEO/MDs who claim (76 per cent) to have changed the strategic direction of their company since taking office in the light of changes in the external corporate environment. CEO/MDs with a stronger functional background, as opposed to the generalist one, are more likely to be managing single product businesses. However, which is cause and which effect is not clear from the evidence. A single business start up by the functionally trained CEO/MD is more likely to keep the SME as a single product business. However, as the enterprise grows it is likely at some point to appoint a professional CEO/MD with a generalist career background with a consequent decline in family influence.

As argued previously CEO/MDs are primarily responsible for appointing members of the top Executive Group. However, it became clearer with SMEs that CEO/MD preferences to a degree are circumscribed by the business strategy pursued. In this regard 11 single product SMEs appointed three personnel directors to the board, 20 product related businesses appointed nine directors and the remaining three conglomerates all had personnel/HR directors. The larger and more multi-product the SME the more likely it is to have a personnel/HR director on the Board/Executive Group. Multi-product SMEs are also more likely to have CEOs with generalist career backgrounds predisposing the CEO/MD to seek a business contribution from all directors including the personnel/HR director.

We return to Frooman's discussion of the interdependency relationship as a means of deepening and developing our analysis of the relationship between CEO/MD and personnel/HR director in SMEs. Progressive management policy developments in SMEs have undoubtedly favoured the growth in numbers, and influence, of personnel specialists and that the main driver of this trend is the CEO/MD who perceives the need for and requires the support of personnel to achieve successful organisational performance. However, Frooman adds to this CEO/MD demand side analysis by offering to the stakeholder (personnel/HR director) the strategic choice of how to supply his/her expertise. At the present time, although a wholly direct usage strategy based on professional personnel expertise has had some limited success with a Board presence of 44 per cent, it remains below that for large public limited companies (73 per cent). In Frooman's terms the relationship of high interdependence between CEO/MDs and personnel/HR specialists is not totally symmetrical as the direct usage strategy (based solely on HR expertise) has not by itself convinced CEO/MDs to value the personnel/HR function by granting more of them formal representation in the top management team.

Regarding Frooman's indirect usage strategy the personnel/HR director has to call on resources, other than professional personnel ones, desired by the CEO/MD, thereby making the latter more dependent on the former. This can be achieved by the personnel/HR director adopting a stronger business orientation and by widening their job responsibilities to include non-HR activities. It has been shown previously that personnel's presence on SMEs Board/Executive Groups and their involvement in business strategy formation is relatively high. Their higher involvement in strategy formation (compared to their presence on Board/Executive Groups) indicates that personnel/HR specialists have more power and influence than their formal Board/Executive Group position would indicate. This greater relationship of dependency between CEO/MD and personnel/HR directors is explained by the greater informality said to exist in SMEs and to the dynamic and emerging situation of increasing numbers of personnel/HR specialists revealed in the evidence of the WERS (1998). Frooman's strategy of indirect usage is a creditable means for personnel/HR specialists to obtain greater leverage from the interdependency relationship between themselves and their CEO/MDs. Finally, as a measure of Frooman's direct and indirect usage, CEO/MDs of both SMEs and PLCs were asked if the personnel/HR directors had proactively negotiated membership of the Board of Directors. The results show that 39 per cent of PLC personnel/HR directors had done so whereas the figure for SMEs was lower at 16 per cent. The lower SME figure may reveal an emerging situation in which personnel/HR specialists still have some way to go with the dependency relationship being more asymmetrical and overly skewed in favour of the CEO/MD.

7 Globalisation and the role of personnel/HR directors in multinational companies

This chapter examines the role of the personnel/HR director in the multinational company (MNC). The focus is on the power and influence which personnel/HR directors exert in the strategic decision-making processes of MNCs. Multinational companies have diverse and complex organisation structures and problems of balancing corporate direction and control (centralisation) with local market responsiveness (decentralisation). Global markets and organisational changes present new opportunities for personnel/HR directors to contribute to the formation and implementation of business and HR strategies.

Globalisation and the rise of the multinational company

The trend to globalisation accelerated in the last quarter of the twentieth century with the deregulation and liberalisation of capital and product markets. By the 1970s the Japanese, then later other Asian owned companies, had helped intensify competition in world markets both in terms of product price and quality. This competition was initially felt in the heavy industries of western economies such as shipbuilding and steel manufacture but subsequently spread into consumer durables, including motor vehicles and then to electronic and software products. By the 1980s pressures arising from competition had altered the political climate, leading in industrialised western democracies to the freeing up of trade, as not to do so would cause such countries to become even more uncompetitive. The pattern of trade has changed markedly from the pre-World War Two pattern of western countries, when buying raw materials and primary produces from less developed countries, to manufacture and then supply mainly domestic markets, to much of the world's manufacturing capacity, has now moved to the developing nations. Concerned to raise the standard of living of their own people these countries offered preferential tax regimes to encourage knowledge and technology transfer. Additionally they offered much lower labour costs, and minimum employee rights and social protection (Moreau and Trudeau, 2000).

To prevent the transfer of work from high cost member states, the European Union contains a mechanism – the social chapter – whereby social conditions can be harmonised across member states. Free trade within the Single European Market

(SEM) takes place within a context of minimum labour standards. It cannot take place on the basis of competing down employment conditions. Juxtaposed to the development of the free trade area of the SEM has been the North American Free Trade Area which has no trade and labour standard provisions. The Association of South East Asian Nations has moved away from trade protectionism, which often followed the gaining of political independence, to encourage direct foreign investment as a means of knowledge transfer and national development. The growth of free trade areas has encouraged foreign direct investment and the development of MNCs as they seek to get behind tariff barriers to obtain access to the free trade area.

Multinational companies have become responsible for an increased proportion of world trade often causing integrated manufacturing systems to cross national boundaries. Hendry (1994) records that one-fifth to one-quarter of the total world production of market economies is performed by MNCs dominated by a core group of 600 firms. In the US and Japan more than 50 per cent of total trade is carried out by MNCs, whereas in the UK it is estimated that 80 per cent of manufactured exports are from MNCs. The US Bureau of Economic Analysis (cited in Cooke, 2000) estimates 85 per cent of foreign direct investment in the US came from seven countries – Japan, UK, Switzerland, France, Canada, Germany and the Netherlands in that order. The Japanese External Trade Organisation (JETRO, 1999) figures on direct overseas investment (as a ratio of GDP) place the UK at the top of a list of five industrial countries including the US, France, Germany and Japan. On the other hand Nagai (2000), using JETRO figures, traces a remarkable decline in the number of newly established Japanese affiliated companies overseas, due to the country's economic recession in the late 1990s, except in Europe where the numbers increased by 47 per cent between 1997 and 1998.

The development of computer and telecomunications technologies has greatly facilitated communications within MNCs making it possible to fax documents, communicate instantaneously through electronic mail and to conduct 'in house' television and video conferences via satellite (IRS Employment Trends, 1999a). This compares with the slower communications systems of the recent past which depended heavily on telephones, letter mail, aircraft, railway, road and ship. Company web sites can dispense information throughout the world and can be accessed easily by subsidiary business units at the periphery of the organisation. These processes have the capacity, not only to speed up the transfer of messages, but to allow more horizontal and diagonal information flows cutting out the necessity for large hierarchies at corporate headquarters for purposes of direction and control.

Development and growth of the MNC

Dowling *et al.* (1999) argue, 'Most firms go through several stages of organisational development as the nature and size of their international activities grow'. The initial move of a company into international markets is through overseas' export to make use of surplus capacity, to sustain profits and to keep prices down for customers. As firms grow in size, an international division in marketing and sales increases its intelligence of overseas markets, and its proficiency of operation in them. At this stage a company usually employs agents who have detailed knowledge of host country markets to promote sales.

The next stage is direct investment to establish a production or service unit combined with a marketing and sales force in the foreign country which has the advantage of securing headquarter's direct control by not being dependent either on marketing from a distance or on agents who may be working for more than one company. The firm is in effect turning into an MNC with outlets in a number of different countries. Several of the small and medium enterprises in our own sample of companies were following this growth pathway. Benefits to MNCs include the ability to shift investment to alternative locations where labour costs are lower and employee rights legislation less burdensome. The establishment of foreign subsidiaries improves supplies and reduces the cost of shipping raw materials to the subsidiary and finished products to the market. Companies can also overcome tariff barriers by setting up production units in an overseas country as many USA, Japanese and Korean MNCs have done within the European Union. Highly educated and trained labour is an attraction to MNCs when deciding to invest in advanced industrial countries (Cooke, 2000).

However, this organisational development process is not followed by all firms as some may encounter difficulties in the search for growth on the international stage. In some cases the MNC may, as a result of host government policy, have to enter a joint venture with a local firm; have to enter by acquisition; have to decide to sub-contract its product and have it produced under licence by a host country producer. The further stage of internationalisation is the development of global production strategies. This is where a MNC sub-divides the production process so that components of it are confined to particular areas of the world. This is especially the case in the motor car industry where component production (e.g. engines and bodies) are located in various countries and all brought together for final assembly to create the car in another country. Hendry (1994), however, reports that for some MNCs growth strategies in foreign markets are more direct than those implied by the organisation development process. Millington and Bayliss (1990), cited in Hendry (1994), argue against the theory of progressive international development placing greater emphasis on levels of market maturity and saturation which may have closed off the gradualist approach of new entrants whilst in other cases, depending on the size and experience of the firm, it may be expedient to participate quickly in foreign markets through joint ventures, acquisitions etc. Barlett and Ghoshal (1988) argue against an overly structural approach, maintaining MNC success is more dependent on the abilities, behaviour and performance of its individual managers.

In the early twentieth century European business established overseas subsidiaries, making use of decentralised structures within which local companies were given a degree of autonomy. This was at a time when communications systems between the corporate centre and its subsidiaries were slow and when managers in far off lands, faced by diverse local circumstances, required authority to make decisions. Large MNCs such as Royal Dutch/Shell developed a highly decentralised organisation for these reasons. Shortly after World War Two, United States-owned firms began a wave of overseas investment bringing to host countries their managerial and technological expertise. Initially host country subsidiaries were normally managed by an American CEO/MD on an overseas assignment to implement corporate policies and culture. By the 1970s a third wave of MNC foreign investment into the UK came from companies with head offices in Japanese and other Asian countries which brought more strongly cultural paternalist and collectivist values than North American owned companies. This also coincided with the advance in computerised and satellite technologies allowing for the development of global strategies, whereby the world could be viewed as a single market in which cost advantages could be achieved through the integration of international operations. Stemming from their national culture the Japanese, in particular, favoured a centralised and paternal approach to HRM strategies by placing expatriates overseas, although Nagai (2000) and Kuan (2000) consider this now to be changing. Kidger (1999) researching into 24 MNEs, located in Britain, concluded they were almost all moving in the direction of global integration and developing, at the top level, international management cadres.

Levels of strategic decision-making and organisation in MNCs

As a company pursues a strategy of international growth the complexity of management control and organisation structure becomes more problematic. Centralised control becomes more difficult to maintain as MNCs develop a wide product range and extend the number of different countries in which they operate. For example IBM has operations in 160 countries. As the trend towards globalisation accelerates MNCs start to 'think globally but act locally' as they are now required to meet the demands of customers who expect the same standard quality service wherever they are located in the world. Some MNCs, with integrated manufacturing systems, can produce semi-finished products in different locations moving these across national boundaries for final assembly, facilitated by advanced communications technology and production systems. Organisations producing disparate multiple products and services, however, are more likely to be decentralised. Nevertheless even in fairly centralised MNCs diversity is important and a degree of local autonomy is necessary for corporate advantages as the following example illustrates.

In this example the business unit of the MNC was located in east Scotland. The MNC corporate head office located in the US decided what was manufactured in the Scottish plant. The corporate business mission was excellence in engineering, product quality and sales service. This began to change in the 1980s as its declining cash register business was replaced by the production of high value automatic dispenser machines for the banking industry. This change of business strategy was not wholly driven by US corporate management, since the Scottish management team, led by a dynamic managing director who was concerned about the plant's survival, convinced the US corporate headquarters to base its worldwide self-product development and manufacture at the Scottish plant (Kelly and Gennard, 1996). The Scottish business unit management saw the need to regain competitiveness through a high value product which contributed significantly to corporate profits. It received corporate headquarter's approval to be run as a centre of product expertise. Corporate head office, however, continued to approve the local business plan and the corporate management style became more open, with more key players participating in strategy formation than in the past. This case is an example of local initiative and decentralised corporate responsiveness which recognises that in the contemporary global market diversity of knowledge and decentralisation of decision-making is of great value, if the overall corporate objectives are to be achieved.

The problem for an MNC therefore is to be sufficiently responsive to local country or regional customer needs, to differences in host country legislation, culture and customer tastes and to the coordination and control needs of the corporate centre (Kamochie, 1996). This presents a challenge of conflicting demands causing the large MNC to configure an organisational structure along either a matrix or transnational lines. The matrix organisation attempts to reconcile both the multi-divisional product structure of the organisation with its operations in various countries. Hence territory managers are often responsible for the delivery of the various products within their areas and the product division management respon-sible for the sales of their division's product across the various countries. However, dual reporting systems and responsibilities do result in communication and internal political problems which have led Barlett and Ghoshal (1992) to conclude that many MNCs have failed to find success with such an organisational structure.

Transnational MNCs are fluid organisations which require a complex process of coordination and cooperation incorporating cross-unit integrating devices such as mission statements, strong leadership and corporate culture as well as a developed worldwide managerial perspective to enhance integration. At the same time this requires relationships between the corporate centre and subsidiaries, and laterally between subsidiaries, which are responsive and can vary between different countries. An example provided by Kidger (1999) shows that the firm might differentiate its marketing strategy when customer preferences vary between countries, but coordi-nate the supply chain in order to achieve economies of scale in purchasing materials. Citing Hendry (1994), 'The true trans-national, by virtue of its flexibility, is able to connect resources, innovations, and entrepreneurship which are spread throughout the company'.

Other less structured and more fluid organisations include the heterarchy and network MNCs. The heterarchy is less hierarchical, recognising that alternative centres of excellence to headquarters exist to input to the strategic direction of the company. For instance some MNCs centralise research and development for the whole organisation, not in corporate headquarters but in a subsidiary in another country where higher education provision is of a higher standard. An example is our case study of the switch control company, employing 13,000 which had 17 centres of excellence within its European region. The network organisation is even more boundaryless, fluid and less hierarchical with greater equality dependent on expertise between various units in various countries. This has been well stated by Dowling *et al.* (1999), 'Such MNEs are loosely coupled political systems rather than tightly bonded, homogeneous, hierarchically controlled systems'.

Integration is dependent upon a lateral network of interpersonal relations and processes reinforced by socialisation and culture. The organisational structure provides loose guidelines within which the processes for achieving efficient performance can vary, depending upon the business and heritage of each company.

In addition to the corporate headquarters and the overseas subsidiary levels of decision-making, it is also the case in MNCs that regional headquarters may direct strategy within whole regions of the world such as Europe. Nagai's (2000) research into regional headquarters provides an insight into how Japanese MNCs allocate HR decisions between different levels of the enterprise. Manufacturing and research and development decisions are normally made at parent headquarters in Japan. However, sales and HR decisions are left to the business unit level within the host country. In the case of HR, cultural differences between the parent and host countries make it imperative personnel management has an important role in the top management team at the subsidiary and regional levels. Nagai argues that the regional headquarters of Japanese MNCs are becoming more important, especially within the SEM. The development of the EU and associated European Works Councils legislation has encouraged greater coordination between company European business units. Regional headquarters have responsibility for developing a database for high performing managers and for their transnational job rotation and development as part of the management education and training system. Notwithstanding these changes, levels of wages, fringe benefits, recruitment and working hours are difficult to harmonise due to different country legislation and cultures and therefore remain at the business unit level.

Levels of organisational decision-making are not cast in stone and change to either reflect environmental pressures, as in the Japanese regional strategy outlined above, or for internal political reasons. One of our case organisations, a Scottish based MNC, employing 3,800 people, manufacturing and distributing collagen, cellulose, fibrous and plastic casings for sausage skins, had business units in Australia, Belgium, USA, Switzerland, Germany, and the Czech and Slovakia Republics. It had a decentralised organisation giving considerable autonomy to host country subsidiaries, but within a corporate level determined planning framework. This had not always the case in its recent history. The company took over a similar firm in the United States and initially the business strategy was to operate with regional accountability. The company then moved to a centralised structure. At this point it established a functional structure with all local functions reporting directly to their respective functional directors at corporate headquarters including the HR function. This strategy aimed to rationalise the organisation and to consolidate power at the corporate centre with regard to direction and control. However, it was discovered that centralisation reduced local responsiveness and performance, diminishing focus on profits and resulting in September 1999 in a move back to a modified regional structure.

The reasons for this reversal in strategy were largely political. When the MNC took over the American subsidiary there was a need for the dominant firm, as represented by corporate headquarters, to show 'who is boss'. The strategy broke up previously established structures and the loyalties surrounding these by bringing in a functional structure through which local heads of function, previously reporting to the host country CEO/MD, now reported to their corporate head of function. This tied power and influence into the corporate headquarters which then found it easier to develop and implement corporate strategies throughout the MNC. At this point if local host country managers resisted the new regime they were removed. After a period, headquarter's management felt relaxed enough to decentralise authority granting, as market circumstances warranted it, a degree of autonomy to the local subsidiaries.

Staffing and development policies in MNCs

In the literature staffing and development models are usually linked to the MNC business strategies and to changes in organisational structures. It reports four management attitudes, the first three of which were articulated by Perlmutter (1969) and the fourth later by Heenan and Perlmutter (1979), which underline international HR strategies and are reflected in organisational design. These are ethnocentric, polycentric, geocentric and regiocentric. Ethnocentric means strategic decisions are made at company headquarters with all key jobs at home and abroad filled by parent country nationals. Polycentric staffing places the management of MNCs' subsidiaries in the hands of the host country nationals, but key headquarters jobs remain with the parent country nationals. The geocentric approach to staffing and development is based on the principle of the best person for the job irrespective of nationality. The composition of the CEO/MD Executive Group is likely to be thoroughly international. The regiocentric approach is a half way house between geocentric and the other two policies with HR policies based on individual competence, but with cross country transfers confined to particular regions of the world. In this case MNC headquarter jobs tend to remain with the parent country nationals.

The organisational development process model does not apply to all firms engaged in international trade and those on a growth path to becoming an MNC. Nevertheless it is illustrative of the way staffing and development policies change as the firm moves through the growth path from exports to fully fledged investment overseas. When MNCs first venture overseas, they tend to manage through an ethnocentric approach by putting in place a managing director, supported by other senior technical and professional employees, from the parent nation, who has worked a long time for the parent company. In this way the corporate headquarters more easily exercises control over the subsidiary by ensuring that corporate culture and financial reporting procedures are implemented properly. This approach has usually been applied to the three phases of internationalisation mentioned above (Dowling *et al.*, 1999) by European, North American and Japanese firms. The downside of ethnocentrically based HR policies is their discrimination on grounds of nationality, religion and ethnic differences, against appointment on the basis of personal ability. Moreover, firms operating in a fiercely competitive international marketplace cannot ignore talent and ability whatever their country of origin, especially in an era of knowledge development and transfer. Polycentric approaches to staffing and development follow as organisations develop more experience of operating in the host countries. This is a less costly option as the cost of sending parent company nationals on expatriate assignments is considerable. At this point headquarters staff, who are generally parent country nationals, are required to visit frequently host countries to become acquainted with the senior personnel and to monitor progress. In this way American MNEs move from ethnocentric to polycentric policies but exercise considerable control over subsidiaries by subjecting them to clear financial reporting procedures.

As a firm becomes progressively more international, staffing and development policy is likely to shift from parent country expatriate assignments and polycentric approaches, to more geocentric and regiocentric policies. The regiocentric is the less costly option, at least for a time. The need to achieve greater decentralised local market responsiveness, and global innovation, often with centres of excellence in subsidiary business units, causes the MNC to adopt organisational characteristics taking it in the direction of more complex matrix, transnational, heterarchical and network structures. Although some of these organisational models may be considered ideal types they do point to the need for MNCs human resource strategies that search for and establish talent banks throughout the corporation. Through these strategies, and organisation changes, more managers are moved across national boundaries including third country nationals working overseas from their national subsidiaries, and also with foreign nationals spending time on assignment at the parent country headquarters. Subbarao (2000) points to wider demographic reasons for the increasing adoption of geocentric policies by MNCs. He argues low birth rates in western countries combined with high birth rates, and an increasing supply of highly educated professionals, and mobility, in developing countries has encouraged a shift towards geocentric polices in MNCs.

One of our case companies was a USA owned MNC producing switch control products. It employed 53,000 people (including 13,000 in Europe) in 95 different countries. The company had a matrix organisation combining strong vertical business units with geographical regions. Products included aircraft cockpit switch controls, lasers, industrial processors, computers in oil refining, thermostats in food processing, heating and ventilating in house building etc. Some of its markets, for example aircraft, were totally global whilst others were national e.g. house building. In the early phase of development the company grew organically, then moved through acquisitions into computers and semi-conductors, but then moved back to its core business. The HR function was represented on the USA corporate CEO Executive Group. Traditionally the MNC had an ethnocentric strategy towards staffing with American managers throughout the world in charge of plants in host countries. As the company became more international this policy changed in favour, first of a more polycentric and later a more geocentric style. It had an international assignees policy which applied globally to facilitate staff moves.

The management development programme required an examination of management stock (including professional engineers) every year to identify new talent and to plan career succession. There was a talent bank for every strategic business unit in Europe. The Vice President Europe, assisted by the HR department, drew up a list of talent who were then sent to a development centre for assessment and if they reached the required standard entered into the corporate management development programme. Nominations had to be based on key business results and on a personal profile of accomplishments in people management. Performance appraisal was 360 degrees with assessors required to provide examples of good and not so good practice/behaviour. The planning side of the process required the identification of future vacancies and organisational gaps to be filled through succession planning to ensure managers had the experience to do the job and that it stretched them sufficiently for career development. This career planning applied within the European region (and others throughout the world) but was replicated at corporate level which surveyed people across the business units, regions and headquarters in the USA.

More generally given the importance of knowledge utilisation in MNCs and the more dynamic technology-based communication systems available, learning, production and functional services are required to be on tap. Project and communication teams are major means of tackling problems and integrating the global company. This network arrangement involved nationals from different countries requiring the CEO/MD Executive Group to give attention to geocentric and/or regiocentric personnel policies in staffing and development (Nagai, 2000). An illustration of the use of project teams by an MNC was seen in our electronic switch control company. In this company project teams were put together continuously to solve management problems and to assist the personal development of managers. For the company it was important its managers were exposed to different country cultures and developed interpersonal understanding by working with people who often saw things differently to themselves. Hence multi-project groups existed across business units, functions and regions of the company.

Although it was the CEO/MD Executive Group pursuing strategies of business growth which led to this metamorphosis in organisation, the structural changes also impacted on the composition of the CEO/MD Executive Group. In a geocentric MNC the CEO/MD Group composition is likely to consist of heads of division or major companies, some of which are foreign nationals, who are located overseas. Such diversity and complexity combined with decentralised innovation was a further factor encouraging the less functional and more open team CEO/MD Executive Group as discussed in Chapter 2.

The personnel/HR director on the MNC board/executive group

Many textbooks convey the impression that MNCs respond solely to changes in international markets as if they had no control over such developments. It is as if an impersonal force had taken over and in order to pursue company goals such as profit and sales growth, or even to survive, the logic of the market must be followed. The pressures of international markets are very real to those who compete in them. Nevertheless the growth of international markets and the MNCs, which operate within them, are created by people who by their actions impose pressures on others, and who interact with and amend such market and organisational structures. It is the leaders of business firms who determine whether or not to grow a domestic business into an MNC to trade competitively on world markets.

It is the CEO/MD and their team who make these strategic decisions, albeit finally approved by the main Board of Directors. It is imperative the quality of the CEO/MD and composition of the Executive Group in terms of knowledge and competence is of a high standard if competitive advantage is to be gained in the market place. Enterprises which have successfully adapted to environmental turbulence have tended to select CEOs who have different professional backgrounds from their predecessors but still recognise the continuous drive to change and improve organisational performance. This fits our research findings reported earlier that CEOs interviewed claimed to have changed their companies' strategic direction to become multi-product organisations which undoubtedly extended to growing into an MNC. Other evidence from previous chapters supporting this contention is the increase in size of Boards of Directors since the 1970s, and the more open project-based style CEO/MD Executive Group both of which reflect the changing complexity of decentralised MNCs, and the large salaries and benefits paid to directors, especially CEO/MDs.

Home-based MNC corporate headquarters

Our questionnaire survey revealed that 23 MNCs conducted 40 per cent of their business through international trade ranging from one company with just 2 per cent to one with 80 per cent. Forty per cent of our MNCs had over 50 per cent of their business conducted in overseas markets. Seventy three per cent of personnel/ HR directors were members of the CEO/MD Executive Group who had the opportunity to participate in international trade and HR decisions. Unlike Marginson *et al.* (1993) and Hunt and Boxall (1998) we made no attempt to relate the involvement of personnel/HR directors to specific business decisions (e.g. merger and acquisitions).

Table 7.1 shows the degree of involvement of personnel/HR directors in the formation of both business and HR strategies in British owned MNCs at corporate headquarters level. It shows a greater proportion of personnel/HR directors in the larger PLC multinational companies participate in the making of HR strategies compared with those engaged in making business strategies. The 'highly involved' category shows personnel/HR directors highly involved in making HR strategies whereas the largest category in business strategy formation shows them moderately involved at 59 per cent. Although personnel/HR directors' involvement in business strategy is lower than their involvement in HR strategies these figures support the views of CEO/MDs expressed in the interview programme that their total involvement in the business decisions of MNCs at corporate headquarters level is significant.

What personnel/HR directors do at MNC headquarters

Purcell and Ahlstrand (1994) in discussing the multi-divisional company concluded that their corporate personnel departments and industrial relations institutions were in decline. Most of the corporate headquarters included in our CEO/MD and personnel/HR director interview programme did not have large numbers of staff in their corporate personnel departments as in the 1970s. The interviews with CEO/MDs and personnel/HR directors at eight head offices of British-owned MNCs displayed considerable diversity as to the organisation of the personnel/HR function. Most common was a corporate headquarters personnel/HR function responsible for strategy formation serving the CEO/MD Executive Group and headquarters staff but also with overall responsibility for co-ordinating in various countries the implementation of corporate strategy by divisional and subsidiary companies. The personnel/HR directors were responsible for, *inter alia*, the configuration of the personnel/HR departments at the lower levels of organisation of the MNC, as well as the slimmed down corporate office. Heads of personnel/HR in subsidiaries normally reported to their MD with a dotted technical line responsibility to the corporate HR director regarding corporate policy. In a minority of cases personnel/HR directors in the divisions had direct-line responsibility to the headquarter's HR director. This diversity of operation was also found in the IRS Employment Trends (1999a, 1999b) surveys into 'employment in the global village'.

This organisational model distinguishes between strategic and operational decisions with the main Board approving the corporate strategy devised by CEO/MD Executive Group and the divisions and subsidiary companies operationalising corporate strategies. Additionally at corporate level the personnel/HR directors were involved with strategy formation, in deciding the pay and benefits of the top 200 executives, and with management training and development initiatives. The decentralised model of the multi-divisional firm still largely equates with a top down view of the organisation, whereas the development of the MNC suggests inputs to strategy have themselves been decentralised, although as some of our case study companies (i.e. the automatic dispensing machines, sausage skin producers and electronic control switch makers) demonstrate, subject to central

Table 7.1 Personnel/HR director involvement in business and HR strategy formation in MNCs

Level of involvement	Business strategies		Human resource strategies	
	Corporate PLC	Percentage	Corporate PLC	Percentage
Highly involved	3	14	17	77
Moderately involved	13	59	3	14
Little involved	5	23	1	5
Not involved	1	4	1	4

Source: PLC CEO/MD questionnaires

Note: One of the 23 CEO/MDs did not answer the question.

coordination and direction. For instance a Canadian owned company in the spirits and entertainment industries dissatisfied with the performance of local company management (over product quality and inflated wage costs) drafted in a senior HR director (Vice President) from corporate headquarters in Canada to ensure corporate HR policies were implemented by the local subsidiary and thereby reduce the power and influence of the UK subsidiary's production management (Kelly and Gennard, 1996). Marginson *et al.* (1995) consider MNCs monitor HR performance across business units in different countries encouraging the dissemination of HR policies from the country of origin to overseas subsidiaries (the so-called host country effect). However, with globalisation, and the growth of MNCs, the need for this integration of HR policies has been demonstrated by Nagai's (2000) study of Japanese MNCs, operating at regional level in Europe.

Data from our own research demonstrates personnel/HR directors have a high presence on the CEO/MD Executive Group and participate in a number of ways in the strategic decision-making process. With regard to the pay and conditions of the top executive directors, the personnel/HR director worked, in the case of a British-owned MNCs, with the remuneration committee of the main Board. They were invited by CEO/MDs to offer advice and technical data on the going rate for different types of office holder including benefits such as top hat share schemes, pensions etc. The main PLC Board remuneration sub-committees were usually made up of non-executive directors (NEDs) and the personnel/HR director had frequent interaction with them. The personnel/HR director also had some input into the nomination of individuals to be invited to join the Board/Executive Group but such input was in no way as extensive as with remuneration committees. CEO/MDs played the largest part in such appointments. Most personnel/HR directors reported that the CEO/MD consulted them most extensively when the appointment to the Executive Group was to be the promotion of an internal candidate(s). The personnel/HR director at a major brewer and leisure group told us: 'On these occasions the CEO does much of the work himself but will ask me for my views'.

Moreover, some MNCs, such as in the sausage skin maker case, gave the host country subsidiary considerable autonomy on recruitment, but interferred to secure the corporate interest in key appointments. When their subsidiary in the Czech Republic was to appoint a new director the corporate personnel/HR director helped decide the appointment to ensure corporate interests were taken into account.

A vital consideration for a global company is management development and succession planning if future senior directors are to obtain a rounded experience of the total business. As the CEO of a steel manufacturing company remarked:

> The CEO group spends a lot of time with the personnel director on career plans of the top 140 to 150 individuals who are in the senior management development programme. They are rotated round the business to gain experience of the whole company.

In the IRS Employment Trends (1999b) survey performance management and staff development were seen to lend themselves to a consistent cross national border approach. The personnel/HR function often sent managers, engineers and some other professionals on overseas assignments to broaden their experience of the business and to develop their personal confidence. Our case study companies offered several examples of managers sent on overseas assignment. The collagen company had several technical people on expatriate assignment, although in their case the determining factor was the nature of the project rather than management development. A Scottish utility, which had taken over a major utility in the USA, seconded senior HR professionals to investigate their personnel systems with a view to their integration into the Scottish company's business values and management development programme.

Our case companies revealed other mechanisms for the integration of corporate personnel policies. These included the staffing of task forces and multi-disciplinary project groups by corporate personnel to tackle specific problems and on which there was a personnel/HR presence. In this way senior managers formed informal relationships which improved communication and understanding long after the task had been completed and the group disbanded. Headquarters personnel departments also carried out formal management audits to monitor performance and the implementation of corporate policy in overseas subsidiaries. However, most important were the HR committees comprising of host country personnel specialists, set up by the corporate centre, as a means of transferring policy understanding, and also through which new policy innovations could be identified and worked up for adoption as corporate strategy. This process included encouraging overseas subsidiaries to raise and present HR innovations introduced in their own locations. In this latter case the corporate personnel department acted as an intelligence agency coordinating local initiatives and evaluating their suitability to the Group as a whole.

Other HR policies in which corporate personnel/HR directors were involved included the design and gaining acceptance of profit related pay/share ownership schemes and new communication systems through the company web site. Moreover, notwithstanding the high degree of decentralisation to business units throughout the world, some corporate HR policies remained important such as pensions and health and safety in oil exploration, transport and steel manufacture. Finally, it is important to remind ourselves that HR policies are seen to be integrated with business strategies and where possible measured (Brewster *et al.*, 2000). This is summed up in the following quote from our interview with a personnel/HR director of a private utilities multinational company, 'The HR director must paint a picture of how personnel/HR can facilitate business success. You must present HR strategy in quantitative terms, when you can, to equate with the sales, production, supplies, finance functions etc.'.

Those MNCs operating in the European Union are required to establish a European Works Council (EWC) as the means of informing and consulting employees' representatives from all their EU subsidiaries on matters which are of concern to them and which are of an EU wide nature. To be covered by the

Directive a company (or group of companies) must have at least 1,000 employees in the European economic area and of these there must be at least 150 employees in each of two member states. The Directive lays great emphasis on establishing that the precise mechanism for information and consultation be by negotiation. Only if negotiations are unsuccessful, or refused by management, do the minimum (or fall back) terms for a EWC come into play. At three of our case study MNCs (brewing and leisure, sausage skins and electronic control switches) the personnel/HR directors had been given full responsibility by the CEO/MD Executive Group, to negotiate the format and composition of the EWC, and to gain the commitment of senior general and functional management as well as management in the various subsidiaries to the EU-wide EWC.

What personnel/HR directors do at foreign-owned subsidiaries

Our questionnaire survey of CEO/MDs recorded an 82 per cent presence of personnel/HR directors on the CEO/MD Executive Groups of 159 subsidiary companies. Of these 15 were foreign owned subsidiary companies operating in Britain of which their parent nationalities were six from the USA, two from Norway, and one each from Japan, Australia, Canada, Ireland, Switzerland, France and Holland. Unlike Marginson *et al.* (1993) we discovered no significant difference between the presence of personnel/HR directors on foreign MNCs subsidiary boards compared to British subsidiaries of MNCs. All these 15 foreign owned subsidiaries had a personnel/HR director with a Board presence and who was confirmed by their CEO/MD as being highly involved in the formation and implementation of business and HR strategies and policies. In addition our questionnaire survey contained data on independent SMEs of which 16 were involved in international trade. These had a mean of 41 per cent of their trade going into international markets. The SME questionnaire, unlike the corporate PLC questionnaire, did not identify MNCs, but has been included here to identify the personnel/HR directors' involvement in international activities within smaller companies. Table 7.2 shows the personnel/HR directors' involvement in both making business and HR strategies.

The table shows personnel/HR directors to be little involved in the international strategic business decisions of SMEs, although their involvement in HR international decisions is higher. This is explained by the smaller employment size of SMEs which were in the early stages of the development cycle (Dowling *et al.*, 1999) engaging in international trade but not yet investing directly overseas and not yet MNCs.

Our interview programme revealed personnel/HR directors of the foreign subsidiaries located in Britain were represented on the local company Board and highly involved in implementing corporate HR policies. However, the important question here relates to the degree of autonomy possessed by the subsidiary companies and the ability of the local personnel/HR directors themselves to initiate

Table 7.2 Personnel/HR director involvement in the formation of international business and HR strategies in SMEs

Level of participation	Business strategy		Human resource strategies	
	Numbers	Percentage	Numbers	Percentage
Highly involved	0	0	5	31
Moderately involved	4	25	5	31
Little involved	4	25	3	19
Not involved	8	50	3	19

Source: CEO/MD SME questionnaires

proactively the development of HR strategies within the subsidiary in the host country.

Ferner and Varul (2000a, 2000b) and Ferner, Quitanilla and Varul (2000) analysed the process of reverse diffusion in German MNCs. They examined organisational learning processes of German-owned MNCs operating subsidiaries in Britain, the USA and Spain. Their argument is that German companies are locked into a social partnership culture enshrined in national legislation and the works council system, both of which emphasise participation and consensus management. Traditionally German MNCs displaying an ethnocentric attitude would decide policy strategically at headquarters and spread or diffuse these out to their subsidiaries. However, as international competition increased, other non-German MNEs have innovated and found ways of operating in less well regulated international labour markets. German MNCs face the prospect of losing business as they become less competitive. They argue German MNCs are thus learning and adopting new and innovative HR techniques, especially from their Anglo-Saxon subsidiaries. As the authors say, 'German managers on returning from spells in the United States were said to have brought with them competency frameworks which they introduced into central departments'.

Reverse diffusion arises when managers from the parent country are placed on assignment overseas and learn at first hand about 'good labour practices' there, and subsequently transfer their learning back to the parent organisation on return from their overseas assignment. The establishment of international functional committees including HR committees, formal HR audits and project teams are also means of transferring within the corporate group ideas and practices existing elsewhere. In this way German headquarters collect intelligence which if found desirable is incorporated into corporate policy and diffused throughout its other subsidiaries in a multiplicity of host countries. This development is aided by decentralisation within MNCs taking on the characteristics of matrix, transnational and networking organisations which, combined with a geocentric staffing and development strategies, accept innovative centres of excellence within the corporate organisation. According to Ferner *et al.*'s analysis the scope for local subsidiaries making, and implementing, their own business and HR strategies and policies is considerable.

Another relevant issue arising out of the Ferner and Varul (2000b) research is the emergence within MNCs of proactive and strategic personnel/HR departments. They illustrate the change by reference to German companies in which personnel/HR management tended to be administrative and reactive within a highly regulated legal and collective bargaining context. German codetermination laws provide employees with rights to be consulted and informed and on some issues the right of veto over management. The personnel department, including the Labour Director, who is also a member of the Executive Group, not the Supervisory Board, implement legal requirements, works councils' decisions and collective agreements concluded outside the firm at sectorial level. However, as MNCs become more organisationally complex the need for HR integration becomes more critical. German MNCs, as do others, require their personnel/HR departments to be strategic and proactive in identifying talent, in management development, succession and career planning and in putting in place the associated processes such as measuring performance management, compensation packages, transfer policies etc., to accommodate an increasingly geocentric management and professional cadre (Subbarao, 2000). They also require them to seek proactively more efficient and effective ways of improving business performance by coordinating and securing the implementation of HR policies developed elsewhere within the MNC. Moreover Nagai's (2000) work on Japanese MNCs realigning their business and HR strategies to intensify the role played by regional headquarters confirms this argument, especially with respect to the European Union.

Our own research unearthed many examples of personnel/HR directors at subsidiary level taking initiatives to develop policies to suit local company needs which were either ahead of the corporate position or filled gaps in headquarters policy. In our Irish brewing company the local CEO/MD top management team took the initiative in devising a plan to improve the productivity and profitability of their subsidiary. The motivation behind this strategy was the survival of the Irish site against a MNC corporate management threat to locate new investment in the UK. The personnel director, in conjunction with the MD, played a substantial part bringing in major changes in technology and associated HR policies to down size the workforce and to establish new working practices to ensure their site's survival.

Our cash register American-owned multinational whose Scottish business was in decline until the local subsidiary board initiated, with the approval of corporate headquarters, a new product – the automatic dispensing machine – provides another example. Two American MNEs operating in Scotland introduced cell manufacture to their whole corporation. In one case, a personal computer company employing 3,000 in Scotland, and 70,000 worldwide, was fast growing with a flat management hierarchy of five/six levels between corporate CEO and the shop floor. The Vice President manufacturing explained to us the local company initiated a business re-engineering process in moving to cell manufacture. The results were exported successfully more widely in the corporation. The HR function played a major part in driving the change process. The HR director had been in place for five years but had previously been production manager for seven. Job rotation was seen as important in meeting the challenge and in sustaining interest in a flat management hierarchy. Our switch control organisation also introduced to the wider corporation cellular manufacturing groups. However, on this occasion, a decision had been made at corporate headquarters that the Scottish plant would pilot the scheme. The local HR department's role was to introduce flexible working methods and training programmes for these cellular manufacturing groups which now operate globally throughout the corporation.

Finally, the Norwegian-owned shipbuilding case study company provided an example of a subsidiary with a large measure of discretion to decide both its business and HR strategies. The Norwegian MNC took over a nationalised shipyard in the late 1980s with the objective of improving the yard's competitiveness to that of European standards. The Scottish shipyard took twice as many staff hours to build a ship as its European competitors. The MDs business plan aimed to win orders at the high value specialist end of the market. The personnel director persuaded the new MD on his arrival at the yard of the significant role a personnel strategy could play in converting the yard from making financial losses, to initially a break even, and then, to a profit position. The new MD lacked an understanding of the traditions and culture of the shipyard but was quick to realise the personnel/ HR director could provide him with this. The personnel director's plans to improve staffing utilisation included the introduction of 'bell to bell' working (working from the start to the finish of the shift) with tea breaks taken on the job, in contrast to the previous indulgent work patterns, a major improvement in welders' rework production rates, reductions in absenteeism (running initially at 25 per cent) and accident rates, the introduction of three shift working in a traditional day working industry, performance-related pay for managers and a quality incentive bonus for welders. In the early to mid 1990s the shipyard broke into profit for the first time prior to nationalisation in 1977.

However, in the late 1990s the original MD left the company and his replacement, initiated a change in business strategy taking the product downmarket from sophisticated ships to simpler structures in direct competition with far eastern ship-builders. This caused a split in the subsidiary's board with the personnel, and other, directors (including the financial director) resigning from the company. The new business strategy sought to reduce the core workforce considerably with greater reliance on hire and fire policies. By the late 1990s the shipyard was in financial difficulties and was sold in 1999 to a new owner. The autonomy of the subsidiary to initiate both business and HR strategies and the role of the personnel director (during the first phase) in contributing to the formulation and implementation of business and HR strategy is illustrated by a letter dated 21 April 1994 from the first MD to the personnel director saying:

> It is very pleasing to see the continued progress of the shipyard in the employee relations field ... Your efforts at the yard were instrumental in turning it around, and I can assure you that even here in Norway the 'social experiment' undertaken there has caught a lot of attention.

However, some of our case study companies had less autonomy, although they did have some (stemming from host country differences in labour laws, history and culture) to initiate at host country level their own business and HR policies. There appeared to be three factors at work. First, where production was highly integrated as in the case of a Swiss chemical MNC the cross border transfers of production within and between product divisions required the application of uniform policies to facilitate the standardisation in technologies and work organisation. Second, two of our companies, one in engineering the other in distilling, had experienced financial difficulties resulting in an attempt by the corporate headquarters to introduce and tighten up on reporting procedures. Third, some American MNCs in the computer industry had strong corporate cultures enshrined in various personnel policies (e.g. non-recognition of trade unions) which were required to be implemented within their subsidiaries throughout the world.

Power and influence of the personnel/HR director in MNCs

Globalisation, changes in business strategies and structures provide opportunities for personnel/HR directors to enhance their power and influence at all levels within MNCs by making the CEO/MD Executive Groups more dependent on their contribution. The changing circumstances give significance to staffing and development processes encompassing a geocentric style. The need to facilitate the movement of people and knowledge throughout the organisation to solve management problems gives greater scope to the HR director and the personnel function generally to influence events. Pettigrew and McNulty (1995) and McNulty and Pettigrew (1996a) in their discussion of power and influence of non-executive directors (NEDs) stress the importance of the Board of Director context (i.e. its history, structure, culture and leadership style) and the NEDs interaction with this context in the exercise of power and influence. They highlight the importance of 'relationship influence' to change events and the NEDs willingness to use it. This is an important distinction as authority and official position are prescribed for the director by the legitimising body, in this case the shareholders. However the exercise of power and influence, although an element of authority, is something more. In a sense power and influence have to be sought, taken and wielded by the director – hence the significance of the individual's 'will' to use it. In support of this point Hunt and Boxall (1998) draw attention to the personal discretion exercised by HR directors at this senior level and which goes beyond the behaviour prescribed by their formal role.

McNulty and Pettigrew's research (1996b) establishes NEDs to have influence in personnel/HR areas concluding, 'No significant difference of opinion existed between executive directors and NEDs over personnel matters'. Our own research findings show heavy involvement of personnel/HR directors in the servicing of sub-committees of Boards. This enabled them to establish a network of interaction, dependence and influence which can be traced between actors. According to McNulty and Pettigrew the social skills deployed to improve Board decision-making are assertiveness, persuasion, collaboration, diplomacy, lobbying, logical argument and the establishment of trust and mutual respect. These generic social skills apply to interactions between all directors, including personnel/HR directors.

Frooman's analysis of power and influence provides an additional insight into how personnel directors use this network of relationships to influence strategic issues. In Chapter 5 it was argued that where the CEO/MD has power over the personnel/HR director the latter is likely to make use of an indirect strategy (as opposed to a direct strategy) to influence events. This is especially the case where the CEO/MD attitude to the personnel/HR function is marginal (or even negative) in terms of a favourable disposition as in the case of the Hospital Trust (see Case study 5.1). Previously examples drawn from various organisations ranging from a multi-utility, brewing and leisure group, engineering, shiprepair and computer manufacturer etc., showed the personnel/HR director widening their portfolio to take on non-personnel tasks salient to the needs of the CEO/MD Group and to the Board of Directors. In these instances the relationships were triangular between NEDs, as chairs and members of the Board's remuneration and appointments sub-committees, personnel/HR directors who service them, and the CEO/MD. The personnel/HR director's power and influence was enhanced by making use of relationships with NEDs, a third party, thereby leveraging their influence with the CEO/MD, providing they have the 'will' to use it. Indeed Ferner and Varul (2000b) highlight dangers to the corporate personnel department as they may be left with a declining administrative function as the more strategic work arising from globalisation is taken on by newly emerging management functions. Personnel/HR directors therefore have to be politically aware, dynamic, proactive and willing to grasp new strategic opportunities as they arise within MNCs.

Personnel/HR processes in MNCs

Overseas assignments

The majority of MNCs in our case studies had formal policies on recruitment and selection for the appointment of senior international management. They employed people on international contracts who then moved on completion of a project overseas to another international assignment. According to IRS Employment Trends (1999b), 'A key criterion for recruitment and promotion to the top jobs is international mobility'.

In the HR policy area decentralisation to national subsidiaries was common given the diversity in national legislation, local host country employee relations institutions and labour market conditions. Nevertheless even in the most decentralised companies pursuing a polycentric staffing strategy there was a degree of central direction, via a policy framework, intervention by corporate personnel/HR directors in local recruitment decisions. The MNC selection literature highlights a number of problems regarding the complexity of overseas assignments. These may cover expatriates from the parent country going abroad, third country assignees to a host country and both host and third country nationals recruited to headquarters in the parent country. Indeed the evidence would suggest that the extent of international transfers has increased with MNC convergence and the adoption of geocentric staffing strategies (IRS Employment Trends, 2000; Kidger, 1999).

Attempts to identify selection criteria for overseas assignments is complex and to date success has been limited. According to Dowling *et al.* (1999) there are three factors which influence the selection process at the individual level. These are the situational requirements of the MNC, language and the host country culture. Empirical studies concerning individual characteristics show greatest weight is given to technical ability. A PriceWaterhouseCooper (1998) survey of 184 European firms established that the most important selection criteria were job related skill (99 per cent) and leadership skill (76 per cent). However, Tung (1981) has shown cultural suitability to be important in achieving effective assignee operation in the host country. Abilities include cultural empathy, adaptability, diplomacy, language, positive attitude, emotional stability and maturity. It is important the expatriate can adjust and relate well to people in other countries, who hold different values and attitudes which affect their interactions as they work with one another. According to Hendry (1994) adjustment is facilitated if the expatriate has a global awareness, 'A strategic outlook which comprehends trends in world business'.

The work of Dowling *et al.* (1999) on selection criterion for overseas assignments shows family requirements to be important. Evidence supports the view that the expatriate's job success is heavily influenced by the spouse's attitude and adjustment to the host country environment (De Cieri *et al.*, 1991). According to the IRS Employment Trends (2000) survey, the most important reasons for success in international assignments are job satisfaction, a happy partner, a happy family and good intercultural skills and training. These results suggest the need for the inclusion of the family in the selection process, but this is rarely the case. Work by Brewster (1988) covering 25 European companies shows some 16 per cent prepare families for overseas assignments. A study of 184 companies by PriceWaterhouse Cooper estimates the figure at 11 per cent.

The preparation and training of people going on overseas assignments is necessary for successful adjustment. Research by Bjorkman and Gertsen (1990), cited in Dowling *et al.* (1999), into 80 Danish companies and Barham and Oats (1991) have shown that MNCs pay most attention to language training, a visit to the host country and briefing by host country nationals. The intensity and depth of the training varies depending on the MNC requirements. For instance Swedish MNCs place more emphasis on language training than do American companies. In industries such as petroleum, airlines and banking, English is the established language, whereas in others (such as electronics and food and drink) there is no common international language. In the latter industries language training is most important. Other non-English speaking MNCs use English as the international company language. In such a case a parent country national needs to be competent in English before going overseas on an international assignment.

However, despite the importance of preparation and training for overseas assignments the evidence suggests that the majority of MNEs give little attention to it. Derr and Oddou (1991), in their study of 135 individuals employed in US MNCs, found over 65 per cent had no preparatory training at all, whilst one third received only reading materials. In one of our sample companies (a large British textile MNC) the personnel director based in London was given one week's notice to agree to a move to a managing director's job in Hong Kong. There is also a problem of a lack of available candidates. In some instances only one or a few people possess the necessary technical skills, whereas more generally the first or second choice candidate may have rejected the offer of assignment.

One of the most important reasons candidates reject overseas assignments is dual careers, especially where the candidate's spouse or partner has a career of their own and is reluctant to give it up. PriceWaterhouseCooper's (1998) survey reported 86 per cent of companies had offers rejected with the main reasons being domestic and family concerns (77 per cent) and dual career issues (58 per cent). At the level of household income an overseas assignment has to be very attractive financially to make up for the loss of a partner's income. Companies manage these problems by seeking alternative employment for the spouse in the host country and if this fails by offering to compensate the person by paying for and facilitating personal development through education and extra qualifications.

Another important constraint is the age of children. Very young children or those of university age can more easily be accommodated than children at an age when school examinations are critical. Depending upon the location of the assignment children of this age might have access to an English-speaking school abroad, or if not, they may be left behind to attend boarding school. In an attempt to accommodate this problem some companies concentrate their overseas assignments on younger and older managers missing out those whose family responsibilities are at their highest. This policy is also less costly to the firm. Finally, managers may be reluctant to accept an overseas posting because it is to an undesirable location in a third world country. They may regard the assignment as detrimental to their career development, as it takes them out of sight, out of mind. Here the manager is concerned with being out of the mainstream, away from the parent country, and with possible re-entry problems on return from the assignment. Evidence on expatriate failures suggests higher rates for the USA than for Japanese managers with Europeans having fairly low failure rates (Brewster, 1988; Tung, 1981). Family difficulties arise through social isolation and a lack of facilities comparable to home country standards.

The American-owned switch control MNC in our sample had sophisticated policies on foreign assignments and experienced few problems in persuading managers to accept overseas postings, although it found it easier to get managers to go to Switzerland and the USA rather than other countries. The company employed consultants to provide pre-departure training to the assignee, usually in languages and orientation to the host country culture. It reported problems did arise, however, where children were established in the school system. In addition there were problems with dual careers when the partner had to vacate a job. In the latter case the company provided financial assistance, training and, on rare occasions, employed the partner in the overseas location. The company had also a re-entry policy for repatriates in that it guaranteed them an equivalent job on return, but not the same job or a better one, justifying this on the grounds the organisation was likely to change rapidly over the duration of the assignment.

Performance management and management development

The trend towards globalisation has caused MNCs to grapple with the problem of achieving corporate integration whilst acting locally by giving subsidiary companies sufficient autonomy to respond quickly to local markets. Kidger (1999) argues top management has become more integrated with MNCs creating a pool of international managers. Hendry (1994) argues career management becomes increasingly significant as the MNC's involvement in internationalisation deepens. The IRS Employment Trends survey (1999a) divided companies into those, like IBM and Eli Lilly, which are highly centralised and others such as GKN and Marconi Communications who decentralise strategic decisions on performance management and management development. In the cases of IBM and Eli Lilly harmonisation has been taken to the point of making use of the same performance appraisal forms across national boundaries, simply translating the form into different languages. This standardised approach receives support from the work of Bjorkman and Gertsen (1990) in that 76 per cent of US firms in their sample used standardised appraisal forms for expatriation evaluation. However. decentralised MNCs are also likely to require corporate policies on performance management and management succession, albeit leaving operational details to the subsidiaries. Of the ten MNCs surveyed by IRS Employment Trends (1999b) eight reported making strategic decisions at the corporate centre on performance management and management development. Here the role of the corporate personnel/HR function was more extensive both in formation and monitoring the implementation of those policies. The survey concluded that performance management and management development policies and practices lend themselves more to central direction and control than some other HR policies such as industrial relations.

Performance appraisal and management development serve several goals for MNCs. One objective is control as corporate headquarters attempt to ensure corporate policies and strategies are adopted and implemented by subsidiaries. In the early phase of internationalisation corporate control is achieved through parent country expatriates on overseas assignments. The corporate centre is concerned to transfer technical skill and management knowledge throughout the corporation. However, as MNCs become more decentralised, transnational and geocentric, other methods are adopted, e.g. use of task/project teams. A further objective is to spot talent within the management group through the assessment of their task achievement as well as identifying their training and development needs. Performance management systems linking individual goals to those of the subsidiary company and in turn the corporate strategy is one way to achieve integration.

Another objective is processing identified talent through the corporate management development programme. Even in decentralised MNCs, where responsibility for succession planning lies with subsidiaries, there is a point when corporate headquarters takes over the management of the development process for strategic reasons. This was illustrated by our sausage skin manufacturer case where the company was moving from a polycentric staffing and development policy to becoming a more geocentric one. Traditionally the emphasis was on local autonomy in the HR area. However, headquarters had intervened in subsidiary decisions as and when required for wider strategic reasons. Examples included, as we have shown previously, the corporate HR director recruiting jointly with the local HR director, a director in the Czech Republic with a view to his further development within the MNC as a whole. It is in the interest of the MNC to develop internationally experienced managers to operate at senior level both within host countries and at parent headquarters. The dynamic of the development process has been greatly facilitated by improved corporate communications based on new computer satellite technologies. IRS Employment Trends (1999a), for example, reported all its eleven MNCs surveyed had set up intranet sites to this end.

There are many methods by which management can gain international experience of their company's business strategies and operations of which the three to five year overseas assignment is only one. There was not a lot of evidence from our case study companies of personnel/HR directors having had expatriate experience, although a few did have as the Hong Kong case cited above shows. Generally, personnel/HR directors developed their international experience through foreign visits, holding international corporate HR meetings and working on international project teams. International experience was not a dominant factor in personnel directors gaining membership of the CEO/MD Executive Group, but it is likely to become more important as globalisation increases and geocentric policies become more common. As MNCs shift in the direction of matrix and networking organisations the need (and cost) grows to train a larger number of international managers. In a fast changing context most of our sample MNCs had entered into contracts with international recognised business schools to educate and train their managers. In other cases MNCs have set up their own training and development colleges, e.g. Elf Aquitaine and British Steel. In this way managers from headquarters and overseas subsidiaries meet to discuss and improve their understanding of business strategies, operations and problems facing the company (Bartell and Ghoshal, 1988).

Another method of broadening international experience was through participation in project teams both of a functional and multi-disciplinary composition. An example of a multi- disciplinary team (i.e. line and HR managers) within our sample of MNCs was the setting up of a project group under the leadership of the personnel/HR director to establish a European Works Council (EWC). These cases (drawn from brewing and leisure groups, switch control and sausage skin companies) entailed international representatives of employees from all their plants within the EU meeting in rotating locations throughout Europe. Another method falling between the long expatriate assignment and the short one or two day project meeting is the assignment lasting two to three months which does not necessitate family transfers and household expenditures. These development methods help to build a network of interpersonal relations as managers from different parts of the MNC get to know, understand and communicate more effectively with each other. As Kidger (1999) says, 'International business is built through networking rather than an enormous cadre of international managers who travel'. In this way the personnel/HR function of the MNC helps to build a culture or mind set of how things are done within the corporate organisation.

Dowling *et al.* (1999) offer a model of expatriate performance consisting of the compensation package, the task itself, headquarters support or absence of it, host country environment and cultural adjustment of the expatriate and family to the host environment. They conclude that headquarters support in the foreign location for the expatriate and family is a powerful explanatory variable in their emotional adjustment and successful job performance.

Compensation and employee relations

International compensation of employees can be considered at two levels. First the individual personal contract, normally applied to senior managers, and second collective or group contracts applied to manual and more junior white collar employees in the host locations. In the case of the individual employee going on an overseas assignment the MNC's compensation policy should meet a number of criteria, i.e. it is attractive enough to encourage employees to take an overseas assignment, will not cripple the company with enormous costs, and fits with other international HR policies of the MNC. Dowling *et al.* (1999) consider there are two approaches to international compensation – the going rate, and the balance sheet. Both have advantages and disadvantages. The going or market rate is where the MNC compensation package is based on the levels existing in local markets of host countries. This has the advantage that expatriates are paid the same as host country nationals performing the same work. The disadvantage is the variation between expatriates of the parent country in different countries doing the same job and for the same employee on assignment in different countries. The going rate approach can lead to resentment amongst expatriates with competition for high standard of living locations with little interest in countries with low standards of living.

The balance sheet approach is the one most commonly used by MNCs. It is based on the assumption that no employee on a foreign assignment should lose financially by accepting an overseas assignment. Adjustments are made to the basic salary and benefits package to compensate for additional expenditure and to make the assignment attractive. It has the advantage of equity between assignments and between expatriates of the same nationality. The downside can result in disparities of different nationalities and between expatriates and local nationals. Differences in taxation, cost of living, social security and exchange rates must be accounted for within the package. In this respect corporate personnel/HR departments liaise with consultancy firms who specialise in such work. Allowances to expatriates are considerable and generally include housing, cost of living, air flights for home leave, education of children, relocation expenses and spouse assistance. These costs vary greatly but are generally put at between two and four times basic salary (Dowling *et al.*, 1999).

Unlike the performance management and management development processes, none of our sample firms engaged in a centralised approach to employee relations. Our MNCs divide into two groups – those who adopted a decentralised approach and those centralising firms which had an overt corporate policy. The corporate personnel/HR function played a larger role in the more centralised organisations. All firms pursued a policy of local pay determination within the host country for manual and junior white collar grades. This is explained by the need to be competitive by making use of cheaper labour costs where they exist, due to diversity in national employment laws (e.g. minimum wage and working hours) and the strength of trade unions and collective bargaining. No company recognised trade unions across national boundaries for purposes of collective bargaining. Collective bargaining, if it took place at all, was within national boundaries in accordance with the country's employment and labour laws. European Works Councils (EWCs) did provide an opportunity for employee representatives from various countries to meet, but these forums are restricted to consultation and information giving purposes.

Notwithstanding this hands off approach to international employee relations, the more centralising companies did have some world policy statements. Common amongst these was a corporate decision on level of pay rates in the host country e.g. to pay in the top quartile. To determine this salary level surveys were conducted within host countries. Another area where corporate policy had an influence on local subsidiary companies was team working and performance-related pay. It would seem MNCs had shifted towards realigning pay more tightly with the performance of the individual through performance assessment (IRS Employment Trends, 1999a). Others, although sometimes with both policies combined, introduced share and/profit bonus schemes to encourage a corporate identity and to provide employees with a share in the prosperity of the MNC as a whole. Previously we discussed reverse diffusion (Ferner and Varul, 2000a) in which employee relations innovations in vanguard host country subsidiaries are adopted by the corporate headquarters. These MNC policies include team working by Japanese firms and performance measurement systems by American MNCs.

Questions and answers

Attempt to answer the following questions based on the text. Indicative answers are provided at the end of the chapter.

Q. 1 What opportunities arise in MNCs for personnel/HR directors to enhance their power and influence at both headquarters and in overseas subsidiaries?

Q. 2 What considerations must be taken into account, both from a company and individual employee perspective, when sending a manager on an overseas assignment?

Your answers should contain some or all of the following points:

A. 1 As MNCs grow to exploit the benefits of expanding international product and financial markets their organisation becomes more complex with the need to balance acting globally with that of acting locally. Management has to find an optimum balance between central co-ordination, integration and control and local autonomy to take account of host country differences in legislation, customer tastes, language and culture. In this context rigid hierarchical organisation structures are replaced by a more open and flexible organisation including matrix, transnational, networking and heterarchical forms. A significant problem relates to the staffing and development of senior management with the shift from ethnocentric and polycentric policies to geocentric and regiocentric ones. The personnel/HR director has an opportunity to be at the forefront of these developments by offering a range of advice and service including establishing a pool of management talent, planning career development and managing succession, introducing HR innovations to overseas subsidiaries, auditing corporate performance through international HR committees, recycling subsidiary HR innovations for corporate consideration, and setting up communication systems to facilitate vertical, horizontal and diagonal information flows by making use of the latest technologies.

A. 2 Personnel has to establish formal policies on overseas expatriate assignments and repatriation. Company policy on overseas assignments is to facilitate the transfer of expatriates and their families to host countries at a competitive price acceptable to the company. Expatriation is costly as the compensation package involves the no worse off principle whereby the assignee receives a basic salary no less than the comparable job in the home country with the addition of allowances for cost of living conversion, taxation and social security, car, visits to home country etc. Consultants can be employed to deliver much of the preparation through pre-training programmes, especially important in the difficult area of compensation.

The employee normally has two main concerns when asked to accept an overseas assignment. What are the implications for his/her career? On repatriation will there be promotion? Second, family problems are a concern for managers going on overseas assignments. These include dual careers and children. With children age and schooling are important. If children are pre-school or at university the problems are likely to be less severe. However, if established in the school system, then it may mean finding an English-speaking school abroad or boarding school at home. Dual careers usually require the spouse or partner to vacate a job to accommodate the transfer overseas. This loss of household income and future career prospects can be a difficult problem to manage. The company may have to provide financial assistance, education and training, find a job for the partner in the host country and on rare occasions employ the partner in the overseas subsidiary.

8 Personnel/HR directors in the public sector

In the 'old' public sector, four main categories of public employment were distinquished. First, there was central or national government, known as the civil service. Employees were paid directly by money raised from taxation and were either manual or industrial workers (found in various maintenance, construction, or manufacturing jobs in government establishments) or non-industrial civil servants (engaged in clerical, executive and administrative duties for government ministries). In 1979, the civil service employed 725,000 employees. Second, there was local government where employees were paid by local taxes (rates), although central government provided a high proportion of local authority finance. Local authority employees were engaged in a wide range of activities delegated by central government, including education, police, fire protection, refuse collection, road and house building and recreational facilities. In 1979, the local authorities in the UK employed 2.2 million employees.

Third, there were the nationalised industries or public corporations, most of which achieved this status in the period 1945–51 when the then Labour Government nationalised the fuel, power and transport industries (electricity, gas, coal, railways), plus road haulage and the airlines. The steel industry and the post office became nationalised industries in the late 1960s whilst shipbuilding gained such status in 1977. In 1979, the nationalised industries employed 1.9 million people. Finally, there was the National Health Service that came into being in July 1948. It was funded out of general taxation, a statutory subscription made by all working adults, dental and ophthalmic and prescription charges plus some limited private services provided by hospitals. In 1979, the National Health Service employed 1 million employees.

The role of personnel/HR in the public sector: pre-1979

The civil service

Until 1969, in the civil service, the crucial management decisions were made by the Treasury. In that year, however, the Civil Service Department was established with a senior executive directly responsible to the Prime Minister. It was responsible for developing policy on all labour relations issues including selection and recruitment, training and development, promotion, pay and conditions, managerial efficiency and pensions arrangements throughout the public sector as a whole. Personnel/HR was seen as one of a number of administrative duties within the civil service.

The government as an employer was concerned to be viewed as a good one. It encouraged its employees to become union members because it regarded collective bargaining as a good and desirable activity. Collective bargaining cannot be sustained without organisation on the employees' side. Compared to the private sector, particularly amongst non-manual employees, the density of trade union membership was high. The central government was also keen that the pay and conditions of its employees should be comparable with those employed in the private sector performing the same jobs. So the criteria or principle pursued in determining pay and conditions in the civil service was 'comparability' with similar work or occupations in the private sector. The government was also concerned that any differences between itself and its employees should be settled by independent arbitration rather than the imposition of industrial sanctions. Its disputes procedure provided, as its final stage, for independent arbitration.

In the pre-1979 civil service, personnel/HR management was highly bureau-cratic, centralised and standardised. Terms and conditions of employment of civil servants were established through a national Whitley Council (and its various departmental sub-committees) with salary bands applied to the same grades throughout the service. The role of personnel/HR was that of an 'establishments' officer administering centrally determined collective agreements and rules, offering advice to departmental managers, policing policies and maintaining staff levels. Line managers had little autonomy to interpret procedures that were applied uniformly and consistently throughout the service. Within this centralised administrative framework, the personnel function had a significant central role, but in a negative, reactive and 'you cannot do it that way' culture.

Local government

Local government had considerable diversity in managerial structure, training and policies amongst its 1,500 or more units. Only the large, urban local authorities had developed any managerial professionalism. Local authorities achieved some degree of coordination via membership of employers' associations. Some unifor-mity in pay and employment conditions was achieved through the establishment of central staff negotiating machinery in 1948. In April 1974, a new two-tier structure of local authorities came into being in England and Wales followed one year later by the introduction of a similar scheme in Scotland.

Personnel/HR was until the mid-1970s the responsibility of an 'establishments' officer working in the Town Clerk's department undertaking administrative policies and procedures, including the auditing of staffing levels. However, the Bain's Report (1974) recommended that in local authorities, personnel management should become a separate function with shared responsibilities for human resource planning, recruitment, termination, discipline and absence, education and training, working conditions, negotiation of wages and conditions and the people implications of organisational change. It recommended the chief personnel manager have direct access to the local authority's chief executive officer. In practice most post-1974 Councils accorded full director status and membership of the top management team (TMT) to the chief personnel director.

Industrial relations aspects of personnel/HR work in local government had been traditionally centralised. Various National Joint Industrial Councils (NJIC) existed for different grades of local authority workers. Trade union membership was high and NJIC agreed terms and conditions were laid down via the sector framework agreement for issues such as incentive schemes. Manual workers had a job evaluated pay structure and non-manual employees, including management and professional grades, had salary grades with pay spines. An important part of the personnel/HR role in the local authority prior to 1979 was to administer and interpret national agreements.

The National Health Service

Traditionally, personnel/HRM in the Health Service centred on the Whitley Council system. Such Councils were responsible for establishing, through collective bargaining and joint consultation, employee pay and conditions. Some professions, however, such as doctors and nurses had Pay Review Bodies to determine their pay and conditions. These Review Bodies, whose members were appointed by central government, recommended to government the pay increases to be awarded to such groups. They were to take pay determination out of collective bargaining thereby avoiding the potential of industrial action by the trade unions concerned. Local Health Boards implemented the Whitley framework for personnel and employee relations policies on recruitment, working hours, training, promotion, grievances and discipline within each hospital and employment unit. Line managers viewed the personnel/HR function as bureaucratic, restrictive and cut off from every day activities. The personnel department was effectively an administrative service to the line.

Nationalised industries

The Labour Government that took office in 1945, greatly extended the area of public employment by a series of nationalisation Acts which established sole provider of a service or source of energy (e.g. coal, gas, electricity) by law. They were legalised monopolies. Public ownership, however, did not revolutionise management approaches to the management of people. At best, it helped to codify and generalise the better practices throughout some of the industries. The traditions that had developed in the industries before their nationalisation continued to influence the prevailing labour management practices. Collective bargaining took place at the industry-wide level and the public corporations were obliged by law to recognise, consult and bargain with the appropriate trade unions.

Pressures for change

By the mid-1970s, it was generally accepted that inflation could not be contained at acceptable levels via the application of productivity, prices and incomes policies that had been implemented by all UK governments, regardless of political allegiance, since the end of World War Two. Government, therefore, turned to the monetarist school of economics for appropriate macro-economic policies to control inflation. Monetarism is associated with the work of Milton Friedman of the University of Chicago and advocates that if inflation is to be kept under control then the overall level of demand in the economy (i.e. the total spending power of individuals, households, firms and governments) must not exceed the total amount of goods and services in the economy available for purchase. In short, the total overall demand for goods and services must balance the overall supply of goods and services. If demand outstrips supply, then a situation arises in which too much money chases too few goods thus causing inflation (rising prices) to occur.

For the monetarist demand in the economy is controlled by interest rate policy. If the government wishes to reduce demand in the economy to prevent inflation from rising, it will increase interest rates and vice versa to raise demand. The supply of goods and services in the economy can be increased by promoting increased product market competition, by increasing productivity, by reducing taxation and by increasing competition in the labour market by reducing the influence of labour market institutions such as trade unions. Increased competition is seen as desirable because it results in an increase in the supply of goods and services (increased output) and a reduction in prices.

The Conservative Governments of 1979 to 1997 sought to increase competition in the private sector by abolishing foreign exchange controls, by the removal of import controls and tariff barriers and by promoting the advantages of free trade areas such as the European Single Market that came into being on 1 January 1993. However, during this period, the public sector was not isolated from the desire for increased competition as the best means of achieving economic growth without undue levels of inflation arising. Monetarists also advocate a reduction in the size of the public sector on the grounds that it competes with the private sector for scarce economic resources. By doing so, it is seen to hold back the wealth creating advantages of the latter without which there could be a reduced source of taxation to fund the public sector. The Conservative Governments of 1979 to 1997 sought not only to reduce the size of the public sector but also to make the remaining smaller sized sector more efficient, effective and economical. This general thrust of policy towards the public sector was continued by the incoming Labour Government of 1997.

The public sector changes from 1979 to date have seen competition introduced into the public sector. The nationalised industries of gas, electricity, steel manufacture, telecommunications, coal mining, airlines, railways, shipbuilding etc. were privatised and their legalised position of sole supplier of the product/service removed. Other institutions can now enter the market to provide these products/services. In the Health Service, internal markets were introduced by the creation of Hospital Trusts to compete with each other. Local authorities were subjected to compulsory competitive tendering (CCT) which obliged them to put some 'in house' departmental services out to tender against the competition of private sector suppliers of these services. In the civil service, the management of public assets, for example naval dockyards, was put out to contract amongst private sector companies, some services were subject to market testing and/or sub-contracting and Executive Agencies managed by a chief executive and a top management team, were introduced to break up and make more efficient large civil service departments.

Another important development was the separation of supplier and purchaser activity. Some public sector organisations (for example the Ministry of Defence) had acted as both customer and producer with work schedules being unspecified and relatively unsophisticated accounting systems with regard to costs and value added. The Ministry of Defence was often prepared with its awarded contracts to pay actual cost plus a profit mark-up to private or public sector suppliers.

Targets designated to improve standards of performance and to achieve value for money for the tax payer were also introduced into Executive Agencies, Health Trusts, local government, higher education etc. Sub-contracting, the adoption of flexible working practices and temporary contracts became the accepted norm as the belief developed that the public sector should adopt the 'best practice' of the private sector, such as the introduction of performance appraisal systems and performance related pay (Farnham and Giles, 1996; Winchester and Bach, 1995). However Boyne *et al.* (1999) based on an extensive study of 909 managers in the public and private sectors urged caution. Their findings show the level of support for 'private sector' HRM practices such as performance related pay, flexible working practices etc., was less developed in the public sector and that the tradition of paternalism, standardisation and collective bargaining arrangements remain strongly embedded.

Similar events as took place in the UK public sector were also observable in mainland Europe, North America and Australasia (Walsh and O'Flynn, 1999; Common, 1998; Flynn, 1995). For example the New Zealand economy had been highly dependent on British demand for its mutton and dairy produce prior to Britain's entry to the European Economic Communities (EEC) in 1973. To adjust to this change major structural changes were required to the New Zealand economy. It considered that this could be best achieved by reducing public expenditure and the state's involvement in its management. Flynn (1995) has shown the generality of such trends throughout Europe with convergence in the solutions adopted to solve public sector problems, despite differences of history, politics and culture.

As in Britain the Australian state of Victoria adopted in 1994–95 a CCT approach with local authorities required to put out to tender 20 per cent of their expenditure, rising to 50 per cent in 1996–97. Walsh and O'Flynn (1999) compared the operation of competitive tendering and contracting in Victoria, Australia with that in Britain and showed conditions of employment to have deteriorated e.g. in Britain manual workers such as street and office cleaners and in garden maintenance suffered from the abolition of or modification to bonus arrangements. Other groups such as part-time workers in school cleaning and meals experienced an increased spreading of their hours of work over the working day and a lengthening of their working week. There was an increase in the use of part-time and temporary workers often with a downward reclassification of their pay rates. Trade unions in both Australia and Britain were faced with the stark choice of a trade-off between sustaining jobs in-house or accepting deteriorating working conditions. The effect has been generally to fragment collective agreements and undermine workers' pay and conditions, although Walsh and O'Flynn point out that some strongly organised groups, such as refuse collectors, due to their improved productivity, experienced gains in bonus payments.

However, despite the drive to reduce the size of the public sector and improve its performance, the sector still retains different goals, purposes and values from the private sector (Moore, 1996). The public sector generally provides services free at the point of delivery, as to charge market prices could/would put them out of reach of a significant number of the population or lead to an inadequate (both in terms of quality and quantity) supply, which would be unacceptable to the public interest, e.g. disease could become widespread if inadequate refuge collection services were available or households could not afford to purchase them. The public sector is always under greater public scrutiny via MPs, local councillors and the media than is private industry. The numbers of stakeholders is larger than within the private sector and thereby the potential for conflicting interests is greater.

The development of the role of personnel in the public sector: post-1979

The civil service

An important change introduced into the management of the civil service via the Management Functions Act 1992 was the creation of Executive Agencies with a high degree of autonomy within devolved budgets for achieving efficiencies and improvement in service quality, to pursue their own HR policies. These Executive Agencies are managed by a chief executive officer and a TMT. According to Newman and Clark (1994) 23 chief executives have been recruited from the private sector. Although Executive Agencies have their own devolved budgets this does not isolate them from the central government's overall policy of financial constraints. The level of pay settlements and the amount of funds available, for example, to fund performance related pay schemes, remain under tight central government control.

The Citizen's Charter of 1991 aimed to improve the efficiency of the civil service by providing for more privatisation, sub-contracting and competition. There was an extended use of performance management standards and targets with an individual's pay related more to their performance than to inflation increases and comparisons with pay movements of other workers.

An important change in the management of the public sector, as we have already noted, was the separation of supplier and purchaser arrangements. Gennard and

Kelly (1992 and 1996) discussed this change in the case of Rosyth and Devonport naval dockyards, which were Ministry of Defence (MOD) owned, supplying repair and maintenance work to the Royal Navy. However, the work to be completed was not specified, in any detail, tendered for, nor subject to proper accounting procedures. It was simply paid for by the Ministry on a cost plus profit margin basis. In 1987 the management of the dockyards at Rosyth in Scotland and Devonport in England were put out to tender (contractorisation), and from then on run by private contractors who had to tender for Royal Navy work in competition with private shiprepair yards. Initially the private contractors employed the dockyard employees but only managed the dockyard facilities which remained in the ownership of the Ministry of Defence. However, at Rosyth the physical assets of the yard were purchased in 1997 by a private company and the yard became part of the private sector. The impact of these changes on Rosyth dockyard has been examined by the authors (1992 and 1996) whose analyses demonstrated the key role of the personnel director, in partnership with the CEO and other directors, in devising and implementing the organisation's key business and HR strategies first under contractorisation and then under privatisation.

The establishment of Executive Agencies with their management possessing a high degree of autonomy presented an opportunity for transforming the role of personnel. According to Gagnon (1996), 'In 1993 government delegated pay and pay-related conditions of service to 21 Executive Agencies and two government departments'.

Other changes included the introduction of performance appraisal systems and performance related pay giving emphasis to individual performance and to a degree threatening the collectivist approaches established through standardisation and collective bargaining. The introduction of more flexible working arrangements, whether of the task, numerical, temporal or financial variety, were aimed at reducing costs and improving performance, but required HR policy initiatives to be supplied by the personnel department, led by a personnel /HR director, if they were prepared to grasp the opportunity presented.

The health service

The post 1979 major changes in health service management commenced with the Griffiths Report of 1983 which advocated the replacement of consensus management by medical professionals with the introduction of general managers. This was followed in the 1990s by a new major restructuring which established Hospital Trust boards and introduced an internal market (Bach, 1998). This restructuring established a separation between supplier and purchaser with contractual relations between the Hospital Trusts and local health authorities (both within and outside their own districts) who purchased their services at an agreed specification and price. The internal market was augmented by the Trust hospitals contracting, in competition with each other, for business including some from general practitioner fund holders and other private medical customers. The Trust Boards gained responsibility for the establishment of business plans and budgets and for the Trust's internal administrative structures. The Whitley Council system which negotiated pay and conditions was wound up and the Hospital Trusts became the employer responsible for pay and other employment conditions.

In the mid-1980s health authorities were required by central government to market test the cost of non-medical services, such as laundry, domestic cleaning and catering, by inviting tenders from private contractors. This continues today. Additionally performance indicators covering improving patient throughput year on year and setting reductions in waiting list targets were introduced. The extent to which these indicators were met was subject to external review by the Audit Commission which conducted audits of all National Health Service (NHS) and local government bodies with a view to improving their economy, efficiency and effectiveness. Most Health Trusts replaced their functional management based structure, centred on professions, by one based on clinical directorates supported by business managers.

In the case of 'Central Scotland Trust' the TMT originally consisted of seven directorates with fourteen heads of various professional disciplines. This created problems of overlapping jurisdictions, co-ordination and control. It was replaced by three clinical directorates supported by three functional directors. The setting up of Health Trusts offered the opportunity for the personnel function under the leadership of a personnel/HR director to break with the tradition of being an administrative, and reactive function to become more directly involved in shaping the Trust's strategy and appropriate policies.

Local government

The two tier system described above in England and Wales and Scotland was replaced in 1995–96 with larger unitary Councils providing comprehensive services within their designated territories. Unitary Councils were allowed to adopt considerable diversity of governance and management models. The debate continues for further reorganisation. A Department of the Environment Report of 1999 proposed new political structures and improvements to financial accountability including directly elected mayors. Although to date the only directly elected mayor under these proposals is in London. Financial accountability was improved by the ending of rate capping and shifting more responsibility for raising taxes locally onto the Council. Central government, however, still retains a reserve power to control excessive Council tax increases as it provides 80 per cent of local authority expenditure.

In Scotland, in addition to the local authority reform of 1995–96, the Commission on Local Government and the Scottish Parliament (the McIntosh Report, 1999) considered the relationship between local government and the Scottish Parliament with devolved powers from Westminister for, *inter alia*, education and health. Local government is also one of the Scottish Parliament's direct responsibilities and therefore relationships between the Parliament and local government had to be clarified following the recommendation of the McIntosh Committee. The Scottish Parliament and the 32 Scottish local Councils set up a standing joint conference to regulate their relationships. McIntosh rejected the concept of an elected provost (mayor) but recommended Councils give particular attention to executive models and simplified committee structures.

A significant change in local government prior to the 1990s under the Local Government Planning and Land Act 1980 was the introduction of compulsory competitive tendering (CCT) requiring local authority departments to tender in competition with private contractors to undertake the services of office cleaning, catering, road and housing repairs. In 1988 central government extended the number of services subject to the CCT requirement to include architecture and information technology. CCT obliges every local authority department when involved in CCT to specify the work to be done (work specification) and to draw up a business plan containing costs of the provision of the service. The process of competing against private sector providers of the same service caused local authority departments to become more cost conscious by tightening up on work specifications, down sizing staff operations, tackling high absence rates and lax management attitudes to discipline.

The Labour Government (1997 to date) moved away from CCT to a best value approach as recommended by the UK Department of Environment and Scotland's Commission on Local Government and Scottish Parliament Reports. Best value entails the setting of performance targets and plans and performance reviews of all local government services. Local authorities drawing up performance plans are expected to take account of national performance indicators (set by government), and to seek continuous improvement by bench marking themselves against leading edge authorities and private firms. The best value inspectorate's role is to audit and ensure local performance plans are realistic and accurate. Although CCT has gone out of fashion, it has not been abolished. The current Labour Government still believes local authorities should not be monopoly suppliers, and that if a service can be supplied more cheaply and effectively from the private sector, then that should be done.

The power and influence of personnel management in the post-1979 public sector

The general view in the academic literature is that the changed context in which the public sector has operated since 1979 has downgraded the power and role of the personnel function. Several authors argue that the changed environment has led to its demise through decentralisation and the devolvement of people management to line mangers (Kessler *et al.*, 2000; Cunningham and Hyman, 1999; Boyne *et al.*, 1999; Oswick and Grant, 1996; Kessler and Purcell, 1996). To quote Boyne *et al.*, 'The emphasis on customer needs and financial performance has resulted in devolution of power to line managers rather then personnel specialists ...'.

Kessler and Purcell argue the changing public sector context created greater uncertainty that resulted in the balance of organisational power shifting against the personnel role. They point to the 1995 local government reorganisation, arguing this resulted in the establishment of smaller TMTs, consisting of CEOs and multi-functional corporate executive directors, and the downgrading of personnel directors as they were now required to report to a corporate director rather than previously directly to the CEO. The study of Brent Local Authority by Kessler *et al.* (2000) also points in addition to the 'stripping out' of personnel specialists from decentralised business units. Oswick and Grant argue environmental changes leading to financial stringency, by central government policy, and a reduction in the priority given to industrial relations has caused downsizing in organisations and personnel departments and as a consequence a shift of HR management from personnel specialists to line managers. The argument is that as line managers become more familiar with personnel work then personnel management as a discipline becomes de-mystified. Oswick and Grant also contend the line manager's authority is further enhanced, and dependence on personnel specialists reduced, by the decline in trade union power. Cunningham and Hyman's empirical study portrays a pessimistic view of personnel's future when they argue, on the basis of four case studies, including two Hospital Trusts, that after devolution of HR activities to line management none of the personnel departments secured an established place within the organisational framework.

Of the 19 public sector TMTs investigated in our research only three did not have a personnel/HR director as a member. Of these, two were in local government and one in a pre-1992 university. All three were in organisations that had adopted the corporate model. The 1995–96 local government reorganisation, establishing unitary Councils, allowed for a diversity of management models (Fenwick and Bailey, 1999). The nine local authorities we observed divided into two models. One allowed for a TMT made up of directors of departments/functions meeting with the CEO. These TMTs were large consisting of between 16 and 22 officials. The other had a smaller TMT consisting of CEO and five to eleven multi-functional executive directors with heads of departments/functions reporting to an executive director and not the CEO (Kessler and Purcell, 1996). The aim of this second model was to establish a greater focus on local government management as a corporate entity compared to the older more professionally based organisation consisting of departmental/functional heads.

In our research there was only a limited relationship between the local government corporate model and the size of authority in that both large and small authorities had adopted it. For example, larger ones adopting the corporate model included 'Large City' and 'Mid Scotland' whereas the smaller 'Clydeside' and 'South West of Scotland' Councils had also adopted the corporate model. On the other hand the relatively larger 'Southwest' authority had not. However, our research showed there was no direct link between the two models and the presence of a personnel director on the TMT. It did establish, however, that the larger size TMTs of the older model had proved unwieldy and were thus accompanied by the existence of a smaller 'inner cabinet' of top officers consisting, usually, of CEO, plus the finance, personnel and corporate affairs directors. This inner cabinet offered support to the CEO. It provided much of the vision and direction of the authority and discussed budget scenarios (and possible allocations) prior to the full TMT meeting and subsequent recommendations to the Council.

In most of our local authority case studies management did initiate and develop policy ideas in pursuit of their own organisation's strategy as well as operational matters such as implementing new legislation etc., and offering advice to councillors. The smaller corporate teams of executive directors in the newer model effectively built this informal cabinet into the formal structure with one significant difference. In several of the councils investigated (e.g. 'South East England', 'Mid Scotland' and 'Large City') the personnel directors role had been broadened to include other business activities. For example, the 'Large City Council' had a corporate executive team of eleven officers including the personnel director who also had extra responsibilities for administrative services. This replaced a TMT of 22. The widening of responsibilities applied to all executive directors on the TMT including finance and not just to personnel. The wider portfolios were designed to create a corporate view of the Authority's business and to gain greater cooperation in agreeing priorities and budget distribution compared to the previous model where heads of departments/functions fiercely argued for and defended their own budgets. It was clear from the research this corporate model has delivered a more business management orientation in local government adding credibility to personnel that is now perceived by other directors as more mainstream to the Council's business. As well as taking on these wider tasks CEO also claimed to value personnel directors for their competencies in handling the trade unions, who although less of a priority than yester year, can still obstruct/delay the implementation of a change strategy and therefore their cooperation in the implementation of change was essential.

Even those personnel directors who had not been selected as members of the executive team, held the view that personnel management had enhanced its power and influence through local government reorganisation. This was confirmed by the CEO at 'South West of Scotland Council' where, for example, the head of personnel reported to the Director of Corporate Support who represented the function in the TMT. However, the head of personnel had direct access to the CEO on various items such as health and safety and the Authority's culture change programme, and would be brought into TMT discussions as required. It is this model arising from changes in management structure in local government which leads Kessler and Purcell (1996), and Oswick and Grant (1996) to conclude that personnel is vulnerable and that its power and influence has regressed. However, their view is anchored in the centralised professional/functional model which fails to take a realistic account of the existence of a 'collective cabinet style', in which personnel/HR, in partnership with the CEO and other directors, plays an important part, in helping the local authority deliver improved services at reduced costs.

An illustration of this analysis is provided by the 'Mid Scotland Council' (although it was replicated by others) which adopted the corporate model of organisation containing a personnel director with widened responsibilities on the TMT. 'Mid Scotland' is the fifth largest Council in Scotland serving a population of 307,000. The TMT consists of the CEO plus seven executive directors including deputy CEO, corporate resources, finance and IT, community resources, education and libraries, housing and technical services and social work. Personnel/HR management is housed in corporate resources which includes responsibilities for legal issues, administration, operations (e.g. births, deaths and marriages), public relations and corporate policy. Prior to the 1996 reorganisation the TMT consisted of 17 directors as heads of departments including a director of personnel services. This mirrored the Council committee structure loosely co-ordinated by the leader of the Council. The director of corporate resources had been the director of personnel services in the previous Council.

In the aftermath of the 1996 reorganisation 'Mid Scotland Council' developed a corporate identity with a stronger focus on a business approach to delivering cost reduction and improved service quality to customers. The TMT was reorganised on the lines outlined above but with a stronger collective team style as opposed to what previously had been largely a functional organisation. The executive directors held broad portfolios to encourage them to take a corporate view of the organisation. The TMT was a collective team with individual directors responsible for functional responsibilities. However, the corporate team had to prioritise decisions regarding the use of resources and all directors had to 'give and take' on their multi-functional budgets for the corporate good. Moreover, each director was given leadership of projects outside their own functions to encourage a Council wide perspective. Notwithstanding this focus it was decided executive directors retain operational responsibilities as to have no functional/service/operational responsibilities carried the danger of the TMT being isolated leaving departments seeing the TMT as an ivory tower. Under the old management structure new developments would have been claimed by different functions to enlarge their budget and empires. Within the new TMT structure, compromise and flexibility was more easily attainable.

In the 'Council' the personnel director as executive director of corporate resources had broader responsibilities. The CEO was asked what he sought in a personnel director. He replied:

> Vision, innovation, to be proactive in the strategic sense, lead on HR matters, to be technically competent, however the latter is secondary as he can get the technical aspects from the 'in house' personnel team. If the personnel director was to leave I would replace him with another personnel director but I would be looking for someone who could develop into a broader role. I believe that this broader portfolio has helped the credibility of personnel with other directors.

This quote reinforces a major theme of this book, namely that to be at the centre of organisational power and influence the personnel director has to be a rounded business person capable of using their HR knowledge and competence and their social/political skills to achieve the main objectives of the organisation. In Frooman's (1999) terms the personnel director can use an indirect usage strategy to enhance power and influence.

Additionally, our local authorities were faced with problems requiring a multi-disciplinary response and could no longer be managed within traditional departmental/functional structures. For example a problem arising in education may require a solution involving the social work and the housing departments. As a result more inter-departmental networking and partnerships between departments and outside agencies are required calling for Councils to put together more readily project teams consisting of appropriate experts in a flexible and responsive manner.

Given the Department of Environment Report of 1999 proposing new political structures and improvements to financial accountability the future of local government is likely to be towards cabinet government. Under the leadership of a mayor or Council leader, a small group of councillors as 'cabinet' members will hold broad portfolios covering a number of departments and are likely to run the Council as a corporate entity. To respond effectively to this management will need to be more generic and flexible. This has implications for the training and career development of not only future personnel specialists but also for the development of all managers within local government. Personnel specialists, along with others, are likely to find themselves engaged in job rotation, as members of multi-task project teams etc., and spending time outside of the personnel function all designed to help them acquire and develop the knowledge and understanding necessary for managing the general business needs of the Council.

We conclude from our research in the public sector that the T-shaped director/manager model (see Chapter 3) is generally required at lower levels in local government and not just at the Board level. Of the nine Councils researched, seven had adopted the corporate model of executive directors and of these five had personnel directors in executive roles. Our research clearly indicated it is the attitude of the CEO, working with the Council's political leadership, which determines whether personnel has a major role and influence in devising and implementing the ensuing change programme. Whether personnel/HR has a presence on the top management team is thus explained (as in the private sector) by the orientation of the CEO towards personnel and the personal quality, skills and proactiveness of the personnel/HR director in interacting with the CEO and the Council's changing circumstances. It is clear from our research that personnel/HR directors exercise power and influence in a variety of forms in local government and not as argued by Kessler and Purcell solely through specialist representation on TMTs. Examples range from the personnel/HR director with the broad portfolio operating as a multi-disciplinary executive to personnel directors on functionally based TMTs, to the case of 'South-West' Scotland, a functional TMT, where personnel was a member of the CEO's informal 'inner cabinet'.

The establishment of Trust Boards as public corporations (Farnham, 1999) in the Health Service took the business model further than in other services of the public sector. The Trust Boards included in our research usually consisted of six NEDs including the part-time chairperson and five executive directors, four of which were mandatory (CEO, finance, medical and nursing). The chairperson and NEDs were appointed by government ministers, a decision in which the Trust had no voice. The Trust Board had freedom to appoint executive directors including the CEO and personnel/HR director. Guest and Peccie's (1994) study of 86 Health Trusts in England, Northern Ireland and Wales showed 80 per cent had a personnel presence on the Board or TMT. Of the five Trusts studied by the authors four had appointed personnel directors to the main Board and who were also members of the CEO Executive Group. However, in a fifth case the personnel director was a member of the CEO Group only, but subsequently negotiated membership of the full Trust Board (see case study in Chapter 5).

As in the private business sector the CEO Executive Group was smaller in size and operated in a less formal manner than the Trust Board of Directors. It met more frequently and was the powerhouse of the Trust initiating and working up Trust policy and strategy for approval by the main Board. The interviews with both CEOs and personnel/HR directors revealed that major organisational changes were on going within Trusts, and that personnel directors participated continuously in the implementation of organisational change. All Hospital Trusts had abandoned the functional model, based on 14 or so heads of professional disciplines (e.g. nursing, medical etc.) and departments such as finance and personnel meeting with the CEO, in favour of three or so clinical directorates supported by internal business managers and other functions such as HR and finance. The CEO Group operated an open collective style of management with all executive directors having both a wider business role as well as a functional one. At the 'Large City' Trust, one of the country's major acute surgery hospital's, strategy formation was separated from implementation, with the personnel director, a full Board member, expected to contribute to the growth and development of the business and to lead on HR matters. For example, the personnel director was involved in the strategic planning and reorganising of theatre staff working arrangements.

The separation between strategic and operational decisions meant that none of the executive directors had neither a budget nor direct responsibility for a department or function. This allegedly assisted a more open dialogue as there was no departmental territory to defend. In this case operational personnel management had been decentralised to the various directorates which had the services of personnel managers organised on a matrix basis i.e. one personnel manager would service two or three operational managers. However, this model was not universal and at South County Trust the personnel director was involved in both strategy and operations decisions. CEOs generally aspired to open and collective team decision-making at the board as it defused internal politics and gained commitment to decisions. Three of the five personnel directors' portfolios included non-personnel activities which assisted their appreciation of the wider needs of the business. In one case personnel had responsibility for the Trust's quality programme, in another for hotel operations and yet in another the clinical waste plant. Additionally as in the private sector personnel directors supplied the CEOs and NEDs in membership of remuneration and nominations sub-committees of the Trust Board with technical data and advice as part of their role of servicing these Boards.

The work of Guest and Peccie (1994) on Hospital Trust's presents a puzzle regarding the effectiveness of the personnel/HR director's contribution to effective people management. On the one hand their survey shows that the presence of the top personnel specialist on the Board or Executive Group is associated with negative qualitative assessments by line managers and personnel specialists themselves of HRM's effectiveness within Trusts. On the other hand, HRM effectiveness is rated highly where there is integration of formal written policy and strategy at Board level (organisational integration) and in the efficient delivery of personnel services (process integration). They argue that where HR policy is owned by top management who have committed themselves to written HR policy, line managers and personnel specialists give higher ratings to HRMs' effectiveness. Although Guest and Peccie argue that the judgement of HRMs' effectiveness is a political one made by those who possess power in the organisation and not an assessment of personnel specialists' worth *per se*, nevertheless as they admit themselves, the two are closely linked. It is our contention that the perceptions of CEOs and other directors are significant to the power and influence of personnel/HRs contribution, but that this is achieved within a collective TMT where personnel places emphasis on both its functional specialism and on its business orientation integral to the Board/TMT. There was little evidence from the Hospital Trust case studies that decentralisation and financial stringency have weakened the position of personnel management. If anything the changes have provided opportunities which some personnel directors as shown by Mid Scotland Trust (see Chapter 5) grasped to enhance their power and influence.

Our research illustrates that the environmental changes in the public sector over the last two decades have generally increased the status, power and influence of the personnel/HR function. This conclusion is in contrast to that of Boyne *et al.* (1999), Cunningham and Hyman (1999), Kessler and Purcell (1996), and Oswick and Grant (1996) all of whom consider that financial stringency, customer orientation, decentralisation of the organisation and the devolvement of HR work from personnel departments to line mangers has undermined the authority and power of personnel management. We accept that personnel's traditional role in the sector grounded in an administrative role has declined if not disappeared. However, any authority, power and influence in this role were largely negative, reactive and based on preventing action contrary to espoused centralised rules. However, this analysis portrays only half the picture. In the last 20 years the role of personnel has changed in the public sector to one that is more positive and proactive, focused firmly on contributing to improved performance in public sector organisations. The major organisational changes of the public sector have provided increased opportunities for personnel/HR directors to take more power and influence and to contribute to improving their organisation's performance. They have achieved this, as in the private sector, by pursuing both direct and indirect usage strategies (Frooman, 1999), to increase their influence with the CEO, for example by broadening their portfolio, taking on responsibilities for non-HR activities, committing themselves to a stronger business orientation and in the case of the Health Trusts by fostering relationships with NEDs.

Changing relationships between personnel/HR function and line management

The changing relationship between personnel/HR and line managers is central to any analysis of the power and influence of the personnel function in any organisation let alone public sector organisations. As shown in previous chapters the decentralisation and devolvement of personnel/HR work from the personnel department to line management has been well documented. It is as well to bear in mind that personnel's role has always been to offer service and advice to line management who have always held responsibility for people management. As Poole and Jenkins (1997) state: 'The shift of responsibility from personnel departments to line managers has been overstated ... in the context of HRM'.

Our research evidence points to a considerable decrease in the numbers of personnel/HR specialists within particular organisations as head offices decentralised and devolve personnel work to business units. However, the quality of contribution required by line managers from personnel specialists has risen (Gennard and Kelly, 1997). Moreover, our research shows personnel/HR directors as members of public sector Boards/TMTs have recommended the devolving of personnel to provide services to line management. Certain HR decisions such as equal opportunities polices and pensions have always been seen as best dealt with by the central employing unit. The Kessler *et al.* (2000) analysis of decentralised and devolved HR within Brent Council reveals some weaknesses of decentralisation in that the Authority still remains legally responsible for the decentralised business units from which personnel departments are absent. According to Kessler *et al.* (2000), business unit managers had been over burdened with work, some had been macho in style thereby creating HR problems and worse still some managers were often unaware of or refused to recognise problems faced in managing people. Our research showed personnel/HR specialist support continued to be required by the line, but it was being delivered in a more flexible and variable manner than before the organisational change.

However, several academics see such developments as a major tenet of HRM, and a threat to the existence of the personnel/HR function. To quote Storey (1992):

> Line managers come to the fore in this regard not only as a crucial delivery mechanism for new approaches in employee relations, but more assertively, as themselves, the designers and drivers of the new ways. Both aspects carry implications for personnel as a separate specialism, but the latter aspect, which suggests invasion of policy making territory by non-specialists is clearly more threatening to personnel managers.

However, it is the work of Oswick and Grant (1996) specifically relating to the public sector which appears most damning of the power and influence of the personnel/HR function in this sector. They argue that environmental changes have caused personnel to change from a specialist to a generalist role to secure partly economies of scale and partly to increase the degree of task enlargement and flexibility. This analysis concurs with the more general evidence of McConville and Holden (1999) and Gennard and Kelly (1997), but is contrary to that of Adams (1991) and work on HR service centres (Reilly, 2000) which argue that personnel has become more fragmented and specialist. However, Oswick and Grant argue that the changing relationships between professional personnel specialists and line managers, contains a real threat to personnel in the public sector. Given the need for cost minimisation, the devolution of HR responsibilities to the line manager is regarded as making them more cost conscious in their use of the HR department, as they may exercise a choice to undertake the activity themselves or sub-contract it out to external consultants, if the organisation's policy permits this. In undertaking HR activities themselves line mangers become familiar with personnel work that de-mystifies it as a separate management profession.

Oswick and Grant's analysis identifies four characteristics determining the exercise of power, namely personal power, expert power, opportunity power and position power. They argue the public sector changes of the last 20 years have had no significant impact on personal power and that position power remains hierarchical in terms of reporting relationships. The two most important variables for them are thus changes in expert and opportunity power. The decline of specialisms (e.g. job evaluation, industrial relations, employee resourcing, training and development) within personnel management combined with the change in the line manager personnel specialist relationship (i.e. de-mystifying personnel expertise) they argue has reduced the power and influence of personnel as a function within the public sector. The decline in opportunity power is seen as the result of changes in the internal client-contractor system whereby the departmental manager is able to dictate the boundaries of personnel's involvement. This is exacerbated they claim by the development of CCT in local government and the health service and market testing in the civil service, although this may now be modified by the emphasis on 'best value practice' rather than CCT. Thus line management dominance limits the opportunities for personnel to control resources including information. Oswick and Grant conclude: 'The current levels of personnel involvement within the public sector are lower than they have ever been at any time in recent years'.

However, Oswick and Grant's analysis contains several weaknesses. First, regarding the demise of personnel's expert power it seems odd that personnel generalists are less professional than the specialists in industrial relations, training and development, pay administration etc. A reduction in the division of labour can give rise to some loss of knowledge in a specific area, but this can be more than offset by the greater ability of the generalist personnel/HR person being better able to integrate the various personnel/HR processes and thereby make the function more effective. Moreover, even if it is accepted that personnel managers are losing expertise it is difficult to see how this is more than compensated for by generalist line managers who reported not to have sufficient expertise, time and inclination and training to do the job properly (McConville and Holden, 1999; Cunningham and Hyman, 1999). Does this mean the total HR resource available to the organisation is depleted or is it being resourced effectively in another way e.g. by external consultants?

Second, changes in opportunity power as defined by the client-contractor relationship is an overly private sector market model with all the weaknesses associated with that system as applied to the public sector. All the evidence suggests that public sector organisations have been made more cost conscious by the introduction of performance indicators, best value practice, market testing etc., but that today's public sector management is not private sector management (Moore, 1996). As Kessler and Purcell (1996) point out in the application of their private sector strategic choice model to the public sector, the sector is subject to central government policy constraints including policy directions to the decentralised public sector units including local government. Therefore despite encouraging decentralised collective bargaining and the introduction of performance related pay (Bach, 1998; Gagnon, 1996) central government pay constraint continues to be imposed in the national interest. Boyne *et al.* (1999) have shown public sector organisations to be less supportive of performance related pay and flexible employment practices than the private sector. The existence of strong trade unions, and most important of professional groups, and their associations, help to protect the values and interests of public sector employees (Carr, 1999; Boyne *et al.*, 1999; Kessler and Purcell, 1996) and make it difficult for government to establish a truly commercial ethos in the sector (Lupton and Shaw, 1999). Other factors include values of fairness and equity in the treatment of employees and the higher political profile of public sector organisations inviting media scrutiny should something go wrong. Moreover, making the personnel department more responsive to market signals does not mean that there is no role for central long-term HR strategies within local government, Hospital Trusts, universities and civil service departments.

Finally the various analysis of the changing line management personnel specialist relationship is restrictive perceiving personnel management as a rigid professional function sitting within well defined occupational boundaries. In Chapter 4 we discussed functional rigidity as applied to personnel management, the limitations of this schema owing to the majority zig zag career pathway of personnel/HR directors, and testing of the flexible hypothesis of personnel management as proposed by Gennard and Kelly in 1997. Our empirical evidence confirms the proposition that personnel/HR management is diffused and dynamic offering a variety of methods by which personnel expertise is delivered within organisations (Ulrich, 1997; Adams, 1991). Although our empirical data included both private and public sector organisations there is no reason to modify our conclusions when applied to the public sector. The important point is that the configuration of the line manager/personnel specialist relationship is decided by the TMT often, but not always, with the personnel/HR director involvement. In this context the personnel/HR director takes decisions in the interests of the whole business reining in functional interests as he/she is exposed to and responsible for total business performance including HR. This is ignored by Cunningham and Hyman (1999), and Kessler and Purcell (1996) and others when they argue that decentralisation and devolvement has made the personnel function vulnerable, and in the case of

Cunningham and Hyman, even in Hospital Trusts, where it had Board representation, being unable to secure additional resources for training and so on.

Our research in the public sector, as in the private sector, shows personnel/HR directors are not functional heads fighting to retain and enhance a personnel budget but are party to a business strategy including HR elements and have to temper HR ambitions in the interests of business as a whole as agreed by the TMT. At levels below the Board/TMT, changes in line manager and personnel function relationship may be moving in the direction of partnership rather than competition. Evidence of the partnership approach can be found in the work of Renwick (2000), Ulrich (1997), Gennard and Kelly (1997), Torrington and Hall (1996), Eisenstat (1996), Hutchinson (1995), Hutchinson and Wood (1995) and Tomlinson (1993).

As Renwick (2000) in his study of a Hospital Trust says:

> In particular we need to move beyond investigating HR–line work relations using existing conflictual theories only but also to consider theories of a more consensual nature (like those of partnership) which seem (at least in the case of the NHS Trust) to provide more power in explaining HR and line managerial actions in practice.

The pace of change requires increasingly multi-disciplinary team working, transition teams, integration production teams, matrix approaches, temporary project teams, greater fluidity of response etc. Functional rigidity is yesterday's problem.

Getting to the top in the public sector

In Chapter 4 we identified and explained the career pathways by which personnel/HR directors secured a place on the Board of Directors and/or CEO/MD Executive Groups of private sector enterprises. This section examines specifically the public sector and compares its findings with those of private sector organisations.

In Table 8.1 the pathways taken by personnel/HR directors in both public and private sectors are compared. It shows the dominance of the zig zag pathway in both public and private sectors, although the vertical pathway scores marginally higher in the public sector compared with the private sector. Additionally the average number of functional moves by personnel directors was less in the public sector at 2.5 compared to the combined private and public sector score of 3.3 suggesting the zig zag pathway to be marginally less important in the public sector. This is perhaps explained by the relative importance of 'professions' in the public sector (e.g. by the Bain's Report, 1974). Nevertheless in the public sector personnel/HR directors are not purely functional specialists in terms of career background and as a result are better able to take an overall view of the business.

Lupton and Shaw (1999) in a study of 186 HR practitioners divided between public and private sectors found little movement of personnel specialists between private and public sectors. They conclude public and private sector personnel management appear to operate as two separate career structures. They explain the lack of movement from private to public sector as a result of personnel specialists

Table 8.1   Comparison of career pathways taken by personnel/HR directors in public and private sector organisations

Sector	Number	Vertical	Zig Zag	Parachute
Public sector	19	7	11	1
Private	41	14	23	4
Total	60	21	34	5

Source: Interviews and questionnaires

being less highly educated and paid in the public sector, to public sector bureaucracy and to the poor image of the sector. The Lupton and Shaw study is of personnel specialists in general and not specifically personnel/HR directors. Nevertheless our research supports their point that the degree of movement between sectors is limited even at the director level. Of the 19 public sector personnel/HR directors only three came to their directorship directly from the private sector with a further four having transferred from the private sector at a more junior level in earlier years. Thirteen personnel/HR directors came to their position from within the sector (e.g. health, local government etc.) of which 11 were promoted to the position. Three came to the directorship from outside the particular sector (e.g. local government to Hospital Trust) but within the broad public sector.

Notwithstanding this absence of movement between public and private sectors our analysis questions the reasons put forward by Lupton and Shaw. Regarding the level of education, public sector personnel/HR directors were well educated with 18 out of 19 holding first degrees or equivalent, with some in addition holding postgraduate degrees or diplomas in personnel management. The Lupton and Shaw study did not see cultural differences between the two sectors as a reason for the absence of mobility. In one of our Hospital Trust case studies, however, the initial personnel director appointed was from the private sector having been recruited to bring in a more commercial oriented style of management. However, this person was so brash in approach they only succeeded in alienating his senior management colleagues gaining little cooperation thereby defeating the purpose of the appointment. He was replaced with someone with a more appropriate style from outside the health service but from within the public sector. Finally centralisation and bureaucratisation is on the wane in the public sector requiring a shift in the personnel/HR role from one of reactive administrator to one of proactive contributor to adding value (Griffiths, 1993). Nevertheless our work confirms the conclusion of Lupton and Shaw when they state: 'The findings are not supportive of a regression in influence of public sector personnel management, although there is little evidence to suggest convergence with the private sector experience'.

Questions and answers

Consider the following questions based on the text. Indicative answers are provided at the end of the chapter.

Q. 1 What impact had the 1996 reorganisation on 'Mid Scotland' Council's management structure and what did this mean for the personnel function?
Q. 2 Discuss the implications of the Department of the Environment and McIntosh (Scotland) Reports for the training and development of personnel/HR specialists in local government?

Your answers should have included some of the following points:

A. 1 The 1995–96 reorganisation of local government abolished the two tier system of district and regional authorities with divided responsibilities replacing them with unitary Councils responsible for the comprehensive delivery of services within their own area. In terms of management organisation Councils could either continue with the existing functional management structure of heads of department forming the TMT with the CEO, or form a new management structure giving a stronger focus to the Council as a corporate entity. This new structure adopted by Mid Scotland Council consisted of the CEO and seven executive directors replacing the 17 heads of department/functions to form the TMT.

They adopted this new management organisation for a number of reasons. First councils were charged with reducing costs and delivering improved services to their communities in an environment where solutions to problems were changing rapidly and calling for greater flexibility of response in deploying professional expertise. Second the older functional structure was rigid and dysfunctional in the sense it encouraged heads of departments to think as professionals whose duty it was to protect and promote the interests of their departments. The TMT required to adopt a collective team style of management in which the Council's mission was brought into sharper focus with its objectives pursued for the benefit of the whole. The smaller TMT allowed for greater cooperation in establishing business priorities with executive directors more readily agreeing to put more resources into, say, education at the expense of housing.

The personnel director was appointed to the role of director of corporate resources with responsibilities beyond those of the personnel function. This new structure could easily be interpreted as a regression for personnel management's power and influence as the function was part of a larger department. Indeed this did happen at two of the Councils researched by the authors because the Councils retained their personnel directors as heads of function and were represented on the TMT by a non-personnel person. In the case of Mid Scotland Council it was the personnel director who became the corporate resource director thereby widening the role of the personnel function to involvement in the main business of the TMT. This happened in the majority of Councils studied. The CEO's view was this change in organisation had increased personnel's credibility in the eyes of other executive directors. Moreover, the CEO said that should the personnel director leave he would replace him with another HR person, but one who would have to be capable of broadening his/her role. This provides further evidence in support of the hypothesis that it is the CEO's orientation that is important in establishing personnel's power and influence. In structural terms all local authorities were similar yet some brought personnel into the TMT whilst others did not, although size of authority had a limiting, but not an overriding effect.

A. 2 The Department of the Environment highlights the move in local government towards cabinet government with a directly elected mayor, or Council leader, being more visible and taking greater responsibility for executive management with a corporate focus. The McIntosh Report for Scotland is more circumspect regarding directly elected Council leaders but acknowledges the need to move in the direction of executive government in the light of developments elsewhere in the UK. It is envisaged that councillors as members of cabinet will have portfolios encompassing several management departments cutting across and reducing the importance of the existing committee structure. Such a development is likely to impact on the management organisation of the Authority by enhancing the role of the CEO and executive directors with a more generic style of management required. Just as some Authorities have executive directors with broader portfolios, so personnel managers, as will other functional professionals, are likely to become broader in terms of their job responsibilities and flexibility. The career planning and development of personnel managers will involve more job rotation and secondment to multi-disciplinary project teams engaged on general management problems.

9 The effective personnel/HR director

Where is business strategy made?

HRM strategy literature assumes that in the private sector, and parts of the public sector (for example Hospital Trusts), the business strategy of the organisation is made at the highest level of corporate governance, namely the Board of Directors. Our research into 60 organisations questions this assumption. In all of these organisations, business strategy was approved but not formulated at this level. The formulation of the organisation's strategy took place in another body namely CEO/MD Executive Group. The research revealed Executive Groups sometimes called Executive Committees exist at various levels in an organisation. In the large private sector conglomerate firms, there were executive gropus at the corporate level, the subsidiary company level and the operating business unit level. In the public sector, Boards of Directors were found in Hospital Trusts whilst in local authorities the peak governing body was the Council serviced by a Top Management Team (TMT).

The PLC corporate boards in our study consisted on average of twelve directors with a range from a low of seven to a high of twenty. The split between executive directors and non-executive directors (NEDS) was almost 50/50. The main functions of such boards were to approve the corporate strategy as devised by the CEO/MD Executive Group, to monitor the company share price, to approve takeover bids and to reassure the institutional shareholders that the business was soundly managed. The boards of subsidiary companies (average number of directors was seven) and business units had some autonomy in developing their business strategy but most were closely monitored by the corporate board. In addition, they were in competition with other subsidiaries to secure funding from the parent company board for new investment, technological innovation and organisational change. Subsidiary company Executive Groups were usually chaired or had at least one other director representing the corporate-wide interests. The Hospital Trust Boards of Directors vetoed, modified or approved the business strategy presented to them by the CEO/MD Executive Group. In the participating local authorities, executive decisions lay with the elected councillors, but policy initiatives stemmed from a top management team led by the Chief Executive.

In all the organisations participating with our research business strategy was devised and formulated in a CEO/MD Executive Group whose members were selected by the CEO/MD. Its function was to generate and discuss options and conduct necessary research to formulate, for approval by the peak body of governance of the organisation, its business strategy to achieve its business goals. Following such approval, the CEO/MD Executive Group in both the private and public sector became responsible for the implementation of the approved business strategy. The CEO/MD Executive Group was smaller than the main board, met more regularly, was less formal and its members were in more regular contact. In addition, the CEO/MD pursued a more open consultative/participative management style in Group meetings than was the case in Board meetings.

Although the main board had formal power to question, refer back for further consideration and to amend the proposed business strategy formulated by the Executive Group, it was rare for it to reject the Group's proposals. Given that half the CEO/MD Group were also full-time executive director members of the PLC (or Hospital Trust Board) and whose other half of membership were part-time, non-executive directors (but usually full-time executive board members of other companies) this should come as no surprise. The CEO/MD Executive Group, and not the peak body of formal governance of an organisation, was the powerhouse (the heartbeat) for growing and developing the organisation.

The HRM strategy literature implies the business strategy of an organisation is determined by the top of that body and then passed down to the lower (bottom) levels of the organisation. Business strategy formulation is seen as confined to the corporate level and the possibility of a bottom-up (e.g. subsidiary to corporate) influence on corporate strategy decision-making is viewed as at best extremely limited. Our research confirmed the dominant view that most of the time formulation and implementation of business (market) strategy in organisations is top down with very close and strict monitoring methods being applied by the corporate level to ensure compliance by subsidiaries.

However, our research also demonstrated that in certain circumstances in the large multi-product, multi-divisional and multinational company, the subsidiary company may be permitted a high degree of autonomy from corporate level strategy to generate their own business and HR strategies for their particular markets. In 10 of our research organisations whose remoteness from financial control by headquarters was very distant, the CEO/MD Executive Group of the subsidiary, committed to the survival of their decentralised business unit, developed their own, but with approval from corporate level CEO/MD Executive Group, an independent business strategy for their particular markets. In these cases, the subsidiary company was motivated by non-economic considerations such as a commitment to the local community, management pride to be successful, a local/regional identity, etc. The overriding objective, however, always remained to gain, and maintain, a competitive advantage over other subsidiaries of the corporation by cost effectiveness and contributing significantly to corporate-wide profits.

Who makes business strategy?

The dominant view amongst HRM academics is that the business strategy of an organisation is made at the Board of Directors level and therefore by implication those who formulate and approve business strategy are the members of the Board of Directors or its equivalent in other organisations. Many UK surveys (for example WERS and CLIRS) report a relatively low presence of personnel/HR directors on Boards of Directors so the conclusion is drawn that personnel/HR management is relatively unimportant as a player in the formulation of business strategy. However, Purcell (1994) and Guest and Hogue (1994) report that where personnel/ HR has a board presence its influence on strategic decision-making is enhanced. Our own research confirms the relatively low presence of personnel/HR directors (15%) on main boards of PLC but reports 100 per cent for Boards of Hospital Trusts.

However, as noted above, our research shows that in both the private and public sectors an organisation's strategy is formulated at the CEO/MD Executive Group level. It is, therefore, the members of such groups who are responsible for the formulation of business strategy. The evidence from our research (see Table 9.1) is that personnel/HR has a significant presence where it matters, namely on the CEO/MD Executive Group. Of all the CEO/MD Groups surveyed only 15 had no personnel/HR presence.

Our interview programme with, and questionnaire survey to, CEO/MDs revealed that personnel/HR not only had a presence where business strategy is initiated and made but were actually involved in strategy formulation.

However, membership of a CEO/MD Executive Group *per se* does not necessarily mean the personnel/HR director is an influential member of that group. They may be a token member whose views are given little weight. Membership of the CEO/MD Executive Group gives the personnel/HR director a position of authority, provides access to resources and to key players, particularly the CEO/ MD. However, power and influence for an individual in the formulation of business strategies is not necessarily given. It has to be taken and initiated by the individual so that others become dependent upon them. The factors explaining how personnel/HR directors take power to influence the outputs of the CEO/MD Executive Group are discussed below.

Table 9.1 Personnel/HR director representation on CEO/MD executive groups

1 Level	2 Number of CEO/ MD executive groups	3 Number of CEO/ MD groups with personnel/HR directors	4 3 as percentage of 2
Corporate	26	19	73
Subsidiary/business unit	159	131	82
Hospital Trusts	7	7	100
Top management teams (TMT) executive group	12	9	75

Source: Interview programmes and questionnaires

The superficiality of judging personnel/HR's influence on business strategy formulation by its presence on Boards of Directors or its equivalent in other organisations is not only shown by the presence of Executive Groups but also in that our research demonstrated personnel/HR directors can influence the strategic decisions of organisations without a presence either on a Board of Directors or a CEO/MD Executive Group. At 12 participating companies, the personnel/HR director was located at headquarters but was not a member of either the Executive Group or the PLC board. However, they were not without influence on the key business decisions of the organisation. Their physical location in a corporate office close to that of the CEO/MD enabled them, via frequent informal contact with the CEO/MD, to influence corporate decisions. In one particular organisation, the Chief Executive made it known to all the Executive Directors on the PLC board and its Executive Group that all people issues would not be considered at either venue unless they had previously been discussed with the personnel director who was not in membership of either the Executive Group or the main board. In this particular case, a close relationship between the Chief Executive and the personnel director had developed because they travelled between London and Wales together at the start and end of the week.

Our research starkly revealed it is the CEO/MD as a member of both the main Board of Directors and as the chair of the Executive Group, who is responsible for achieving the organisation's success. The CEO/MD is the most powerful person in the organisation selecting the composition of their Executive Group and playing a major role in the appointment of executive directors to the main board and the TMT in consultation with the chairperson of the board or its equivalent. Our research revealed they were often members of the board's nominations committee despite Cadbury's recommendation to the contrary. The CEO/MD thus selects the business strategy makers. In this regard, our research showed that, in general, if the CEO/MD does not have a strong people orientation, then the probability of the personnel/HR function having a strategy-making role is extremely low. If the CEO/MD holds a favourable attitude towards the personnel/HR function then it is likely a personnel/HR director will be a member of the CEO/MD Executive Group and/or the main board and the TMT. The large majority of personnel/HR directors in the research worked in organisations whose CEO/MD had a positive attitude towards personnel/HR's contribution to the achievement of business success. All CEO/MDs interviewed stated they selected a personnel/HR specialist to serve on their board or in their TMT because they recognised people management competency was one of their lesser strengths but appreciated 'getting the people quotation right' was crucial to business success. They had invited a personnel/HR person to work in partnership with them, thereby providing the necessary skills they lacked themselves.

Our research also demonstrated that CEO/MDs with a negative attitude to the role of personnel/HR in adding value to the organisation could be persuaded to the contrary view. Our work revealed two examples (one at a Hospital Trust and the other at a shipbuilding firm) of personnel/HR directors persuading newly appointed CEO/MDs who were not particularly people centred to promote them to CEO/MD Executive Group membership and/or to the Board of Directors. They had, in effect, negotiated themselves into a position of having the opportunity to influence the strategy decisions of those organisations.

The importance of the CEO/MD in the appointment of a personnel/HR director cannot be over emphasised. Just as the 'star' of a personnel/HR director can rise dramatically under a CEO/MD, favourably disposed to its contribution to 'value added' and 'bottom line' etc., so it can decline almost overnight with a change of CEO/MD to one who is less favourably disposed to the role of personnel/HR as source of added value to the organisation. In five of our 60 organisations, a change of CEO/MD led the personnel/HR director to lose director and/or Executive Group status in one of two ways – early retirement or voluntary resignation accompanied by an appropriate financial package. In all cases the personnel/HR director was not replaced, however, the personnel department continued within the company but without a boardroom presence. In this regard, our research confirms the Purcell (1995) view that the decision of an organisation to have a personnel/HR director is linked to the values and beliefs of CEO/MD and only partly related to the organisation's structure, size and strategy.

What career paths to the board/executive group do personnel/HR directors take?

Our research identified three career pathways – vertical, zig zag and parachute – by which personnel/HR directors had gained Board, Executive Group or Top Management Team status (see Chapter 4). The dominant route in both private and public sectors to the top was the zig zag pattern which involved vertical and horizontal occupational movements between, and within, management specialist functions including entry, exit and return to personnel/HR. The CEO/MD selects the skill mix and composition of their TMT/Executive Group. Our research showed that in accordance with the Spence (1973) theory of 'signals' they signal via various HR processes (e.g. characteristic of staff promoted, performance appraisals, career planning and development, etc.) the requirements they demand of personnel/HR directors. These consist of professional HR competence, a wider understanding of the business and interpersonal team working and networking skills. These qualities were found in all the 34 personnel directors who had taken the zig zag route to the top. They had been acquired and developed by multi-management functional job changes, by involvement in company development programmes, by self-development activities, by building networks and by seeking and gaining more challenging jobs.

Twenty-one of our personnel/HR directors had acquired Board, Executive Group or TMT status by vertical occupational mobility within the personnel/HR function. However, they did not display markedly different priorities or patterns of behaviour from those who had followed the zig zag route. It was thought these directors would give relatively greater weight than zig zag careerists to professional standards and values. This turned out not to be the case in that they held a strong sense of the need for personnel/HR to contribute to solving business problems and thereby help the organisation achieve its objectives. These vertical route directors had also picked up CEO/MD signals that having business awareness was a relatively high priority in selecting individuals for directorships. They accepted personnel/HR must contribute to cost reduction, to improved business performance and add value to the business. They were more likely, relative to the zig zag careerists, to have broadened and deepened their knowledge and understanding of the business by self-development activities (such as gaining formal qualifications) and by volunteering, or being selected by senior management to participate in multi-management project teams assembled for a particular purpose. In this way, there was convergence between those who had pursued the vertical and zig zag pathways. In selecting a personnel/HR director for the Board, Executive Group or TMT the CEO/MDs had preference for the zig zag experience but the choice between pathways was not so stark. Other considerations, for example the composition of the existing board and organisational circumstances, were also significant in their selection of a director.

A feature of the parachute pathway was the absence of experience in the HR function. The five personnel/HR directors involved, nevertheless, had detailed knowledge of the business and possessed the required social and teamworking skills. Their lack of HR expertise, however, was not a problem as they learned quickly and drew on personnel/HR expertise already available in the organisation. This is a significant research finding on our part because it places personnel/HR expertise not wholly with the individual manager but with a departmental team, where continuity lies. Moreover, where company policy and culture was one of functional rotation, other managers in the personnel/HR team gave support to the new (non-personnel/HR director) on the basis of reciprocal dependency as they knew they would experience a similar entry problem when next rotated into another function.

It is not clear from our research how long term a view personnel/HR directors have with regards to achieving director status. For most of them it was a mixture of circumstances and willingness to take opportunities presented. For those taking the zig zag route to the top, it was sequenced development, albeit with no long-term plan, mastering their present job and seeking new challenges at a more senior level by either applying to another organisation or by negotiating elevation to the Board or Executive Group with the CEO/MD. All the personnel/HR directors involved in our research had demonstrated in previous situations their comfort with exercising high levels of responsibility, influence and power.

What do personnel/HR directors do?

Our 'typical' personnel/HR director was male, aged 47, possessed formal higher education qualifications, was in membership of the Chartered Institute of Personnel and Development and had been a Board and/or Executive Group member for three and a half years. They were younger than their Board, Executive Group or TMT colleagues. The average age of PLC board members was 54 compared to that of the Executive Group's 50 years. Our 'typical' personnel/HR director held more formal higher education qualifications than UK managers in general. Ninety-five per cent of our sample held a formal higher education qualification compared with 42 per cent for UK managers in general. They also had a relatively shorter length of tenure of Board and Executive Group membership than their other director colleagues. The average length of Board and/or Executive Group membership for personnel/HR directors was three and a half years compared with five and a half years for other directors. With respect to membership of the CIPD, some 50 per cent of our sample were at the membership grade of Fellow and a further third at corporate grade of membership.

Turning to the question of what personnel/HR directors do, our research shows they are heavily involved in the making of business decisions and that they fit their expertise to facilitate business strategy. Their role on the CEO/MD Executive Group and TMT was to lead on personnel/HR issues and to configure the function's expertise and policies to the business requirements of the organisation. Their business orientation put them into a strong position to argue for personnel/HR's contribution to improving business effectiveness.

In addition to involvement in business strategy formulation, personnel/HR directors undertake personnel/HR activity, service the sub-committees (remuneration and nominations) of the PLC board and enhance their business acumen by broadening their portfolio to taking on non-personnel/HR tasks and by involvement in multi-disciplinary projects. The main personnel/HR responsibilities undertaken by the personnel/HR directors were training and development, recruitment and employee relations. Over 75 per cent of the personnel/HR directors interviewed or surveyed by questionnaire were involved in these activities. Management training and development was seen by the CEO/MD interviewed, as a particularly important activity in achieving a change of attitudes amongst managers and the workforce, in the face of the need to restructure organisations and employment working practices to improve competitiveness (the private sector) and efficiency, effectiveness and economy in the case of the public sector.

Another contribution personnel/HR directors make at corporate PLC board level is their involvement, with non-executive directors, on main board remuneration and nominations sub-committees. Our research revealed these committees were highly dependent on the personnel/HR directors to conduct research (for example into the level and rate of change in directors' salaries in other organisations) to provide information and to offer advice. This access of personnel/HR directors via these activities to non-executive directors, including the chairperson of the Board, is an important avenue for enhancing their power and influence within organisations.

An important activity of personnel/HR directors was the broadening of their understanding of the wider concerns of the business by their engagement with the higher business decision-making process through extending their portfolios to take on non-personnel tasks and by involvement in multi-disciplinary management projects. Of the 41 private sector organisations included in our study, 16 had personnel/HR directors who had widened their job portfolio to include both personnel and specific non-personnel/HR responsibilities. In the 19 public sector organisations, nine personnel/HR directors had taken on wider portfolios. In one case, the personnel/HR director had taken over responsibilities for the hotel operations at the Health Trust whilst in a large local authority a personnel/HR director also had responsibility for corporate resources. At a large brewers and leisure group, the corporate personnel director held responsibility for information technology and security whilst at an engineering group the personnel/HR director held responsibility for buying and for contracts, including legal aspects. Our research also revealed contributions by personnel/HR directors in multi-functional task force teams, particularly in merger and acquisition situations.

Some may argue that if personnel/HR directors need to extend their job into non-personnel/HR activities it illustrates that personnel/HR is not important enough to justify a full-time position on the Board of Directors, or the Executive Group or the TMT. However, this was not the view of the CEO/MDs interviewed who all said they had deliberately, as part of the management training and development of their directors, encouraged their personnel/HR directors to deploy themselves in this way. This reinforced the view that personnel/HR directors are heavily involved in the general business of the Executive Group as team players. It facilitated the business focus of the Executive Group and was not confined to personnel/HR directors but applied to other directors.

What factors explain the power and influence of personnel/HR directors

Our research shows that the probability that personnel/HR directors will exercise significant influence over the formulation of an organisation's strategy is likely to be high where:

1   the organisation has a CEO/MD who is positive in their attitude towards the contribution that personnel/HR can contribute to the 'bottom line' and to the success of the organisation;

and if the personnel/HR director:

2   is business focused, and not management function based, in making business decisions;
3   has a proven record of success in the implementation of personnel/HR matters;
4   has the ability to be a team player;
5   possesses good interpersonal and group skills;
6   is proactive in achieving board/Executive Group status;

All these factors increase the dependency of the CEO/MD, Board of Directors, CEO/MD Executive Group and TMT on the personnel/HR director delivering for the organisation if its objectives are to be achieved. The first of the factors outlined above (i.e. the attitude of the CEO/MD) has been discussed above and there is nothing more to say.

Business focused

Our researches, however, revealed that CEO/MDs seek a broader contribution to devising the Board's/Executive Group's/TMT strategic decisions from personnel/HR directors than just a personnel/HR input. They expect the personnel/HR director to be, as board, Executive Group or TMT members, first and foremost business people engaged in devising strategies and policies to achieve corporate and business objectives rather than as personnel specialists. Like other members of the board or Executive Group they are expected to be interested in the 'bottom line', the 'added value' and 'efficiency/effectiveness' and 'economy' of the business in implementing their decisions. As Executive Group members the overall business performance of the organisation was uppermost in their consideration and their primary role as director was to achieve business objectives. In short, the personnel/HR director was a business person first and a personnel/HR director second. They were all-round business people who were able to combine their management specialisms with the requirements of the business.

The personnel/HR directors participating in our research had acquired their business acumen in a number of ways, including by networking and by spending time in a line management role. Wider business experience was also, as we have noted above, acquired and developed by personnel/HR directors broadening their portfolio at board, CEO/MD Executive Group and TMT levels by taking on a general management role or by participating in multi-management teams. As we saw above, our research revealed the most common career pathway of personnel/HR directors to broaden their business experience was by spending a period of time in line management. The dominant pattern was that personnel/HR directors had worked in two or three functions other than personnel/HR. Business acumen had been developed and acquired by some of our personnel directors either by company sponsored management development programmes or by self-development. A typical personnel/HR director career pathway was as follows: commences in line management; moves to a second function, usually personnel; a third move to general management as managing director, often of a subsidiary company and fourth back to personnel.

This sharing of business values by personnel/HR directors has caused some academics (Tyson, 1995; Storey, 1992) including the authors (1996 and 1998) to state that successful personnel/HR directors are business people first and personnel/HR specialists second. However, a more detailed consideration of this issue, based on our research, has led us to shift our view somewhat. Our findings confirm the view that personnel/HR does not rule or dominate private and public sector organisations strategy formulation but can only secure power and influence if personnel/HR strategy is seen to contribute to improving business performance. Nevertheless HR is an important ingredient contributing to distinct competency (knowledge, skills and attitude) to business decision-making. The authors have demonstrated this through the concept of the T-shaped manager (see Chapter 3 and below) with the stem of the 'T' representing functional expertise combined with the bar of the 'T' representing wider business competency. Effective personnel/ HR directors ride both horses finding a synthesis between them.

Team players and networkers

Personnel/HRs ability to deliver for the CEO/MD is explained from our research by their social competencies in areas of interpersonal skills, team working, political acumen and networking with others both inside and outside the organisation. Board of Directors, CEO/MD Executive Groups and TMT are made up of a mixture of knowledge, technical skills and individual talent which have to be fused together to achieve effective performance. In sport, team games offer numerous examples of highly skilled individuals who underperform as a collective because they fail to work for each other. Teamworking in business, hospitals and local authorities is no different. In an environment of enhanced competition and quickening pace of change, the requirement in organisations for collective team and project working has become more necessary. Projects and problems requiring new ideas and solutions come ever faster to the fore. Chief Executive Officer/Managing Director or Personnel/HR directors are unlikely to have a monopoly on ideas. Today's Boards of Directors and Executive Groups and TMT devote more time and energy to discussing future development of the organisation. This requires greater openness and collective awareness as a team.

Kotter (1982) identified a key factor making general managers effective was their networking and lobbying activities through others. In his study of senior general managers they knew hundreds of people from whom they could obtain information to help them overcome obstacles to improved performance. The personnel/HR directors in our study had created an extensive network of personal relations as source of data available to them when formulating the organisations' strategy. They were widely known in industry and management circles via networks of established contact with superiors and subordinates, with managers in other functions, with members of cross functional project teams, with attending general management and personnel/HR conferences, with officials and officers of employers' organisations, including the Confederation of British Industry (CBI) and with links into the wider, academic and consultancy communities. This network of resources could be called upon at the appropriate time to help make difficult decisions. The research revealed in this regard a relationship of dependency with both the CEO/MD and the personnel/HR director working closely together exchanging information, not only about what was happening in their organisation but in the wider industry.

Professional competency

Our research programme revealed that if personnel/HR directors are to have a significant influence on the formulation of an organisation's strategy then they require not only a strong commercial (business/value for money, etc.) orientation but to earn the respect of other Board, Executive Group of TMT members as competent professionals in the area of personnel/HRM. It is essential personnel/ HR directors are competent and have a record of achievement in their own basic field. Their competence in solving personnel/HR problems establishes their credibility and standing with other directors and with it their influence on board and/or Executive Group or TMT decisions. The importance of a proven personnel/HR record for a director to be effective is illustrated by the following comment from a Chief Executive of a multinational, multi-utility supplier:

> There were a number of factors in his favour. He was an engineer, had an MBA, understood business, had private sector know-how, had a strong back- ground in HR and had a proven track record, having successfully put in a similar change at a major car manufacturer, albeit on a smaller scale.

The personnel HR directors were all described by their CEO/MD as 'doers' who delivered for the Board, etc. on personnel/HR strategy and associated policy. In terms of their personnel/HR technical competence, the personnel/HR directors were generalist rather than a specialist, for example in training and development, in pensions, in equal opportunities, etc. They were all seen by their CEO/MD as competent in HR planning, employee relations, training and development, pay and benefits and employment law and had demonstrated they had the skills to apply their knowledge and understanding in these areas to the solution of business problems. The personnel/HR directors participating in the research were all well- rounded personnel/HR professionals.

Interpersonal and group skills

The interview programme and questionnaire survey of CEO/MD and personnel/ HR directors revealed that to be effective as directors individuals require inter- personal and group skills. In our study, the personnel/HR director possessed the courage and confidence to engage in debate with the CEO/MD and other directors on a wide range of business and personnel issues. They were tuned into the political sensitivities of small group dynamics, offering both support and constructive criticism of strategic proposals. The effectiveness of the personnel/HR director was much dependent on congruence between their interpersonal, social and group working skills in relation to the CEO/MD and other board members. This impor- tance of social skills in exercising influence matches Kotter's 1982 study of senior general managers in which he showed good inter-personal and group skills were necessary to develop relationships with others to persuade them to move in a desired direction. Our personnel/HR directors had the 'will' and the 'skills' to make use of sources of power in and around the board, the Executive Group and the TMT.

Although our own research points to personnel/HR director effectiveness depending on congruence with the CEO/MD's requirements, the relationship between the two was not one of mutual admiration. It was one of dependency with each getting from the relationship what they wanted. The personnel/HR directors shared loyalty and commitment in the best interests of the organisation and its chief executive/managing director. This did not mean blind allegiance but a willingness to be constructive in helping the Board (or TMT or Executive Group) to operate positively by suggesting solutions fee of negative attitudes.

In summary, the effective personnel/HR director combines high functional expertise with a wide business orientation and effective skills, all of which bring something extra to boardroom deliberations. In building credibility with their fellow directors, it is important personnel/HR directors establish a reputation for competency in their own field (the well rounded personnel/HR professional) for getting matters completed in a successful manner and having a willingness to widen their responsibility outside the personnel/HR area. All this shows that for a high level of power and influence to exist for the personnel/HR director, effective relationships with key players (especially the CEO/MD) are more important to business success than functional organisational structures *per se*. Indeed, some of the personnel/HR directors interviewed regarded formal structures as a constraint on the influence of personnel/HR on business performance.

The 'T'-shaped manager

Our research findings demonstrated that personnel/HR directors in both the private and the public sector undertake a combination of both business and HR roles. On this basis, the effective personnel/HR director can be described as a 'T'-shaped manager. The stem of the 'T' represents their core competency (technical knowledge and understanding) in personnel/HR matters as that of a generalist personnel/HR professional. A high level or generalist professional competency has been acquired and developed through work experience and by gaining higher qualifications in personnel/HR. They have a proven record in personnel/HR matters which aids their credibility with their fellow directors and CEO/MD.

The bar of the 'T' denotes a general understanding of the business/organisation as a whole acquired and developed by operating successfully in other management functions, by strengthening inter-personal skills, by working in a project team including representatives from other management functions, and by self-learning and development. This understanding of the business and/or organisation as a whole also enabled them to enhance their credibility with their fellow directors by their ability to justify personnel/HR strategic and policy initiatives on business/organisational improvement grounds rather than a sectional management interest perspective.

By being 'T'-shaped managers, the successful (effective) personnel/HR director has a bundle of skills which enables them to integrate business and personnel/HR strategies and related policies. Our research suggests that it is personal influence, plus personnel/HR expert power, plus business/organisation acumen that gives personnel/HR directors their power and influence rather than just personal corridor power as suggested by Purcell and Ahlstrand (1994).

References

Adams, K. (1991) 'Externalisation versus specialisation: what is happening to personnel?', *Human Resource Management Journal*, Vol. 1:4, pp. 40–54.

Anthony, P.D. (1986) *The Foundation of Management*, London, Tavistock.

Aram, J.D. and Cowen, S.S. (1995) 'Reforming the corporate board from within: strategies for CEOs and directors', *Journal of General Management*, Vol. 20:4, pp. 23–39.

Armstrong, M. (2000) 'The name has changed but has the game remained the same?' *Employee Relations*, Vol. 22:6, pp. 576–89.

Armstrong, P. (1995) 'Accountancy and HRM', in Storey, J. (ed.) *Human Resource Management: A Critical Text*, London, Routledge.

Arnold, J. (1997) *Managing Careers into the 21st Century*, London, Paul Chapman Publishing.

Bach, S. (1998) 'NHS pay determination and work re-organisation: employee relations reform in NHS Trusts', *Employee Relations*, Vol. 20:6, pp. 505–76.

Bacon, N., Ackers, P., Storey, J. and Coates, D. (1996) 'It's a small world: managing human resources in small businesses', *International Journal of Human Resource Management*, Vol. 7:1, pp. 83–100.

Bain, G. (1967) 'Trade union growth and recognition', Research Paper 6, Royal Commission on Trade Unions and Employers' Associations, London, HMSO.

Bain, G. (1970) *The Growth of White Collar Unionism*, Oxford, Clarendon Press.

Bain, N. (1995) *Successful Management*, Basingstoke, Macmillan Business.

Bantel, K.A. and Jackson, S.E. (1989) 'Top management and innovations in banking: does the composition of the top team make a difference?' *Strategic Management Journal*, Vol. 10, pp. 107–24.

Barclays Bank (1994) 'Bridging the skills gap', London, Barclays Bank plc.

Barham, K. and Oats, D. (1991) *The International Manager*, London, Economist Books.

Barlett, C.A. and Ghoshal, S. (1988) 'Organising for world wide effectiveness', *California Management Review*, Fall, pp. 54–74.

Beardwell, I. (1998) 'Wanders, wavers and clean home runs', CIPD discussion paper, pp. 1–18.

Beaumont, P.B., Hunter, L.C. and Sincliar, D. (1996) 'Customer–supplier relations and the diffusion of employee relations changes', *Employee Relations*, Vol. 18:1, pp. 9–19.

Berle, A.A. and Means, G.C. (1932) *The Modern Corporation and Private Property*, New York.

Bjorkman, I. and Gertsen, M. (1990) 'Corporate expatriation: an empirical study of Scandinavian firms'. Conference proceedings of the 3rd Symposium on Cross-Cultural Consumer and Business Studies, Honolulu, December.

Bolton Committee Report (1971) Report of Commission of Inquiry on Small Firms (chaired by Bolton, J.E.) Cmnd 4811, London, HMSO.

Boon, S. and Ram, M. (1998) 'Implementing quality in a small firm', *Personnel Review*, Vol. 27:1, pp. 20–38.

Boxall, P. (1994) 'Placing HR strategy at the heart of the business', *Personnel Management*, Vol. 26:7, pp. 32–5.

Boyne, G., Jenkins, G. and Poole, M. (1999) 'Human resource management in the public and private sectors: an empirical comparison', *Public Administration*, Vol. 77:2, pp. 407–20.

Brannen, P., Batstone, E., Fachett, D. and White, P. (1976) *The Worker Directors*, London, Hutchinson.

Brewster, C. (1988) 'The management of expatriates', *Human Resource Centre Monographs* Series, No 2, Cranfield School of Management, UK.

Brewster, C. (1995) 'HRM the European dimension', in Storey, J. (ed.) *Human Resource Management: A Critical Text*, London, Routledge.

Brewster, C. and Hegewisch, A. (1994) *Policy and Practice in European Human Resource Management*, London, Routledge.

Brewster, C., Larsen, H.H. and Mayrhofer, W. (2000) 'Human resource management: a strategic approach', in Brewster, C. and Larsen, H.H. (eds) *Human Resource Management in Northern Europe: Trends, Dilemmas and Strategy*, Oxford, Blackwell.

Brookes, C. (1979) *Boards of Directors in British Companies*, Department of Employment.

Budhwar, P.S. (2000) 'Evaluating levels of strategic integration and development of human resource management in the UK', *Personnel Review*, Vol. 29:2, pp. 141–57.

Burnham, J. (1942) *The Managerial Revolution*, London, Putnam.

Burns, T. (1961) 'Micro politics: mechanisms of institutional change', *Administrative Science Quarterly*, Vol. 6, pp. 257–81.

Cadbury Report (1992) *Committee on Financial Aspects of Corporate Governance*, Moorgate.

Carr, F. (1999) 'Local bargaining in the National Health Service: new approaches to employee relations', *Industrial Relations Journal*, Vol. 30:3, pp. 197–211.

Carroll, M., Marchington, M. and Earnshaw, J. (1999) 'Recruitment in small firms', *Employee Relations*, Vol. 21:3, pp. 236–50.

Charkham, J. (1994) *Keeping Good Company: A Study of Corporate Governance in Five Countries*, Oxford, Clarendon Press.

City of London Stock Exchange (1998) Committee on Corporate Governance, final report, (chaired by Sir Ronald Hampel), Gee Publishing.

Common, R.K. (1998) 'Convergence and transfer: a review of globalisation and new public sector management', *International Journal of Public Sector Management*, Vol. 11: 6, pp. 1–8.

Confederation of British Industry (1995) 'Remuneration of directors' (chaired by Lord Greenbury).

Conyon, M.J. (1994) 'Tenure and contracts: the experience of UK CEOs', *Personnel Review*, Vol. 23:5, pp. 25–33.

Conyon, M.J. and Mallin, C.A. (1997) 'A review of compliance with Cadbury', *Journal of General Management*, Vol. 2:3, pp. 24–37.

Cooke, W.N. (2000) 'Human resource management strategies and foreign direct investment in the US'. Conference proceedings IIRA 12th World Congress, Tokyo, Japan, May–June.

Coulson-Thomas, C. (1991) 'What the personnel director can bring to the boardroom table', *Personnel Management*, Vol. 23:10.

Cromie, S., Stephenson, B. and Montieth, D. (1995) 'The management of family firms: an empirical investigation, *International Small Business Journal*, Vol. 13, pp. 11–34.

Cully, M., Woodland, S., O'Reilly, A. and Dix, G. (1999) *Britain at Work*, London, Routledge.

Cunningham, I. and Hyman, J. (1999) 'Devolving human resource responsibilities to the line: beginning of the end or a new beginning for personnel?', *Personnel Review*, Vol. 28:3, pp. 9–27.

Dalton, M. (1959) *Men Who Manage*, New York, Wiley and Sons.

De Cieri, H., Dowling, P.J. and Taylor, K.F. (1991) 'The psychological impact of expatriate relocation on partners', *International Journal of Human Resource Management*, Vol. 2:3, pp. 377–414.

Derr, C.B. (1986) *Managing the New Careerists*, San Francisco, Jossey Bass.

Derr, C.B. and Odden, G.R. (1991) 'Are US multi-nationals adequately preparing future American leaders for global competition', *International Journal of Human Resource Management*, Vol. 2:2, pp. 227–44.

Department of the Environment, Transport and Regions (1999) 'Modern local government: in touch with the people', www.local-regions.detr.gov.uk/lgwp/3.htm.

Department of Trade and Industry (1999) Statistical Bulletin: Small and Medium Enterprises, Statistics for the United Kingdom, 1998, Government statistical service, URM.

Development Dimensions International (1999) *National Human Resource Directors' Survey*, High Wickham.

Dooley, R.S. and Fryxell, G.E. (1999) 'Attaining decision quality and commitment from dissent: the moderating effects of loyalty and competence in strategic decision-making teams', *Academy of Management Journal*, Vol. 42:4, 389–402.

Dowling, P.J. and Boxall, P. (1994) 'Shifting the emphasis from natural resources to human resources: the challenge of the new competitive context in Australia and New Zealand', *Zeitschift für Personalforschung*, Vol. 8:3, pp. 302–16.

Dowling, P.J., Welch, D.E. and Schuler, R.S. (1999) *International Human Resource Management*, Cincinnati, ITP.

Drucker, P. (1989) *The Practice of Management*, Oxford, Heinemann.

Eisenstat, R.A. (1996) 'What corporate human resources brings to the public picnic: four models for functional management', *Organisational Dynamics*, Autumn, pp. 7–22.

Elsik, W. (1992) *Strategisches Personalmanagement: Konzeptionen und Konsequenzen*, Munich, Mering

ER Consultants (1992) Who's managing the managers?, *Institute of Management Report*, 4:12.

Farnham, D. (1999) 'Human resources management and employment relations', in Horton, S. and Farnham, D. (eds) *Public Management in Britain*, Basingstoke, Macmillan Press.

Farnham, D. and Giles, L. (1996) 'People management and employment relations', in Farnham, D. and Horton, S. (eds) *Managing the New Public Services*, Basingstoke, Macmillan.

Fashoyin, T. (1998) 'Into the unknown: managing human resources in small medium enterprises: a review'. Conference proceedings of IIRA 11th World Congress, Bologna, Italy.

Fenwick, J. and Baily, M. (1999) 'Local government reorganisation in the UK: decentralisation versus corporatism', *International Journal of Public Sector Management*, Vol. 12:3, pp. 249–59.

Ferlie, E., Pettigrew, A., Asburner, L. and Fitzgerald, L. (1996) *New Public Sector Management in Action*, Oxford, Oxford University Press.

Ferner, A. and Varul, M. (2000a) '"Vanguard" subsidiaries and the diffusion of new practices', *British Journal of Industrial Relations*, Vol. 38:1, pp. 115–40.

Ferner, A. and Varul, M. (2000b) 'Internationalisation and the personnel function in German multinationals', *Human Resource Management Journal*, Vol. 10:3, pp. 79–96.

Ferner, A., Quitanilla, J. and Varul, M. (2000) 'Country-of-origin effects and management of HR/IR in multi nationals: German companies in Britain and Spain'. Conference proceedings IIRA 12th World Congress, Tokyo, Japan, 29 May–2 June.

Fisher, C., Dowling, P. and Garnham, T. (1999) 'The impact of changes to the human resource function in Australia', *International Journal of Human Resource Management*, Vol. 10:3, pp. 501–14.

Flynn, N. (1994) 'Control, commitment and contracts', in Clark, J., Cochrane, A. and McLaughlan, E. (eds) *Managing Social Policy*, London, Sage.

Flynn, N. (1995) 'The future of public sector management', *International Journal of Public Sector Management*, Vol. 8:4, pp. 59–67.

Fox, A. (1971) *A Sociology of Work and Industry*, London, Collier Macmillan.

Frooman, J. (1999) 'Stakeholder influence strategies', *Academy of Management Review*, Vol. 24:2, pp. 191–204.

Gagnon, S. (1996) 'Promises v. performance; pay devolution to next steps executive agencies in the British Civil Service', *Employee Relations*, Vol. 18:3, pp. 25–47.

Gennard, J. and Judge, G. (1999) *Employee Relations* (2nd edn), London, CIPD.

Gennard, J. and Kelly, J. (1992) 'Human resource management and managing change: the case of Rosyth Royal Dockyard', in Towers, B. (ed.) *The Handbook of Human Resource Management*, Oxford, Blackwell.

Gennard, J. and Kelly, J. (1994) 'Human resource management: the views of personnel directors', *Human Resource Management Journal*, Vol. 5:1, pp. 15–32.

Gennard, J. and Kelly, J. (1997) 'The unimportance of labels: the diffusion of the personnel/HR function', *Industrial Relations Journal*, Vol. 28:1, pp. 27–42.

Gordon, R.A. (1966) *Business Leadership in the Large Corporation*, Los Angeles, University of California.

Grant Thornton Consultants (1999) *Family Businessess: How Directors Can Manage Key Issues in a Family Firm*, London, Institute of Directors.

Grant, D. and Oswick, C. (1998) 'Believers, atheists and agnostics: practitioners views on HRM', *Industrial Relations Journal*, Vol. 29:3, pp. 178–93.

Greenbury Report (1995) *Remuneration of Directors*, CBI.

Griffiths, W. (1993) 'A leaner, fitter future for HR?', *Personnel Management*, Vol. 25:10.

Guest, D. (1987) 'Human resource management and industrial relations', *Journal of Management Studies*, 24, pp. 503–21.

Guest, D. and Baron, A. (2000) 'Piece by piece', *People Management*, Vol. 6:15.

Guest, D and Hoque, K. (1994) 'Yes, personnel does make a difference', *Personnel Management*, Vol. 26:11.

Guest, D. and Mackenzie Davey, K. (1996) 'Don't write off the traditional career', *People Management*, February, Vol. 2:4, pp. 22–5.

Guest, D. and Peccie, R. (1994) 'The nature and causes of effective human resource management', *British Journal of Industrial Relations*, Vol. 32:2, pp. 219–42.

Haddad, C.J. (1998) 'Labor participation in modernization at small mid-sized firms: research findings from the USA'. Conference proceedings IIRA 11th World Congress, Bologna, Italy.

Hall, P. (2000) 'Feel the width', *People Management*, Vol. 6:1.

Hall, L. and Torrington, D. (1998) *The Human Resource Function*, London, Financial Times Publishing.

Handy, L., Holton, V. and James, P. (1995) 'Creatures of change', *Ashridge Journal*, April, Vol. 4:8.

Hay Group (1998) 'Hampel – much ado about nothing', *Boardroom Remuneration Review*, Spring.

Hay Group (2000) Hays' boardroom survey – top pay moving ahead, Winter.

Heenan, D.A. and Perlmutter, H.V. (1979) *Multinational Organisation Development*, Reading, MA, Addison-Wesley.

Hendry, D. (1994) *Human Resource Strategies for International Growth*, London, Routledge.

Herriot, P. and Pemberton, C. (1995) *New Deals: The Revolution in Managerial Careers*, Chichester, Wiley.

Hickson, D.J., Hinings, C.R., Lee, G.A., Schneck, R.E. and Pennings, J.M. (1971) 'A "strategic contingencies" theory of intra organisational power', *Administrative Science Quarterly*, Vol. 16, pp. 216–29.

Hill, R. and Stewart, J. (1999) 'IIP in small organisations: learning to stay the course?', *Journal of European Industrial Training*, Vol. 23:6.

Hoque, K. and Noon, M. (1999) 'Counting angels: the personnel/human resource function in the UK. Evidence from the 1998 Workplace Employee Relations Survey'. Conference proceedings, BUIRA, July 1–3 1999, De Montford University.

Hornsby, J.S. and Kuratko, D.F. (1990) 'Human resource management in small businesses: critical issues for the 1990s', *Journal of Small Business Management*, July, pp. 9–17.

Horton, S. and Farnham, D. (1999) *Public Management in Britain*, Basingstoke, Macmillan.

Hunt, J.W. (2000) 'Untapped resources: people may be a company's greatest asset, but HR still has a poor profile'. *Financial Times*, 9.2.00.

Hunt, J. and Boxall, P. (1998) 'Are the top human resource specialists "strategic partners"? Self perceptions of a corporate elite', *International Journal of Human Resource Management*, Vol. 9:4, pp. 767–81.

Hutchinson, S. (1995) 'Variation on the partnership model', *People Management*, November.

Hutchinson, S. and Wood, S. (1995) *Personnel and the line: Developing a new relationship*, London, Chartered Institute of Personnel and Development.

IIPUK (1998) 'What is investors in people?, www. iipuk.co.uk/iipuk/indexz.ptml.

Institute of Management (1999) 'Struggle for a seat at the top', *Financial Times* 23.3.99.

IRS (1999a) 'Employment in the global village', *Employment Review*, 689, October, p. 5.

IRS (1999b) 'Employment in the global village: 2', *Employment Review*, 691, November, p. 3.

IRS (2000a) 'People management has a low profile in small and medium-sized businesses', *Employment Review*, 709, August, p. 3.

IRS (2000b) 'Working all over the world', *Employment Review*, 699, March, p. 3.

Janis, I.L. (1983) *Group Think*, Houghton Mifflin.

Johnson, G. and Scholes, K. (1993) *Exploring Corporate Strategy* (3rd edn), Hemel Hempstead, Prentice Hall.

Kakabadse, A. (1991) *The Wealth Creators*, London, Kogan Page.

Kamochie, K. (1994) 'A critique and a reformulation of strategic human resource management', *Human Resource Management Journal*, Vol. 4:4, pp. 29–43.

Kamochie, K. (1996) 'Strategic human resource management with a resource-capability view of the firm', *Journal of Management Studies*, Vol. 33:2, pp. 213–33.

Katzenbach, J.R. (1998) *Teams at the Top*, Boston MA, HBSP.

Keenoy, T. (1999) 'HRM as hologram: A polemic', *Journal of Management Studies*, Vol. 36:1, pp. 1–23.

Kelly, J. (1988) 'Labour utilisation and industrial relations at Scott Lithgow 1967–1987', *Industrial Relations Journal*, Vol. 9:4, pp. 296–309.

Kelly, J. and Gennard, J. (1996) 'The role of personnel directors on the board of directors', *Personnel Review*, Vol. 25:1, pp. 7–24.

Kelly, J. and Gennard, J. (1996) 'Business and HRM strategies at Rosyth Dockyard', in Towers, B. (ed.) *The Handbook of Human Resource Management* (2nd edn), Oxford, Blackwell.

Kelly, J. and Gennard, J. (1998) 'The effective personnel director' *Employee Relations Review*, Vol. 4, March, pp. 17–24.

Kelly, J. and Gennard, J. (2000) 'Getting to the top: career paths of personnel directors', *Human Resource Management Journal*, Vol. 10:3, pp. 22–37.

Kessler, I. and Purcell, J. (1996) 'Strategic choice and new forms of employment relations in the public service sector', *International Journal of Human Resource Management*, Vol. 7:1, pp. 206–29.

Kessler, I., Purcell, J. and Shapiro, J.C. (2000) 'Employment relations in local government: strategic choice and the case of Brent', *Personnel Review*, Vol. 29:2, pp. 162–83.

Kidger, P. (1999) 'A study of structure and management in multinational enterprises'. Conference proceedings BAM, Vol. 1, pp. 479–95.

Kinnie, N., Purcell, J., Hutchinson, S., Terry, M., Collinson, M. and Scarbrough, H. (1999) 'Employment relations in SMEs: market driven or customer shaped', *Employee Relations*, Vol. 21:3, pp. 218–35.

Kotter, J.P. (1982) *The General Managers*, New York and London, The Free Press, Collier Macmillan.

Kuan, W.K. (2000) 'An exploratory framework for glocalizing human resource management: implications for Japanese MNCs under transformation challenge', Conference proceedings IIRA 12th World Congress, Tokyo, Japan, May–June.

Legge, K. (1978) *Power, Innovation and Problem Solving in Personnel Management*, London, McGraw-Hill.

Levinson, D.J., Darrow, C.N., Klein, E.B., Levinson, M.H and McKee, D. (1978) *The Seasons of a Man's Life*, New York, Alfred A. Knopf.

Loan-Clarke, J., Boocock, G., Smith, A. and Whittaker, J. (1999) 'Investment in management training and development by small business', *Employee Relations*, Vol. 21:3, pp. 296–310.

Low Pay Commission (1999) 'The national minimum wage: the story so far', second report, www. lowpay.gov.uk

Lupton, B. and Shaw, S. (1999) 'Across the great divide? HR careers in the public and private sectors'. Conference proceedings BAM, Vol. 2, pp. 1338–9.

McConville, T. and Holden, L. (1999) 'Filling in the sandwich: HRM and middle managers in the health sector', *Personnel Review*, Vol. 28:5/6, pp. 1–12.

McDonald, J. and Wiesner, R. (1998) 'Organisational change and HRM strategies in Australian SMEs'. Conference proceedings IIRA 11th World Congress, Bologna, Italy.

McKiernan, P. and Urquhart, J. (1996) *Corporate Governance: A Psychoanalytical Approach*, University of St Andrews.

McNulty, T. and Pettigrew, A. (1996a) 'The contribution, power and influence of part-time board members', *Corporate Governance: An International Review*, Vol. 4:3, pp. 160–79.

McNulty, T. and Pettigrew, A. (1996b) 'Part-time board members: their influence on strategy in UK firms'. Conference proceedings BAM, September, pp. 2–45.

MacKay, L. and Torrington, D. (1986) *The Changing Nature of Personnel Management*, London, IPM.

Marginson, P., Armstrong, P., Edwards, K.P. and Purcell, J. (1995) 'Extending beyond borders: multinational companies and the international management of labour', *International Journal of Human Resource Management*, Vol. 6:3, pp. 702–19.

Marginson, P., Armstrong, P., Edwards, P., Purcell, J. and Hubbard, N. (1993) 'The control of industrial relations in large companies: an initial analysis of the second company level industrial relations survey', IRRU, University of Warwick, pp. 29–37.

Marginson, P., Edwards, P., Martin, R., Purcell, J. and Sisson, K. (1988) *Beyond the Workplace*, Oxford, Blackwell.

Marlow, S. (1997) 'The employment environment and smaller firms', *International Journal of Entrepreneurial Behaviour and Research*, Vol. 3:4, pp. 143–8.

Matlay, H. (1999) 'Employee relations in small firms: a micro business perspective', *Employee Relations*, Vol. 21:3, pp. 285–95.

Mileham, P. (1996) 'Boardroom leadership: do small and medium companies need non-executive directors?', *Journal of General Management*, Vol. 22:1, pp. 14–28.

Miles, R. and Snow, C.C. (1978) *Organisation Structure, Strategy and Process*, New York, McGraw-Hill.

Millward, N., Bryson, A. and Forth, J. (2000) *All Change At Work*, London, Routledge.

Ministry of Labour (1961) *Industrial Relations Handbook*, London, HMSO.

Mintzberg, H. and Waters, J.A. (1985) 'Of strategies deliberate and emergent', *Strategic Management Journal*, Vol. 6, pp. 257–72.

Monks, K. (1993) 'Careers in personnel management', *Personnel Review*, Vol. 22:1.

Moore, C. (1996) 'Human resource management in the public sector', in Towers, B. (ed.) *Handbook of Human Resource Management*, Oxford, Blackwell.

Moreau, M. and Trudeau, G. (2000) 'The social effects of globalisation on labour law'. Conference proceedings IIRA 12th World Congress, Tokyo, Japan, May–June.

Nagai, H. (2000) 'HRM strategy of Japanese MNCs in the European Union'. Conference proceedings IIRA 12th World Congress, Tokyo, Japan, May–June.

Negrelli, S. (1998) 'Participation and decentralisation of collective bargaining in Italy'. Conference proceedings IIRA 11th World Congress, Bologna, Italy.

Newman, J. and Clarke, J. (1994) 'Going about our business? The managerialisation of the public services' in Clarke, J., Cochrane, A. and McLaughlin, E. (eds) *Managing Social Policy*, London, Sage.

Newton, J. and Hunt, J. (1997) 'Employment relations in small service organisations', *Employee Relations*, Vol. 19:1, pp. 67–80.

Niven, M.M. (1967) *Personnel Management 1913–63*, London, IPM.

Oswick, C. and Grant, D. (1996) 'Personnel management in the public sector: power, roles and relationships', *Personnel Review*, Vol. 25:2, pp. 4–18.

Pahl, R.E. and Winkler, J.T. (1974) 'The economic elite: theory and practice', in Stanworth, P. and Giddens, A. (eds) *Elites and Power in British Society*, Cambridge, Cambridge University Press.

People Management (2000) '… end of an era for HR at troubled Marks and Spencer', *People Management*, Vol. 16:19, September.

Perlmutter, H.V. (1969) *The tortuous evolution of the multinational corporation*, Columbia Journal of World Business, Vol. 4:1, pp. 9–18.

Personnel Manager's Year Book (1998) AP information services.

Pettigrew, A. and McNulty, T. (1995) 'Power and influence in and around the boardroom', *Human Relations*, Vol. 48:8, pp. 845–73.

Pfeffer, J. (1992) *Power in Organisations*, Marshfield.

Pfeffer, J. and Salanick, G.R. (1978) *The External Control of Organisations*, New York, Harper Row.

Poole, M. and Jenkins, G. (1997) 'Responsibilities of human resource management practices in the modern enterprise', *Personnel Review*, Vol. 20:5, pp. 333–56.

Porter, M.E. (1985) *Competitive Advantage: Creating and Sustaining Superior Performance*, New York and London, The Free Press / Collier Macmillan.

PriceWaterhouseCoopers (1997) *International Assignments: European Policy and Practice 1997/ 1998*, Europe.

Purcell, J. (1988) 'The structure and function of personnel management', in Marginson, P. *et al*, (eds) *Beyond the Workplace*, Oxford, Blackwell.

Purcell, J. (1991) 'Impact of corporate strategy on human resource management', in Storey, J. (ed.) *New Perspectives on Human Resource Management*, London, Routledge.

Purcell, J. (1994) 'Personnel earns a place on the board', *Personnel Management*, Vol. 26:2.

Purcell, J. (1995) 'Corporate strategy and its links with human resource strategy', in Storey, J. (ed.) *Human Resource Management: A Critical Text*, London, Routledge.

Purcell, J. and Alhstrand, B. (1994) *Human Resource Management in the Multi-divisional Company*, Oxford, Oxford University Press.

Purcell, J. and Gray, A. (1986) 'Corporate personnel departments and the management of industrial relations: two case studies in ambiguity', *Journal of Management Studies*, Vol. 23:2, pp. 205–23.

Rainnie, A. (1989) *Industrial Relations in Small Firms*, London, Routledge.

Ram, M. (2000) 'IIP in small firms', *Personnel Review*, Vol. 29:1, pp. 69–91.

Reilly, P. (2000) 'Called into question', *People Management*, Vol. 16:14, July.

Renwick, D. (2000) 'HR-line work relations: a review, pilot case and research agenda' *Employee Relations*, Vol. 22:1/2, pp. 179–98.

Report of the Committee of Inquiry on Industrial Democracy 1977, (Chairman Lord Bullock), London, HMSO.

Reward Group (2000) 'Remuneration of company directors'.

Royal Commission on Trade Unions and Employers' Associations 1965–1968 (Chairman Lord Donovan), HMSO, Cmnd 3623.

Scottish Office (1999) 'The Commission on Local Government and the Scottish Parliament', www.scotland.gov.uk/library/documents-w10/clg-01.htm.

Schein, E.H. (1978) *Career Dynamics*, Reading, MA and London, Addison-Wesley.

Schein, E.H. (1993) *Career Anchors – Discovering Your Real Values*, San Diego, Pfeifer.

Schuler, R.S. and Jackson, S.E. (1999) *Strategic Human Resource Management*, Oxford, Blackwell.

Schumacher, E. (1973) *Small is Beautiful*, London, Abacus.

Sisson, K. (1993) 'In search of HRM', *British Journal of Industrial Relations*, Vol. 31:2 , pp. 201–10.

Sisson, K. (ed.) (1994) *Personnel Management* (2nd edn), Oxford, Blackwell.

Skinner, W. (1987) 'Big hat – no cattle: managing human resources', *Harvard Business Review*, Vol. 59, pp. 106–14.

Smith, K.A. (1995) 'Managing without traditional planning: The evolving role of top management teams', in Flood, P.C., Gammon, M.J. and Paauwe, J. (eds) *Managing Without Traditional Methods*, Cambridge, Addison-Wesley.

Smith, M. and White, M.C. (1987) 'Strategy, CEO specialisation and succession', *Administrative Science Quarterly*, Vol. 32, pp. 317–36.

Spence, M. (1973) 'Job market signalling', *Quarterly Journal of Economics*, Vol. 83, pp. 355–74.

Storey, J. (1992) *Developments in the Management of Human Resources*, Oxford, Blackwell.

Storey, J. and Sisson, K. (1993) *Managing Human Resources and Industrial Relations*, Guildford, Oxford University Press.

Storey, J., Okazaki-Ward, L. and Gow, I. (1991) 'Managerial careers and management development: a comparative analysis of Britain and Japan', *Human Resource Management Journal*, Vol. 1:3, pp. 33–57.

Subbarao, A.V. (2000) 'Management development of professionals of a diverse workforce in global corporations' Conference proceedings IIRA 12th World Congress, Tokyo, Japan, May–June.

Tomlinson, J. (1993) 'Human resources – partners in change', *Human Resource Management*, Vol. 37:4, pp. 545–54.

Torrington, D. (1991) 'Human resource management and the personnel function', in Storey, J. (ed.) *New Perspectives on Human Resource Management*, London, Routledge.

Torrington, D. and Hall, L. (1998) *Human Resource Management*, Hemel Hempstead, Prentice Hall.

Trades Union Congress (2000) 'Winning at work', General Council Report.

Tsui, A. and Gomez-Mejia, L. (1988) 'Evaluating human resource effectiveness', in Dyer, L. (ed.) *Human Resource Management: Evolving Roles and Responsibilities*, Washington, DC: BNA.

Tung, R.L. (1981) 'Selection and training of personnel for overseas assignments', *Columbia Journal of World Business*, Vol. 16:1, pp. 68–78.

Tyson, S. (1985) 'Is this the very model of the modern personnel manager?', *Personnel Management*, Vol. 17:5.

Tyson, S. (1995) *Human Resource Strategy*, London, Pitman Publishing.

Tyson, S. and Fell, A. (1986) *Evaluating the Personnel Function*, London, Hutchinson.

Ulrich, D. (1997) *Human Resource Champions*, Boston, MA, HBSP.

Ulrich, D. (1998) 'HR with attitude', *People Management*, August, 1998.

Walsh, J. and O'Flynn, J. (1999) 'Managing through contracts: the employment effects of compulsory competitive tendering in Australian local government'. Conference proceedings BAM, Vol. 2, pp. 1025–41.

Walton, R.E. (1985) 'From control to commitment in the workplace', *Harvard Business Review*, Vol. 63:2, pp. 77–92.

Watson, T.J. (1977) *The Personnel Managers*, London, Routledge, Kegan Paul.

Weber, M. (1964) *The Theory of Economic Organisations*, New York, Free Press.

White, M.C., Smith, M. and Barnett, T. (1997) 'CEO succession: overcoming the forces of inertia', *Human Relations*, Vol. 50:7, pp. 805–27.

Wilkinson, A. (1999) 'Employment relations in SMEs', *Employee Relations*, Vol. 21:3, pp. 206–17.

Wilkinson, A. and Marchington, M. (1994) 'TQM: instant pudding for the personnel function', *Human Resource Management Journal*, Vol. 5:1.

Winchester, D. and Bach, S. (1995) 'The state: the public sector', in Edwards, P. (ed.) *Industrial Relations Theory and Practice in Britain*, Oxford, Blackwell.

Yarnall, J. (1998) 'Career anchors: results of an organisational study in the UK', *Career Development*, Vol. 3:2, pp. 56–61.

Index

9 780415 217606

For Product Safety Concerns and Information please contact our
EU representative GPSR@taylorandfrancis.com Taylor & Francis
Verlag GmbH, Kaufingerstraße 24, 80331 München, Germany